WE LIVE IN

QUEEN CREEK

ARIZONA

By

Alden F. Rosbrook

Table Of Contents

~

ACKNOWLEDGMENTS

Cover photo © and page one photo © by Bernadette Heath
Memorial Photo© by Liz Guy

To those that have served within the San Tan Mountains PRIDE Association as officers and directors and those that did outstanding works in helping us with our Community wide mission:

Gordon & Nonda Brown, Fulton Brock, Silvia Centoz, Sue & Larry Cox, Kathy & Donald Denton, Sharon & David Dobbs, Robert & Rebecca Dotson, Cathleen & Dr. William Gunderman, Ed, Reece & Kristen Guerra, Bernadette & William Heath, Michelle Heckman, Janie Hanlon, Kaye B. Howell, Ron & Donnis Hunkler, Wendy Feldman Kerr, Gene Kilber, Thomas Huggy Bear Lang, Ron & Karen McCoy, Gerhardt & Pat Obrikat, Deb Perry, Joan & Bill Perry, Georgia & Ralph Peterson, Anne Reed, Valerie Reed, Caroline Rosbrook, Sandie Smith, W. Van Vandenberg, Regina Whitman, Diane & Charles Wilson and all the many hundreds that helped us with our clean-ups.

Editor In-Chief Deb Perry, Associate Editor Caroline Rosbrook, Book Cover Graphics Designer Katie Perry.

Interviewee: Steve Sossaman, Wendy Feldman Kerr, Sandie Smith, Ed & Kristen Guerra. Interviewer, Alden F. Rosbrook

DISCLAIMER:

All statements of apparent fact in this book are empirical inferences based on observational data. These are idiosyncratic in nature and have not necessarily been subject to verification.

*PLEASE NOTE THAT SOME OF THE NAMES IN THIS BOOK HAVE BEEN CHANGED.

INTRODUCTION

Maybe this book should have the title "We live in Queen Creek Arizona....finally!"

This story begins a few years before 1957. It would be in November 1957 when the Mafia influenced Alden and Caroline's lives in a way that sent their family--later our three boys and one girl--on a path leading to Phoenix, Arizona in 1969. It would take them another seventeen years before they would finally immigrate to Queen Creek.

This memoir recounts scores of fascinating and remarkable stories covering their family's lives for over 58 years. It begins with a mind-blowing blunder made by a then secret crime syndicate, which later turns out to be the Mafia (La Cosa Nostra), that profoundly affects a newly married couple and changes their lives forever.

After finally reaching Queen Creek, twenty-nine years later, they would discover that they wound up right in the middle of some more very disturbing criminal activities. The author and his wife bought a house on 3.45 acres that lies near the base of Goldmine Mountain that has fantastic 360 degree views. The land is on the outskirts of the Town of Queen Creek, with most all their nearby neighbors living on 3 + acres north of them. Their land borders a 10,000 acre park. It took a while to find out, shockingly, that their new home overlooked: a drug dealer/manufacturer/fence's house, a drug and human smuggler's house and a vehicle chop shop house. Then later, they found out that there was another drug manufacturer and another drug dealer that deals from his house of prostitution within one mile of them.

To combat these criminals, the author forms the San Tan Mountains PRIDE Association. He invites a group of citizens to join the organization and enlists help from their county supervisor. After a while the county supervisor meets with the PRIDE members and she thereupon enlists the help of her sheriffs department.

It took some time but with the help of the Border Patrol, the Pinal County Health Department and her sheriff's department, a neighboring county sheriff', all five illegal businesses were shut down within a couple of years.

It was very hard to believe that these criminals practically worked right out in the open. All they lacked were signs advertising what they were selling or the services they offered.

It was very interesting for them to be able to see, on two different occasions, swat teams raid the drug dealer and the human smuggling house down the street from them right from their front deck.

Forming the PRIDE helped them get the attention of all the people in government that had the ability to finally clean up this crime ridden area.

IN MEMORY OF:

Carl E. Touhey

Gene Kilber

Pauline Fitzsimmons Rosbrook Bergren

Rachel La Grange Ransford Nelson

David Ellis Ransford

Frederick Terrance Rosbrook Sr.

Edmond Leroy Ransford II

Alden Eugene Rosbrook

PART ONE: THE FIRST 30 YEARS
1956-1986 CHAPTER 1

Because Of The Mafia

My wife and I were both born in Albany, NY in the same hospital, on the same day, one year apart. Both of our birthdays are on November 7th. Growing up, Caroline's parents bought a dairy farm in Couse Corners, NY. My parents bought a new home in nearby East Greenbush, NY. I went to a parochial school, Saint Johns Academy, that was about twenty-five miles from my home and Caroline went to a public school that was about three miles from her home. My father was a plumbing and heating contractor who needed extra space for all his equipment and Caroline's mom was a widow with no livestock who had lots of extra space in her barn. My dad rented that space and that is how I got to meet Caroline.

My father suffered a great deal for the last three years of his life because of being misdiagnosed by a doctor before he finally passed away from cancer in March 1954 when I was sixteen. My brother Fred was thirteen and Richard was ten. Times were rough on all of us then.

When dad was unable to work, I started working when I was fifteen at Bill Sullivan's Shell gas station. Bill worked in the New York State Police when my dad was a Trooper. I believe that Bill hired me because he knew our family wasn't doing very well financially. Bill didn't really need me but kept me on just so I could get some kind of pay check on a weekly basis.

After dad passed, I went to work at Hepinstall's Esso (now Exxon Mobil) Service Station located in Couse Corners, NY, which happened to be about one mile from my future wife's home.

Working for "Hepy" inspired me a great deal. Esso had several training programs that dealt with selling the many automotive products that Esso had to offer.

Hepy took me to these sales training and servicing programs. In those days of full service gas stations, sales and customer service were a big part of how busy the inside service department would be. I learned very quickly that having the right knowledge and using it with customers worked very well. Gas at that time was about twenty-three cents a gallon.

Me, Leah & George Hepinstall & Caroline

Our full service approach was (1) suggesting a fill up instead of "$3.00 please" that customers usually asked for and (2) asking to "may I check your oil and water sir?' while washing the windshield led to more sales. Getting under the hood was a good opportunity for selling a filter and oil change or a new fan belt. Showing the driver his oil dip stick that showed dirty oil was a good way of getting the car inside for that oil change and lube job.

Offering to check the air in the tires gave you a chance of selling a set of new tires and on and on it went. Hepy offered a lot of contests related to numbers of sales that really motivated me to do a better selling job. I won a great many of those contests and every time I won it encouraged me to try harder on the next sale.

Everyone that worked for Hepy had to be a multi-tasker, and we had to have clean clothing and freshly washed hands while doing it. We did everything from pumping gas to pricing and stocking shelves, checking out customers, serving fresh dipped ice-cream, greasing and changing the oil in customers cars or trucks, hand washing their vehicles, changing and/or fixing car and large truck tires. When I think about it now I see that this experience helped shape my life and was the college I never enrolled in and I got paid to do it, even though it was only 80 cents an hour at that time.

My dad was very well known in our community and while he was sick our neighbor's and friends helped us a lot. Their generosity continued after my dad died. Thinking back on that, our East Greenbush, NY community was a very special one that helped keep us in our home and our family together.

By the time I was seventeen I was the manager of Hepy's gas station/grocery store while I attended Saint John's Academy in Rensselaer NY. In the summer I often worked sixteen hours a day, five days a week.

I joined the USMC between wars in 1956 and by the time I fulfilled my six year Ready Reserve commitment, I received my Honorable Discharge papers as a Corporal E-4 in June of 1963. In 1965 the Marines were the first large U.S. combat group to land in Vietnam and by the end of that year there were 38,000 Marines there. By this time we had four children and I was very lucky not to have been called up.

I witnessed something that was very strange to me. When I was in Beaufort, South Carolina in the 1950's, I saw first-hand what segregation was about. I guess growing up in the north we were somewhat insulated from how the blacks were treated in their daily lives in the south. I saw the signs that read "blacks water fountain" and "no blacks allowed" at the bus stop. I asked a young black boy to step into the cool waiting room at a bus station to give me a shoe shine and he refused because blacks were not allowed inside. In stark contrast many of our USMC drill instructors were black and were not nearly as reserved as any of the black male citizens of South Carolina that I saw. Thanks to President Harry S. Truman and Executive Order 9981, on July 26, 1948 racial discrimination was abolished in the US military. This led to the end of segregation in the services and what I saw on and off base seemed like two worlds apart.

One of my customers at the gas station was the vice president of a major soft drink bottling company in nearby Albany. He asked me to apply for a job with his company, which I did with the blessing of my first full time boss and friend, George Hepinstall. I started as a truck driver delivering Canada Dry soft-drinks and soon moved up to a sales position. Joe was about 12 years older than I and was always a fun person to work with.

Joe Rapp

When I was eighteen and while I was still working for Hepy my good friend Jimmy Anderson and I stopped at Jevens Bar and Restaurant in East Greenbush very late on a Friday night after a party.

Joe and his wife Jackie were there and asked us to sit with them.

The main restaurant area had been closed and there was a big plastic type folding door that closed that area off.

It was about 12:30 a.m. when we saw a car and then a NY State police car drive into the back parking lot.

Soon after that we heard some female laughter and other noises coming from the closed off dining area.

Joe was a Marine who served as an Embassy guard during the Korean War or Police Action as it was called. When we saw some lights going on in the closed off area Joe became somewhat agitated but Jackie kept him in check as best she could. The only person working then was the owner, Mrs Jevens. There were about five other patrons sitting where were at that time which was just before closing time and last call which was just before 1:00 a.m.

Joe continued to become somewhat loud about the State Police having a party while on duty and so forth but not that loud that the officers and the two women could hear. When the owner said last call, Joe ordered another round that would last until after 1:00 a.m. At about 1:15 a.m. the owner took a tray of drinks into the back room being very careful not to open the door too much. When she came back Joe ordered another round and the owner said that is was past the 1:00 a.m. time to legally serve alcohol. Joe protested and Mrs Jevens walked away. This made Joe very angry.

Joe then got up and was headed for the big doors ready to expose these Troopers and their dates. Jimmy and I along with the customers there and Jackie were getting ready for the worst when the owner turned off all the lights just as Joe had his hands on the doors. All we could hear was tables and chairs falling over and people yelling and then we heard the back door slam shut and saw two cars leaving the parking lot in a hurry. Jackie grabbed Joe because he wanted to chase the Troopers down the road. After that the place closed and we all went home.

I had to open the Gas Station/Grocery store the next morning at 6:30 a.m. I was a little still a little groggy from all that happened a few hours earlier, when there was a telephone call for me about 8:00 a.m. The man said he was from the New York State Police Internal Affairs Division. He said that his name was Sergeant Bill Wright and he told me that he was told that I witnessed two Troopers doing something that was punishable by a jail sentence. He asked me what had taken place this morning and I told him that I did not see anything. He kept pressing me for more of what I knew. I did know who the one Trooper was and it happened to be a friend of my fathers so I continued to say that I did not see anything because the lights were out.

He finally told me that there was going to be a grand jury hearing at the capitol on next Monday morning and if I did not come to the hearing he would put out a warrant for my arrest. He told me where the court house was in Albany and hung up.

First I called my friend Jimmy and asked him if he had a call from Sergeant Wright and he said he had not. Then I called Joe and he said that he could not help me because it would hurt his reputation, then he told me that he was afraid that I would have to handle this problem by myself.

My father was gone and I didn't want to give my mom any grief so I just sucked it up but I was extremely worried about appearing before the Grand Jury. Then about 4:00 p.m. I got a call from Joe and instantly I thought he was going to help me out with my big problem. When Joe told me that it was him who called me and not the New York State Police, I could hear his wife Jackie laughing in the background. Boy was I so relieved that anger was not in the equation at all.

Years later, before we decided to move to Arizona Joe was given a brand new Ford convertible as a company car that he offered his wife Jackie to use. In Rochester NY they use a lot of salt in the winter on the roads to melt ice and snow that dried out a lot of the rubber grommets that was used then in the suspension system and shock absorbers used in the undercarriage of cars and trucks. The salt would cause the rubber to dry out and cause them to squeak. It was May and Joe had the new convertible that had a lot of squeaks. He drove the car to the plant and asked me to have our mechanic spray the grommets with the lubricant we used for our fleet of cars and trucks. We had a fifty gallon drum of this stuff. There was a balcony that was outside our offices that overlooked the entire production area and the mechanics work area.

I felt like this was a perfect opportunity for a little pay back so I went to a nearby grocery store and bought a small brick of Limburger cheese. Which is a very smelly cheese when it is cold but when it gets hot it really stinks. I took it to our young mechanic and told him to put half on each top sides of the V-8 engine. He thought that it was a great idea.

The engine was still very warm from Joe's drive from his home that was about twenty miles away. The day was quite warm and sunny and all the doors were open in the production and mechanics area. The wind happened to be blowing from the back of the plant towards the balcony when Joe stepped out there as he often did.

He saw and heard the mechanic spraying the underside of his wife's car when he got a whiff of that incredibly smelly cheese that was melting away. I was in my office when Joe came in to tell me that he thinks that the oil that we use to spray the rubber grommets must have gone bad. I told him that I didn't think that oil could go bad. He said it must not be any good because it really smells like hell and he then left for his drive to Endicott.

Later he told me that he had very puzzling stares from drivers that pulled up along side of him at almost every stop light.

The next day all the managers of our corporation had a meeting in Endicott, which is about 110 miles away. Joe wanted to get down there a day ahead to set up the meeting in advance. After Joe left, our young mechanic came into my office to tell me that he did an even better job with the cheese by putting a small chunk on the spare tire in the trunk and then he said that he wiped the steering wheel with the wrapper. After he told me these things I thought that maybe this prank was now a bit overkill. You betcha it was!

When Joe got to Endicott he gave me a call. He was very upset. He told me to get rid of that drum of oil because it is definitely spoiled. He said that he didn't care how much it cost but just get rid of it. He went on to say that the mechanic must have gotten some oil on his hands and the smell transferred on to the steering wheel and he now has it on his hands. Oh, this is a little bit more than I wanted to happen but it is was still very funny...... especially when I think of the Grand Jury story he put me through years before.

When I got to Endicott the next day Jackie's car was sitting in the parking lot with: The doors open, with the top down, the hood up, the trunk open and the seats and the spare tire lying on the driveway and the trunk stripped. It looked like everything had been thoroughly washed. Joe believed what he had seen and smelled as the vehicle was being sprayed with the lubricant and it was very hard for me to convince him that I had Limburger cheese put in his car and that was what he smelled.

After he had the engine and spare tire steamed cleaned and the steering wheel cleaned five times, the smell of Limburger Cheese still lingered. Jackie never drove the car again so Joe put it on the Orange Motors car lot to sell that Carl Touhey, our Chairman, owned and where we purchased all our company vehicles from.

Everyone thought that the story was hilarious even Joe. Jackie got another convertible so she was happy too. There were a lot of practical jokes that we played on each other over the years we worked together.

One time we were on a trip and stayed at a fine hotel in Chicago that gave us a suite with two bedrooms at no extra charge. After we went to dinner Joe told me that he had a meeting for later in the evening and he might not get back to the hotel until late. He had a smirk on his face so I had to guess who the meeting was with (I heard rumors that he was having an affair) but I didn't know for sure. After he left I asked room service for some Saran Wrap which I used to carefully cover his toilet bowl with. Then I short sheeted his bed and put hangers in the pillow cases. It was about 2:00 a.m. when he finally came noisily in.

He went right into the bathroom and all I heard was swearing because he would tell me later that he thought he had gone blind. When he got into bed there was a loud "What the hell!" And that was when I started to laugh out loud. He then came running into my room laughing loudly and tipped me and the bed upside down, crash. It didn't take long for the phone to ring with the night manager asking, "is there something wrong going on in your room?" I told him everything was fine, then we had a big laugh together but I had to sleep on the mattress on the floor that night and all was good. I never asked him where he went that night but I would find out later that the rumors were true.

Sometimes practical jokes backfire. This one did, big-time! One night, Joe Rapp and I were out with a customer in Endicott. We were walking home from a restaurant by a Catholic Church and saw a discarded black ribbon funeral wreath near some trash cans next to the Church. Joe Rapp grabbed the wreath and thought it would be great to put it on a Town Council member's front door that we knew very well. His house was on the way to our hotel where we were staying .

We hung it on the Councilman's door knocker and thought he would find it very funny when he found it the next morning. Wrong! When Joe called him the next day and before Joe could tell him that we/he put the wreath on his door, he told Joe that he had called the police because he thought it was from the gangsters. He went on to tell him that it was an obvious death threat and he was scared out of his mind. Joe asked the man not to tell the police who did it because it was put there by him as a joke. He had thought that it was very funny at the time and was very sorry for what had happened.

The Apalachin Gangland Convention

On November 14, 1957 there was a very large meeting in Apalachin, NY of a then secret crime organization that would later be known as the Mafia or Cosa Nostra. The host of this meeting was Joseph Barbara Sr, the owner of Canada Dry Bottling Company of Southern New York, located in Endicott.

I did not know that much about "Joe the Barber" Barbara until recently when I started doing research for this book. Joe Sr. was born Giuseppe Maria Barbara on August 9, 1905 in Castellammare del Golfo, Sicily, which is a fishing village dating back to ancient times. The small town is noted however for having been the birthplace of many other American mafia figures, including Stefano Magaddino and Joseph Bonanno.

Joe Barbara Senior came to Endicott, NY in 1921 at the age of 16. With the help of his brother that lived there, he got a job at the Endicott Johnson shoe factory. Soon after he moved to Old Forge, PA and got into the bootlegging business. During the 1930s he was arrested a few times for suspicion of murder. In 1933 he was arrested for the murder of a rival bootlegger, Sam Wichner. Mr. Wichner went to Joe's home for a business meeting where Joe allegedly strangled Mr. Wichner to death.

However, as with the other murders that Joe was suspected of committing, the police were never able to get enough evidence to convict him. On May 24, 1934 Joe married Josephine in Endicott, NY and fathered three sons: Joseph Maria Jr., Peter, Angelo and a daughter, Angela. Sometime between 1936 and 1940 Joe bought the franchise rights to bottle and distribute Canada Dry and acquired a beer distributor liquor license.

The area where the Apalachin Gangland Convention and Joe Barbara's bottling company is located is called the New York State Southern Tier but certainly is not in southern New York State. If you were to look at a map of NYS Endicott, the home of Canada Dry of Southern NY is due south of Rochester NY on the northern edge (tier) of the Pennsylvania State line. Apalachin NY, where the meeting was held, is just west of Endicott. Southern New York City is about four hours drive and about 200 miles south-east of Apalachin NY.

A local newspaper (Apalachin Community Press) stated that there were about 70 men that attended this so called meeting. It was the idea of Vito Genovese, aka Don Vitone, to have the meeting at Joe Barbara's home. One account says that the meeting was held because a high ranking member of a Mafia family in New York City, Albert Anastasia, was murdered on October 1957 while he was having his very last haircut and shave. Don Vitone wanted this meeting of all the families of the country's Mafia to see who would get the murdered victims territory. They were also going to deal with the banning of anything to do with drug sales and its distribution and the heralding of Don Vitone as the Boss of the Bosses in New York City.

Another account tells a story about Vito wanting to build a casino in Cuba and he would need financial help to do so. It goes on to say that he wanted all the Mafia families to come together in this venture as a way for all to safely launder their misbegotten Mafia money.

Before this Mafia meeting the Director of the FBI J. Edgar Hoover said that there was not any organized crime in the USA. This would become a blow to his then stalwart creditability when one New York State Trooper and one New York State Bureau of Criminal Investigation (BCI) investigator would trip over one of the greatest newspaper stories of 1957-1958. It seems that two State Policemen were checking out a misdemeanor crime at a local Endicott/Vestal motel when they overheard Joe Barbara Jr. order six rooms for people that would be attending a Canada Dry Bottlers convention. Joe would not give the names of the people that would be staying there and took the keys to the rooms with him. This made the troopers suspicious. Before this incident they also saw a lot of large black cars with out of state license plates in the area, which seemed out of place for that time of year.

The local state troopers had known for a long time that Joe Barbara was involved in criminal activities but they were not sure exactly what his involvement was. These two must have suspected that something big was going to happen because they called in two Treasury agents from Albany to help them investigate further.

At about lunchtime the next day the four officers were parked within sight of Joe Barbara's large home which was situated on fifty acres in Apalachin. Joe was having a gangster cookout at the side of his large home with 25 large expensive cars parked nearby. After seeing that, they had set up a road block and the fun began when the troopers were spotted by Josephine, Joe's wife. Even though the guests were not doing anything illegal, some of these well dressed gangsters panicked and began running through the woods in every direction, leaving some cash and a couple of guns in their wake. Sixty of those that chose to get stopped at the roadblock were questioned and detained. Most all of them had criminal records and some had served time.

Many of the cookout party people were subpoenaed to testify before the newly established New York State Investigation Commission for the purpose of finding out what the meeting was about. The one person that they were not able to subpoena was Joseph Barbara Senior.

It is interesting to note that no one in the FBI or any other police organizations really knew who these people represented until six years later in 1963 when Joe Valachi, a low level Mafioso, sang before John McClellan's Federal subcommittee on crime investigations. It was then that the FBI realized that the Cosa Nostra aka Mafia was an organized crime unit working with their own special rules and regulations throughout the USA.

One of Joe Barbara's guests at the Gangland Convention was a mob boss by the name Joe Bonanno. Joe was born in the same fishing village as Joe Barbara Sr. in the same year, 1905. Joe Bonanno and his son moved to Tucson four years after we moved to Phoenix/Scottsdale. I was not able to find any direct connection between the Barbara's and Joe Bonanno. There was a story in the Arizona Republic newspaper by Charles Kelly entitled; "Mobsters Never Did Control Arizona". In this story it does mention a few unsolved car bombings in the Phoenix, AZ Metro area before and after Joe Bonanno arrived in Tucson and there were no connections to him that were ever found for these crimes.

Rumors About Endicott Canada Dry

Caroline and I were newly married and without children when I was a salesman for Albany Canada Dry when there were all kinds of rumors going around at the plant. The media was having a ball with the story about the meeting in Endicott and how the owner of the Canada Dry bottling company was involved. The rumors were about the possibility of our company buying Joe Barbara's Canada Dry Endicott operation. In those short weeks prior to the actual purchase, Caroline and I talked about my being selected as a sales supervisor (dreamer!) and having to move there, which was about 150 miles from Albany where we lived. We both agreed that it would be quite an adventure to move there and be right in the middle of all those gangsters that ran the bottling company, or so we thought. Caroline was nineteen and I was twenty by just a couple of months and I was a salesman for the company for less than a year. Some youngsters just have no fear!

I was washing my company car in the plant on a Saturday and, unknown to me, a meeting between my sales manager Joe Merhige, my vice president Joe Rapp and Chairman of the Board Carl Touhey was being held about 100 feet from where I was located. Joe and Carl were trying to talk my sales manager into moving to Endicott but he was older and would only move if they would give him a much higher salary. They told my sales manager that they could not take on any larger salaries at that time. They then asked my sales manager, "who in his sales force would be best suited to move down there and take over the sales supervisors position?"

He must have answered, "Why don't you ask Rosbrook, who is right outside in the plant washing his car?", because Joe Merhige came out with a big grin on his face and asked me to come into the meeting room to talk with Joe and Carl.

Carl told me that there was a position open in Canada Dry Endicott that they had just purchased it. He emphasized that going there would be a one-way street and if the operation failed, there would be no promises that I would have a job back here in Albany. Little did I know that the Endicott plant had not made a profit in many years and none of us knew, at that time, that Mr. Barbara ran it that way on purpose for unknown reasons.

Without telling them that my wife and I had already discussed moving there, I just answered "When do we have to move?" everyone in the room was momentarily dumbfounded to say the least.

Then unknown to me at the time, is that I "seized the moment (Carpe Diem), big time!" It would be years later when I would realize how those six words had so much impact on my superiors. The first question Carl asked was, "Don't you have to ask your wife before you make this decision?"

I never asked about money or benefits or expenses or anything logical like that, just those six words, I repeated again. "When do we have to move?" Carl shook my hand, as did Joe and finally my sales manager, who was still in complete shock. I think he assumed that I would be uncertain and that they would have to reconsider giving him a big salary to move there.

Life In Endicott NY Starting In 1958

In addition to Endicott being known for shoe manufacturing it is also the birth place of IBM. In the apartment we lived in, there were two IBM families that we socialized with quite a bit. The apartment design was called "railroad flats". There were six apartments, three on one side of the stairwell and three on the other. Our company mechanic Ralph and his wife and daughter lived on the first floor right side and we lived on the third floor right side. The staircase ran alongside Ralph's living room wall.

One day Ralph was at home on the first floor, sitting in his living room watching his TV. I was in the middle of my third bound up the first flight of stairs when I heard a very loud voice, Ralph's voice, screamed X*%# *@&*^$st almighty. I stopped just as Ralph opened his door and told me in a very large way that I was knocking knickknacks off his walls and the rabbit ears off his TV and scaring the hell out of his cat, Tobie.

I apologized to Ralph who was staring up at me where I was standing near the second floor landing. Needless to say, I did not run up those stairs again. I must have really upset him for the first three months that we lived there. He was no friendlier to me from that day on. No one else complained and that might have been caused by gravity and my strength slowing me down the higher up the stairs I went.

The Frosting On The Cake!

Each flat had a front porch that was a big spacious area where you could sit and watch the all the activity in the neighborhood. The deck was slightly slanted with a three inch by twelve foot long opening at the bottom of the front half wall that had a ledge at the top where you could put a flower box.

One beautiful sunny day Caroline decided to mop the deck. It was a good idea, Caroline thought, to wash the deck because it had not been washed since we moved in some months ago, and It was filthy. What she did not know was that Ralph's wife Sadie was having her hair done by her daughter on the first floor porch which was two floors directly under our porch.

Caroline also did not know that they were right up next to the front porch opening and had a lot of their hair styling tools on that shelf. Everything was fine until it was time to rinse the deck. So Caroline got a full bucket of water after she mopped it and commenced to flush the deck, sending all that dirty water cascading down on that first floor ledge and immediately all over Sadie and her daughter. OMG!

That is when Caroline found out that Sadie and her daughter could scream profanities just as well as Ralph, only twice as loud. Even though Caroline tried to apologize, they moved out three weeks later. We then moved in to their first floor apartment. Some people thought that we did those things to Ralph and his family on purpose, that was definitely not true.

I worked at the same place Ralph continued to work which at times was uncomfortable. He never talked to me for all the six years I was there. He worked directly for Angelo. I really think that he and his family thought that we did those things to them on purpose but that was not the case at all. Ralph was a great mechanic and an asset to our company and the last thing I wanted to do was be the fault of our losing him. So I avoided any confrontation with him.

THINK

The IBM'ers that were our neighbors were mostly engineers that worked in the new product development testing department. When we would play bridge with them they often talked about their work. They mentioned that they were having a problem with a new huge punch printer and IBM had been working three shifts a day for many weeks in order to solve the problem. It had to do with the machine punching two letters inadvertently and at random every two or three cards at a time.

They were telling us that the average pay for their engineers working on this problem was about five to six dollars an hour, which at that time was a very high wage. One night they asked me to come with them down to the IBM facility even though it was on their own time, they were really interested if any progress with fixing the problem was being made. I thought, "Wow, sure!" After we got through the main gate the three of us marched into the building where the huge machine was. There were about ten men sitting all around this brand new giant IBM machine.

They acknowledged us and went right on thinking. We stood there in silence and every once in a while one engineer would say out loud, "Did anybody try such and such?" Answer came back, "Yes two days ago."

The IBM motto back then and for many years was "Think", and these guys were doing large amounts of just that. There were not any diagrams lying anywhere, no one was working on the machine, no one taking notes or looking at any schematics, they were all just sitting around thinking. I thought to myself, "At five to six dollars per hour per person, that is some kind of expensive thinking." We stayed only for about a half hour because it was getting kind of boring for us watching all these guys thinking.

They told me stories about the founder of IBM, Tom Watson Jr., and how he detested alcohol consumption, especially when his employees did the consumption, even in their homes or in restaurants.

IBM was big at that time but grew even more massive over the years. Tom did not want any of his personnel drinking alcoholic beverages, to the point of firing them if he saw them in public drinking. They told me that he went with a group of IBM salesmen on a train for a meeting in New York City from Endicott. While on the train Tom was told that some of his men were drinking in the bar car.

He went there, found about twenty IBM men drinking and fired them on the spot. He then ordered the train's conductor to stop the train, whereupon he had all the now former IBM'ers get off the train in the middle of nowhere.

Tom told all his aspiring middle entry employees to take advantage of every company-paid learning program that IBM offered or they might not be promoted. Our apartment friends were at IBM classes at least three nights a week throughout the work year. They told us that there was a great deal of pressure to grow within the Company or else.

The Italian Influence

As soon as we got settled in and we all were found to be a compatible working team by my vice-president, Joe Rapp, I officially became sales manager and co-manager of the bottling company. My co-manager was Angelo Alimonti, who had worked for Joe Barbara Sr. when he owned the plant. I was told that Angelo's full name meant "Angel of the Mountain" and it may not be a coincidence that one of Joe Barbara's sons has the same first name.

In fact all of Joe's production and sales employees, were Italian, and they all stayed on. I got to know all of them and most were very nice hard working people. It should be noted at this point that there were some mysterious incidences pertaining to product tampering immediately after we took control of the company.

For several months and maybe up to a year after Joe Barbara Sr. was forced by Canada Dry to sell his bottling company we had continuous product calls about foreign objects in bottles bought by consumers from stores, some bars and restaurants. At first consumers found small nails and bolts in bottles. Some were found before the customer opened the bottle and others after the bottle was opened. At that time the only product that we sold, that was not a deposit product was canned soft drinks. All deposit bottles had to be washed and sanitized before being refilled. We had two quality control people stationed on each line where every bottle had to go past a bright light to protect the consumer against getting anything with foreign items in the product.

We realized soon after the complaints started that it was virtually impossible for most of these items to be in the bottle unless someone put it in there after the bottle was washed because all the bottles were washed upside down with hot jets of water going directly into each bottle. We got calls from consumers that had beetles, cockroaches & mice in their bottles.

After a couple of months it became clear that someone or more were trying to sabotage our business. Joe and I answered every complaint call, went to their home, and offered a case of ginger-ale for the contaminated product. Two people tried to sue the company after they found mice in their bottle's. One was open and the judge threw out the case because no obvious harm was caused. The other one was thrown out because the bottle was unopened and again no harm was done. But a lot of these complaints made the newspapers, radio and TV. A few months after Joey moved his family to Detroit the complaints started to drop off. When it started we were getting up two or three complaints a week. A few months after Joey moved, it was down to one every other month or so. There is absolutely no evidence that Joey or anyone on our production line had anything to to with this problem. We were very glad that it eventually went away.

The only non-Italian people that I worked with were the office staff, Joan Sinclair and Noreen Eldridge. Noreen was probably 15 years older than I and often dyed her long hair blue. She also had a tattoo on the inside of her wrist that consisted of about six numbers that looked like a serial number from a German prison. She never hid her tattoo but would rather not discuss anything about it, at least to me. She was always very prim and proper although she never joined in any social gatherings that we had. Joan was a couple of years older than me. She was an attractive intelligent blonde that would eventually become the plant manager after Angelo passed away and after I moved to Rochester. In order to make a smooth transition between the Barbara ownership and my company's takeover we hired Joey's sister Angela to do part-time office work.

When my wife and I moved to Endicott we were in our early twenties and had never lived within an Italian culture or environment before. It was a totally new world to us and we soon enjoyed how the family and their children were everything to them.

We certainly savored their acceptance of us and our children to be a part of that culture. In addition to the high Italian population that came there from Italy to get jobs in the shoe factories in those days, there were many excellent Italian restaurants that followed.

Our favorite one was Lib Fuscos, that sold spedis among many other fantastic Italian menu items. Spedis are made from marinated lamb pieces cooked on a skewer over hot coals. It is then served upright on the skewer with a large slice of fresh Italian bread on the top of the skewer. After the waiter hands the skewer to their customer, they then could take the bread off and grab the lamb pieces with the bread while pulling the skewer downwards.

There are so many separate regions in Italy that had a different emphasis on food fare. In Endicott the food styles that were available were: Abruzzese, Florencia, Sicilian, Roma (Laziale) and Calibrese. We got to try many kinds of recipes like Baccala (salt dried cod) and Green Peppers and Pasta Fazool (beans, pasta, vegetables and ham). Some Endicott restaurants would offer tripe (cows stomach lining) in marinara sauce that was a one day a week special. We took a pass on that one.

The small Italian grocery stores were something we had never seen before. They had smoked hams, cheeses (provolone) and dried fish (baccala) hanging from the ceiling and big barrels of different kinds of olives in the store aisles. With the smell of fresh baked bread all mixed together in a delicious wafting combination of smells, those stores were out of this world. It is something that I still always vividly remember.

The store where I always shopped made pizza every day that was sold at room temperature. The large pans on display were rectangular and the baked pizza in them consisted of 2 inch thick squares of fresh baked bread covered with melted cheese and marinara sauce. This store was near an elementary school so a lot of kids would stop by for a piece to eat on their way home in the afternoon.

The apartment we rented was close to the bottling plant and was owned by Vincent Colona. Vince married Marie, an American citizen as his pathway to America. Vince started each day off with a raw egg in a glass of wine for breakfast. He worked for the Endicott Johnson Shoe Company in their tannery, lifting large wet cow hides out of tanks, and he also worked in our bottling company on the production line. He and his wife Marie owned three apartment buildings in the Endicott and the Endwell area. They were wonderful to us and often invited us over to their home, which housed many of their relatives as a part of their huge family. Every time we went into their home we heard the word "mangia, mangia".

We were accepted into the various Italian families that we met, always honored by their gracious hospitality. The Italian word "mangeria", was used to say "join us and enjoy some great food and wine".

Angelo invited us to his home for dinner a few months after we arrived in Endicott. The meal was served and we had, of course, spaghetti with marinara sauce and sausage. For us this was considered a full meal, but there were 2 more courses that we did not expect: veal, chicken and finally a forth course, desserts.

One of the desserts was cannoli, which consisted of a crispy pastry tube filled with a sweet ricotta cheese mixture. When we were served two of these wonderful looking things that we had never seen before, I noticed all six of Angelo's children intently watching me. When I got about halfway into this dessert, I ran into a material that was unlike the creamy great-tasting stuff that was at the beginning of the cannoli. I had never eaten one of these things before so I just thought it was a part of the dessert. When they knew that I had reached the center I was asked what I thought of the cannoli. I said, not wanting to be disrespectful of their hospitality, "it is great!." It was about that time that I realized that cotton was in the middle of the cannoli and I was a major part of a practical joke. Because everyone but Caroline was laughing out loud. Her cannoli did not have cotton in hers.

It was the third year after Carl bought the plant that Angelo got caught stealing from the company. He had been stealing about $12,000 a year. Joan the office manager, Angelo and I all received bonuses based on profits made by the company. Therefore the office manager and I were given the job of making the decision whether Angelo be fired or allowed to stay, as long as he made full restitution. It wasn't a hard decision because we knew his wife and children so well, that we decided, and after talking with Angelo, that he be allowed to stay.

Angelo Alimonti & Me

During our six years there one of Angelo's daughters got married. It was the first Italian wedding we had ever been to and it was a lot of fun. At the reception there were as many children there as there were grown-ups.

We all, grown-ups and children, danced the tarantella, which is a rapid whirling dance originating in southern Italy. The music is written in fast time as is the style of this dance. Of course, after we were taught by several laughing Italians who had a little to much vino to drink, we did quite well even though we might have had a little to much vino to drink too.

The bride's father, Angelo, had way too much wine and was telling a few people around him how much he loved Joe Barbara Sr. and started to say some very good things about the organization Joe had belonged to.

That was when Joey Jr. helped him into a private room where Angelo could sleep it off.

When Joey came back I suggested that we go to Angelo's home and short sheet all the beds and do similar pranks. There were three of us that got into Joeys black Cadillac, including our Vice President, Joe Rapp. We rode over to Angelo's home that afternoon. Much later we would think, "What if we were being followed by the FBI?" Me and others believed that our phones were tapped during that period.

The only window that was open in Angelo's house was the kitchen window that was directly over the sink. Joey, even though he was the heaviest of us all, volunteered to climb in. Before he did, he had to move a lot of fragile kick-knack's, which by the way, were never put back in place. We tied knots in all Angelo's shoestrings, short-sheeted all the neat beds, put clothes hangers in all the pillows and pulled toilet paper down the halls. It was about two months later before I had the nerve to ask Angelo about the condition of his home after the wedding reception. He said no one ever said anything to him except that there were some hangers inside the pillow cases, but that was all. I did not press the issue and just let it pass.

A few years later when we were living Rochester, NY I got a call from Joan who was co-manager with Angelo then. She told me that Angelo passed away. I asked her what he'd died from. She said, in a kind of satirical way, that he overdosed on butter. I then asked her for an explanation. She said that when they went to lunch together almost every day he would always say that he was on a diet and would order a salad but he would then eat one cracker after another until all the butter and more was gone. His cracker and butter diet killed him, plain and simple, Joan said. It clogged every artery around his heart that caused him to have a severe heart attack. To this day I do not know why I wasn't told of Angelo's funeral. It might have had something to do with the embarrassment to Angelo's family regarding his dipping in the till.

Giuseppe Maria Barbara Sr.

There were quite a few stories about Joe Barbara Sr. that were told to me by the employees that worked there when Joe Sr. owned and operated Canada Dry. He was first generation Sicilian and spoke with broken English. He was holed up in his home after the infamous barbeque aka "The Apalachin Gangland Convention" so I never met the man and in all the general transition transactions I had with two of his children, their father was never discussed. It was like Joe Sr. did not exist.

One of the stories that was told to me about Joe senior's sense of humor went like this: One day Joe Sr. hired a day laborer to move pallets of empty soft drink bottle cases up to the bottle washer when Angelo, who oversaw production, was not there. The man used a pallet truck that has two legs with wheels that are parallel to the floor that is pushed under the pallet. The handle is used as a hydraulic jack to lift the pallet up a few inches above the floor. A pallet of empty bottles in their wooden cases can weigh several hundred pounds each depending on the size of the bottles and their wooden cases. Joe told the man to get 20 pallets of 7 ounce bottles from the warehouse and take them to the bottle washer. This poor guy spent about three hours dragging those pallets to the washer. The production supervisor was working out of sight setting up the production equipment for a run of 12 ounce bottles and did not see what bottles were being set up to be washed. Unfortunately the production line was now all set up for a different size bottle. Joe was told by the production supervisor that he was not set up for the bottles in line. Joe went out to the man and told him to put the 20 pallets back where he got them and bring 20 pallets of 12 ounce bottles instead. The laborer became infuriated and started yelling at, unknown to him, a suspected hit-man for the Mafia, Joe Barbara. Sr.

There was Joe, in his suit and topcoat, in his fedora, smoking an expensive Cuban cigar who then puffed really hard while the man continued to scream at him. He took the cigar out of his mouth and jammed it into the man's face.

Now the man is screaming for a different reason, and in a lot of pain. While the man is bent over still screaming, Joe told him the he was fired.

Joe Barbara Sr.

Another story about Joe "The Barber" Barbara that most everyone in the production area of the plant knew about was about Joe's driving. After a very heavy rain storm, a bridge that was over a small stream on the road from Joe's home in Apalachin was washed away.

Joe was normally among the first people to show up for work every day. Within an hour after the plant opened Angelo figured that something was wrong, that maybe the Caddy broke down.

He called Joe's home and his wife, Josephine, answered the phone and was surprised that Joe had not made it to the plant because he had left about an hour before as usual. Angelo sent his truck mechanic Ralph and a helper from the production line to go towards Joe's home.

They get to where the bridge used to be and found Joe sitting on his newspaper on a tree stump smoking a cigar. The caddy was nose-first into the stream.

The mechanic asked Joe what happened? Joe said, "I see the hole where the bridge was so I backs way up, then I go very fast to jumps the hole, but she no makes it."

Joe Sr. died in his home of a heart attack a week after the court sent a Doctor in to check and see if he is able to travel to Washington to testify about what the Apalachin Gangland Convention was all about.

Shortly after Joe passed away Joey, his son, made the news one day when he took his sister, Angela, whom we knew quite well, to an Endicott jewelry store so that she could pick out a wedding ring. It seems that she was supposed to marry some guy from Detroit that she had never met. It was a prearranged marriage that was set up by her father which was common for some European cultures then.

Joey Barbara Jr

She had told us about this several times before but she also told us that she was in no way on board with it, at all. After Joey drove up to the store, she refused to get out of the car. Joey lost his temper and commenced to drag her out of the car.

She started screaming and then he supposedly slapped her. This brought the police but she would not press charges and she denied that her brother hit her, even though there were witnesses there that said differently. Soon after that Joey drove away with her in his car.

I do not know what happened with Angela after that. Right after Joey's father passed away, he sold his pre-hung door and window business and then quickly sold the family estate at a loss of about $120,000, then packed up and moved to Detroit.

Joey Barbara joined his father in-law Peter Vitale and his brother Peter in Detroit and formed the Tri-County Sanitation Corporation. According to Wikipedia accounts, this Detroit outfit would eventually gain a monopoly over the refuse business that would last for over thirty years.

It looks to me like Joey had this plan to move his family to Detroit in his head before his father died. With the money he left on the table in Endicott he had to have known that there were much greater financial opportunities available to him and his brother in D town. Wikipedia mentions his "father-in-law" but a marriage did not happen in New York State or it would have surely have been in the Endicott newspaper at that time.

My rather brief encounter with Joey Barbara led me to believe that he did not know that much about what his father's history really was, at least that is what I wanted to believe. Further research shows that Joey was entrenched in the Mafia before he even reached Detroit.

Joey forced himself out of the trash business when he was arrested in 1968 at the age of 36 for rape and extortion charges. Barbara was acquitted of the rape charges but was sentenced to a 7 to 20 year term for extortion. Joey was able to stay out of prison for several years by appealing his conviction but eventually had to serve the minimal sentence.

Then In 1979 he was arrested for income tax fraud. Barbara was sentenced to five years in 1980 for racketeering and probation violation. Joey did become a mafia mobster and is now in his eighties.

I tried a few times to make contact with Joey a few years after he moved to Detroit. I called Angelo who told me that he bought a Canada Dry Franchise someplace along the east coast but he said he was not sure where. Angelo must have been in contact with Joey and he was trying to steer me away from him because I told him that I thought he was in Detroit, Angelo said that he was not in Detroit anymore but that story was not true. I believe that this was at the time that Joey was fighting rape and extortion charges.

I finally got a call from some unknown man that told me in no uncertain terms that Joey did not want to talk with me. To say the least it was a kind of breathtaking experience to say the least so I gave up and did not know what his criminal record was at that time until recently.

Living In Upstate New York

This display using an Grumman aluminum canoe won a national first prize. Grumman loaned us fifteen canoes that we put in major super markets throughout the Rochester, NY.

When I was asked to join the new division in Rochester I was given a promotion to Executive Vice President of Sales and Marketing for Canada Dry Seven Up Bottling Company of Rochester New York.

The money that I spent on my expense account was never questioned. I spent a lot of money on the buyers that worked for all the major supermarkets.

Very soon I was able to get big sales promotions working in all the stores in our division, almost at will. In time I soon became the number four person in the entire corporation.

When we moved to Rochester a new production and distribution plant was already on the drawing boards that would replace the much older facility

Carl had originally purchased. The new plant was going to be built in Pittsford so we eventually moved into a new home in nearby Fairport-Perrington. The new plant would be located just five miles away via expressway which was very convenient for me. After a few years, in my new position within the company I had a lot more responsibility and with that came much more freedom to make major decisions for the Rochester division.

The Paratrooper

In addition to my many other duties including being in charge of selling to all the buyers of all the supermarket chains that were in our division, I was also in charge of six truck drivers and five salesmen. I hired Steven, a former paratrooper to be a truck driver after I checked him out with the US Army, they told me that he had a good record. He was a well built man that stood about five foot seven. He had just been married to a very pretty young Greek lady. She came with him on his interview with me, which I thought was a little unusual.

After about two months Steven was doing a fine job delivering our products. I held meetings once a month with the sales men and I thought that I should do something similar for the drivers as well.

To kick off this new approach I thought it would be nice to hold the meeting at a fine restaurant in nearby Pittsford. I told the owner of the restaurant that I wanted to use their private dining room for this special occasion.

It turned out to be a mistake on my part that I had an open bar in that private room. I asked the men to behave themselves in this upscale restaurant and arrive in a suit and tie. Everything went very well during and after dinner until we all heard a thunderous breaking of glass and loud screaming. It was coming from the main bar at the front of the building. We all went there to see what was happening when we saw Steven fighting with the bartender. The bar area had been about half full with patrons about one hour before, now it was completely empty. The bartender had Steven pushed to the back part of a booth that was across from the heavily damaged back bar.

There were parts of a very large broken mirror and a lot of broken liquor bottles on the floor.

Steven was trying to bite the bartender's hand when our guys traded places with the bartender. I told my guys to get a hold of each arm and leg and drag him onto the floor. He was fighting all our moves and he was yelling venomous nasty words. The bartender and now the owner, who were very upset, said that Steven was sitting alone in the booth and just threw two large heavy glass ashtrays at the back bar mirror and liquor shelves. The bartender said that Steven was like a crazed animal. All the patrons had run out the front door with some of the women screaming.

I told the owner, who was a very good customer of ours, that I would take care of everything and that I would return after we got Steven out of there. Our guys had Steven spread eagle and face down on the floor with one holding each arm and leg and one sitting on his back. "The paratrooper" was still yelling obscenities and struggling like a wildly. There was a small crowd of people outside looking in the front window. Luckily the front doors were wide enough for everybody to get him out to the sidewalk where my company station wagon was parked. Somehow we got him on the back floor of the car and we had two guys sitting on his still failing body.

I asked one of my drivers that knew Steven and his wife if we should take him to the hospital to be evaluated for possible psychiatric care as Steven was still yelling, struggling and kicking the inside of my door. His buddy, Jimmy Meralilo, calmly said "Nah, he will be OK after we get him home to his wife." All the way there I kept asking Jimmy if he was sure that it was a good idea to take Steven home because Steven was still putting up a fight. I asked, "What if he beats up his wife?" Jimmy just said the same thing. "He will be OK when he gets home." When we got to his apartment building, Steven had not stopped yelling and struggling. We all carried him up the stairs to the top of the second floor and stood him up. We were still holding on to both legs and arms and one man had his arms wrapped around Steven's chest from behind.

He was a total mess, with his face all bloody and his suit was now filthy and all torn up. I looked at Jimmy and he still said everything would be OK. The door opened with Steven's wife standing there in a white negligee, holding a frying pan in her left hand. All of a sudden Steven relaxed so that we could all let go. This mess of a man who was a fierce animal a few minutes before, said "I'm sorry" in a loud hoarse voice.

The angel dressed in white grabbed him by the arm and pulled him inside the apartment without saying a word and slammed the door. It was about 1:30 in the morning and we had lot of onlookers in the hallway watching us all the way back to my car. The following Monday I talked with Steven and he told me that it would never happen again. I warned him that if it did, I would have to fire him. I felt a little guilty providing the open bar.

Two months later I got a call from a bar owner that said one of my drivers was drunk and he was outside walking one of his customer's little dog. He said our driver made a delivery to him and the delivery truck was in front of his place. I took a warehouse man with me to drive the truck back to the plant.

We found Steven sitting at the bar telling stories about his being a paratrooper. My warehouse guy found the keys in the truck and took off for the plant. I walked up behind Steven and tapped him on the shoulder, not knowing what I was going to get in return. He turned and asked me what I was doing there. I told him that it was against the rules to be drinking on the job and he said he hadn't had a drink. I then said that the truck was gone and I would take him back to the plant. I helped him to my car and there was no trouble whatsoever. We didn't talk very much all the way back to the plant. I especially did not want to upset him in the condition he was in. I called his wife and told her the story and I told her that he was fired. She called me a few names and hung up. She got someone to come and get him and I thought that was that.

Two days later Steven and his wife came into our front lobby and asked to see the President, Joe Rapp. Soon they both went into Joe's office and that was when I got a call from the receptionist telling me what was going on. After a while Joe called me into his office where I found the Paratrooper and my boss Joe, a Marine crying because of Joe's father being an alcoholic. Joe, still whimpering, said he was going to overrule my firing of Steven and wanted me to give him a third chance. Steven's wife was very stoic and never said a word.

About three months later Joe burst into my office yelling very loudly that I fire that SOB immediately. I didn't even have to ask who it was, I somehow knew. Then I asked Joe what had happened. He said that when he was at the stop light up the street, when Steven came around the corner on three wheels in the big company truck and a whole bunch of cases and bottles came off the truck and almost hit him and his car. He said I had better get a crew up there and get the mess cleaned up before somebody got a flat tire. It sure could have been a lot worse but that was the end of the paratrooper working for the Rochester Canada Dry-Seven-up Bottling Company.

Joe Rapp, Jackie and their two children finally moved from their home in Couse Corners N. Y. to a beautiful home in an up-scale neighborhood in Rochester. Joe Rapp had been commuting between Rochester and Endicott to Couse Corners on a weekly basis for about three years.

This move soon led to another practical joke. Jan, who was Jackie's sister from Las Vegas, was visiting the Rapp's at their new home. She was there to help the Rapps decorate their two-story spacious ten room castle. I had only met Jan once a year before. She was a very attractive lady that was in her early forties.

I called the house to speak to Joe. I knew that Jan was there and she answered the phone. I asked for Mr. Rapp and she told me that he and his wife were out shopping and wouldn't be back for several hours. I told her that I was Claude Bronson, service manager from the New York Telephone Company, and we were doing our annual telephone line cleaning.

She politely asked me why this should affect the Rapps? I told her that "we use high pressure air to clean the dust out of our telephone lines, that increases the quality of our customers telephone conversations. Without our customers help, dust would come out of the phone receivers and may get all over the Rapp's nearby furniture and floors." "She asked me what she could do to prevent this dust problem." "I told her that all she had to do was to take the telephone receivers off the hook and put them into a paper bag, then put a rubber band around the open end to seal the bag around the receiver." She then told me that "this was the most ridiculous thing she had ever heard of and said that her telephone company in Las Vegas never did this kind of thing" but she said that "she will do this for her sister." I then told her that "our company was a little more advanced than her Las Vegas telephone company." I told her that she "could take the phone receivers out of the bags at 4:00 p.m."

It turned out that Jackie and Joe had been trying to call Jan to get some measurements for about two hours without any luck. Joe was furious by the time they reached their home. Joe asked Jan "why she was on the phone for so long." She told Joe and Jackie about the call from the telephone company. Joe saw one of his four phone receivers in a big grocery bag tied up with one of his neckties. Joe, not Jackie, got a big smile on his face and said "This was Ros, I know it is Ros that did this!" Then Jackie saw the receiver in the big bag and started to laugh. Jan unfortunately did not see any humor in this joke at all.

Joe Rapp and Jackie visited us many years later when we lived in Scottsdale. It was great to see and be with the person that was responsible for us eventually moving to Queen Creek.

One More Blizzard

On January 30, 1966 there was a very bad blizzard that our whole family was in after we visited our mother's homes in East Greenbush, NY. It was about noon when the snow started slowly falling as we left my mom's home to get on the New York State Thruway for a two hundred and seventeen mile journey home to Rochester. As the snow fall increased in volume and the wind increased as well we saw many cars that had slid off the Thruway and down embankments. Soon it was snowing so bad that it took us over six hours to go eighty miles.

There near Herkimer, NY, my wife and I, Mark, Matt, Cara Lee, & Kevin were marooned along with one-thousand others, scattered along that part of the Thruway when it closed for nearly five days. We wound up in a motel room from Sunday to Thursday. Talk about a close family.

I had twelve dollars and no credit cards in my wallet (I think that the only credit card back then was Diners Club and we were not members). Caroline's mom,

Rachel, sent us money via Western Union to a truck stop that was located about three hundred yards from our motel room. I believe that we all lived on the twelve dollars for a day and a half until Rachel's money got to us.

Junior Chamber Of Commerce

I was encouraged to become involved in my community so after we moved to our new home in Pittsford I found a group of men that lived in our new neighborhood that wanted to start a Junior Chamber of Commerce chapter. I was about three years younger than the thirty-year-old age limit that Junior Chamber of Commerce membership allowed when we started the Fairport-Perrington Junior Chamber of Commerce.

I was voted to be the master of ceremonies for our Charter banquet celebration dinner. It was a semi-formal event held in the grand ballroom of a large nearby hotel. Everybody that was anybody was invited to the dinner, including our county supervisor and his wife. Most of us, except me, all in our twenty's, were college grads. Most like me were in the upper tier of the companies they worked for. Our County supervisor and his wife were ancient, probably in their fifties, at least that was what I thought then.

The job of being the master of ceremonies included introducing our NY State JC President and I wanted to make a big impression on him...which I did, but not necessarily in a good way. I wanted to do something that everyone would remember, so.......I made a imitation stick of dynamite out of a paper towel cardboard tube covered with bright red paper, with a real piece of fuse about the thickness of a pencil inserted into the top of the tube.

After a very nice chicken dinner and after I introduced all the primary speakers, it was now time for me to introduce the JC

President. Our supervisor was seated on the dais and his wife was seated to my left at one of the front tables. There were about seventy-five people in the audience that fateful evening. My plan was very simple. I set the faux dynamite stick in front of me and say, "Before I introduce our special guest speaker, I would like to start his speech off with a bang." I had a blank pistol in my pocket. I lit the fuse and held my ears until the smoking sputtering fuse stopped. Then I carefully picked up the faux dynamite in one hand and shook it next to my face while pulling the blank pistol out of my pocket with the other hand, shooting the gun behind my back. BANG!....When this happened the supervisor's wife who was leaning back in her chair straining to see what was going to happen fell over backwards showing most of all her undergarments including her girdle, that was in fashion then, don't you know? Several people ran over to help the poor, very embarrassed lady up to her feet.

From the dais I apologized to her in a big way and then introduced the now flustered New York State JC President, which gave the last speech of the evening, that no one remembers. She kept her seat after his speech but seemed not in a very good mood. I hustled over to her after the ceremony was completed which was about the same time my wife and other JC members got there. My wife Caroline said, "Ros, great presentation! Was this lady a part of it?" Then the now irate lady and her smiling County Supervisor husband made a determined retreat to the door. The next day I sent a letter to her telling her how sorry I was for everything that happened.

The next year we had our first birthday Annual Charter Dinner, the same place, the same cast but fewer people. I was the master of ceremonies again and I thought I would personally invite our supervisor and his wife to this celebration. It was an election year for our supervisor and they said, they would let bygones be bygones and that they would be there with bells on or something to that affect. One of the highlights of the evening was to be my presentation to the supervisors wife for bring such a good sport the previous year. I came up with a great idea, or so I thought, that the gift be a live full size rabbit that would be replaced by a beautiful expensive necklace after the laughter stopped.

I really don't remember much about the rest of the evening but I clearly will never forget what happened after I gave her the gift wrapped box, with holes in it, that held the big white rabbit. She was wearing a fancy blue velvet dress and when she opened the box at her table she let out a, very good sport lady, "Oh isn't this cute" and held the rabbit close to her chest.

When I offered to exchange the gift she refused and was gushing to everyone that came over to pet the now very frightened rabbit how happy she was to receive such a wonderful gift. This was a dinner dance and the three piece band was about to play when I noticed a very strange look on the supervisor's wife's face and her husbands face was somewhat distorted as well. It seems that the rabbit peed all over the top of her dark blue velvet dress while she was holding it and she refused to hand it off but still kept the rabbit clutched to her as the big wet stain grew along with a whole bunch of white rabbit hair that came loose with everybody petting it. She and hubby then left abruptly again without explanation.

As JCs we did a great deal of very good things within our community. Many of our projects revolved around all things to help children. While serving on the board I was given the job of providing a program for our regular monthly membership meetings. I was able to line up speakers that were in the news at that time. Some of them were in the slightly radical persuasion category which always drew more of the community to those meetings so that they could hear for themselves what makes these people tick. It was the sixties and we had civil rights and Vietnam issues to hear about. With those people the question and answer part that followed their speeches were always very entertaining.

Rochester, NY was a very special city back then. Eastman Kodak was the biggest employer, with Bausch & Lomb, Xerox, Western Union and French's Mustard following. When we lived there, Rochester was at it's pinnacle. Since we moved from there in 1969 the population has declined each year due to loss of industry and jobs. The University of Rochester is now its largest employer. We traveled through there a few years ago and it was sad to see how it has transformed into a very less robust place than when we lived there.

CHAPTER 2

A STOP ON OUR WAY TO SAN FRANCISCO

Now at about thirty-one years old, the challenge in my present job was gone. Joe Rapp and Carl Touhey were not moving out of the way to enable further advancement; it was a closed corporation, so we, as a family were ready for a new adventure. Caroline's uncle and his wife would visit us every summer and always brought pictures of their lives in Tucson, AZ. They showed us pictures of them watering their lawn on Christmas Day and other beautiful scenes throughout their winter that was so foreign to us in upstate NY. Our whole family of four children are outdoor types that liked to hike, hunt, fish, camp and ski. Caroline's Uncle Clifford told us that in Arizona you can do all those things almost all year around. Although snow skiing is available only in the winter months. Because of what we heard I took out a Phoenix newspaper subscription. In one of the issues we saw an ad about Mary Moppets Day Care Center franchise.

Rochester was known as the "land of the white clouds". Sometimes there were months that went by without a day of sunshine. In the summer it would be normal that there were only three, maybe four, good weekends for outdoor activities.

I had an international Seven Up convention scheduled for February 1968 to be held in San Francisco. I was to be a small part of the international convention that required me to be there two days prior to the convention. I was interviewed on camera about a new product that we had test marketed for Seven Up in Rochester that would be launched at the convention. I took Caroline with me and we stopped on the way in Phoenix to visit with the Mary Moppets Day Care

Center people. What we saw we liked and then continued on to San Francisco. After doing a considerable amount of research we decided after our meeting with Jerry Spresser, President of Mary Moppets that we would indeed buy a franchise from him and move to Phoenix.

We were going from the land of white clouds and blizzards to the land of sunshine and warmth. Okay, sometimes it gets really HOT, but it is a dry heat after all. At least that is what everyone that visited Arizona told us before we moved there said. The other nine months is mostly very nice except for about three weeks of winter when the temperature gets way down to the sixties during the day. Please don't forget it is a dry heat in the summer.

Easter 1969

Extraordinary Scene At Church

In July 1969, Two days before we left Pittsford, we had what you might call a "Spiritual Awakening" that would be one of two more that has affected me to the core of my beliefs. Because we were headed into the caring for children business, it was like a hint from God as to how we should treat all children and that we should teach them every day in a kind and gentle manner.

Pittsford was a fairly new upscale community then and it had a new Catholic church that was very avant garde for that time. Some of the members of our parish would take in disadvantaged children from the urban Rochester area for a portion of each summer, but it seemed that each one of those that shared some of their good life would try to "out Christian" the other by taking in more than one or two and by taking in three or four and so on.

Something really special happened on a Sunday when our family went to the earlier children's Mass. We always spread our children out in the pew between us because they would sometimes get rambunctious with each other during the celebration of the then Latin Mass. The early morning sunlight shone brilliantly through the stained glass windows onto the altar area like something out of a surreal religious painting.

Our celebrant that morning was a visiting Jesuit priest that was dressed in all white vestments except for his brown Jesuit hood that laid down onto his vestments behind his head. The church was set up in a way that had all the pews in a close semi-circle around the altar with three marble steps leading up to the main altar. The priest was a young soft spoken man that had pure white hair and soft pink albino eyes. Just before the mass started he asked all the children, that wanted, to come up and sit on the steps at the altars feet so that he could talk to them during the mass. Without hesitation about twenty to thirty children from all over the church quietly assembled all around the priest displaying a mixture of ages and color that could not have been placed any better than those in a Norman Rockwell painting.

This priest really had everyone's attention that morning. Even the two youngest remaining in our pew with us were quiet. The sun was shining in on this wonderful scene in a most glorious fashion, a mixture of quietly attentive, Asian, brown, black, white, some very young, some older children, listening as the albino Priest began teaching these kids all about the mass and the teachings of Christ. Everyone else in the church that witnessed this "happening" had tears streaming down their faces, including us. Even though this happened some 44 years ago I still get emotional as I write about it. This Priest conversed with the kids as if we were not there. It was a joyous event that had the children asking questions throughout the celebration of the mass. There was communion, there was the collection, but in my mind all that was a blur and it was the teacher that divinely inspired us. I believe many others that shared this "happening" were overjoyed to remember the teachings of our lord Jesus Christ. It has reinforced what we would continue to do in all the years since that day but I had not realized this until I started writing about this wonderful spiritual memory.

Night Before We Left Pittsford

Our neighbors, the Heislers and the Smiths with their dog Victory. Top row in the VW van is Cara, a friend, and Kevin. Next row down, Harry Heisler, Mark, a friend, Matthew. Caroline is behind Victory and I am holding him so he wouldn't bite me.

A few weeks before this picture was taken little Harry got stuck in a small cave that the kids had dug in the woods next to our home. Caroline was away shopping and I was mowing the lawn when I heard the boys calling for me to, get Harry out! Harry's head and one arm were sticking out but the rest of him was buried. I ran to get a piece of plywood to put above him so that the top of the cave would not bury his head. I told my son to go across the street and get Harry's mom. She is the one smiling (thank God these people are moving) in the upper right in the picture. She ran back to her house to call the Bushnell Basin Fire Volunteer Department which was about a mile away. I stayed in place to protect Harry who was not the least bit upset until the firemen got there. We had a two rail split rail fence that was about three feet high. When the firemen pulled up the first thing they did was cut both rails of the fence with their chain saw, which they could have stepped over, then they ran up to the accident scene that was about 30 feet from the fence. The three firemen carefully dug Harry out of there just as my wife got home. By this time there were about 40 people watching and she asked what was going on. We will never forget little Harry Heisler who was thankfully unscathed except for his very dirty clothes.

Go West Young Man

My wife and I were in our early thirties when our family moved from a suburb of Rochester New York in July 1969 first to Phoenix and then to Scottsdale, Arizona. Our oldest of four children was ten and our youngest was four. We were involved in the Scouts in Rochester and we continued when we got settled in Scottsdale. Caroline was a Brownie leader and I was a Cub Scout and Webelos leader. Caroline became a Girl Scout Leader later in Scottsdale as our daughter grew older.

We sold our home and almost everything except our furniture. We then hopped into our new VW seventy horsepower bus with no air conditioning and headed west. Our trip took us from Rochester to Cleveland, Columbus, Louisville, Nashville, Memphis, Little Rock, Dallas, El Paso, Deming New Mexico and then on to the Promised Land.

We stopped at about seven or more Holiday Inns coming across the country, taking our time and seeing the sights as we went. The highlight of our trip was our stop at Six Flags Over Texas which was fun for everyone. It wasn't until we got near El Paso that we really felt how hot it was going to be in July in the Southwest. Our last stop before getting to Phoenix was in the Holiday Inn in Deming, New Mexico, which was a lovely place with a lot of oil rigs pumping oil and natural gas burn off pipes puffing black smoke but the real kicker was that there was a very unpleasant sulfur odor permeating all around the motel. Even the swimming pool water smelled strongly of sulfur.

We started early the next day for the dry heat country of Arizona. On the way we had to stop a couple of times to get bags of ice that we put on the floor of the van for the feet of all the passengers but, of course, none for the driver. By the time we neared the Salt River Bridge, near the last Holiday Inn we would visit for some time to come, it was one hundred and ten degrees, and the dry heat blowing in our faces from the open windows was hardly refreshing. I told my passengers at least Phoenix has a river running through it, or so our gas station road map showed us.

It was indeed disappointing to everybody that afternoon to find out that there was not a drop of water flowing in that river, nothing there but, what must have been very hot rocks down there as we drove over the bridge and I wondered out loud if there was a drought here or something. We later found out that there is rarely water in that river. We were told by a grinning Holiday Inn clerk that it only runs when there is excessive amounts of rainfall all at once but with a yearly rainfall average of around seven or eight inches, that doesn't happen very often. He went on to say that the water is held back by reservoir lakes many miles away in the mountains north of Phoenix.

Our furniture was scheduled to arrive by Mayflower (not the ship but it took almost as long!) a week after we got to Phoenix. We stayed at the Holiday Inn by the Airport for that week while we looked for an apartment. We found one in four days and slept on the floor there until we found out much to our dismay that our furniture would not be in Phoenix for another seven or eight days. By the time we were getting used to sleeping on the floor, our furniture showed up.

When we contacted the President of Mary Moppets Day Care Centers Company, Jerry Spresser, who told us that the construction of our school was not completely finished. He asked me if he could meet with us that day because he said that he had another possible option he wanted to discuss with us. We were hoping that our school would be ready for us to open for the September school year and we hoped that there was something that he might be able to do for us.

Incredible good luck and another blessing we would have in our lives was about to happen again. We went to the Mary Moppets headquarters to talk with Jerry who had a big smile on his face when we went into his office. He explained that the school in operation right next door to the headquarters had been open for about three months and was owned and operated by two retired school teachers, a husband and wife. They had been through most of the hottest part of the Arizona summer and did not think that they wanted to continue in the Day Care business. They wanted to sell it just for what they paid for the franchise, even though they already had some students in place and had good enrollment prospects for September which was about a month away. Jerry took care of everything and within a week we owned Mary Moppets of Scottsdale. As it turned out we had a full school by the end of that September. It could not have worked out any better. It was a win/win for everybody.

Teaching

I left a great job with a large company with very high rank. I would soon find my wife and I in the March 1970 issue of Fortune magazine with a story that had to do with the burgeoning franchise market. We then found ourselves on the cover of Franchise magazine. Fortune Magazine sent a photographer to take pictures of us for two days. It said in the March 1970 issue: "Alden and Caroline Rosbrook opened their Mary Moppets Day Care School in Scottsdale, Arizona last August. Alden, thirty-two---or "Uncle Roz" as the kids call him----was vice president in charge of sales for Canada Dry and Seven-Up's Rochester, New York, bottling plant." In an article called Eight Lives fulfilled by Franchising.

With the Mary Moppets national Franchise headquarters next door to us and within a short time we became the training facility for the Mary Moppets Day Care Corporation. After a while I was asked to manage another Mary Moppets franchise facility that was about twenty miles away. I included a Montessori teaching program their that eventually became very successful.

Owning and operating these day care centers proved to be immensely rewarding, more so with working with young children than financially. I took children from the ages of six to eleven on monthly field trips to the Zoo, dairy farms, restaurant kitchens, botanical gardens, short desert hikes, soft drink bottling plants, etc. One day I had about 10 children in our company van when I stopped at a nearby photo-mat booth in a shopping center to drop off film to be processed. These booths were a about double the size of a telephone booth. I asked the your lady that was the lone attendant if I could bring over about twenty of our students for a tour of her facility. Her mouth opened in amazement and she told me that she was not qualified to allow that. I then told her that I was only kidding.

Lois & Her Young Lady Teachers

Lois Markis

Lois is a wonderful "CRAFTY" person who is also a kind, soft talking, loving teacher that went skydiving on her seventieth birthday.

We were very fortunate to have a Mormon family living nearby. There were three young ladies in that family that we immediately hired who also had friends that needed work. Eventually we had mostly Mormon ladies working for us, some part time and some full time.

In addition I hired a lady that had a vast amount of experience in teaching arts and crafts by the name of Lois Markis, who became our head teacher who was the best possible person to head up our preschool program.

We continue to have a relationship with her and her family to this day.

We enjoyed the very best team of people to help us work with and teach our children ages from 3 years and up. I think it was a very wonderful experience for everyone. In addition to our Mormon ladies we also had four young ladies from the Scottsdale School District Hero program for seniors who received school credit working for us during a part of their school day. Lois created a combo arts-crafts-foreign foods luncheon every month. An example would be having the children make Chinese hats, clothes, paper table cloths, drawing Chinese letters and art on them, even teaching the children a Chinese song and then winding up the project with a Chinese luncheon. We did this using a lot of different countries as our focus for this program, like Russia, Italy, Poland, Greece, France, Spain/Mexico, Ireland, Japan, England, Norway, Scotland, Germany, etc. We always tried to give our children clients a chance to exercise their minds, their bodies and feed them healthy wholesome foods and snacks that they liked every day.

We tried very hard to make sure all enjoyed their stay with us. To do this we had a team of people that liked their work and liked to provide learning experiences that was fun for everyone. On our families children's days off from their school they would often help us by working with our preschoolers in their classes.

Getting In The Headlines

Five months after we opened our Mary Moppets Day Care Center we had a visit at our Phoenix apartment from one of our son Mark's best friends from his elementary school, who stopped by with his mother. It was a beautiful February Saturday with the temperature in the 70s. I was about to take our three oldest children on a short hike and I asked Mark's friend if he would like to go along with us. He asked his mom who said it was OK. Little did we all know that this short hike would last for over eight wet cold and very frightening and dangerous hours.

I was told that there was a great hiking trail going up to the top of the "head" of Camelback Mountain which wasn't that far from our apartment so I thought it would be fun to investigate what it looked like. I did not think that we would be hiking the whole trail but just go up it a short distance. Mark and his friend were twelve, Matt was ten and Cara Lee was six years old.

The hike that day was supposed to be from the parking lot up to the start of the trail which was about a forth of a mile away. Right after we parked Mark and his friend started running up towards the trail-head. I hollered to them to wait for us there. It was about 1:00 p.m. when we got to the trail-head because of young Cara walking slowly.

The boys had not waited and instead had climbed up a crevasse towards the top of the camel's head that was about 500 feet above us. They were using a garden hose that someone had fastened there and by this time were about 100 feet up the very steep slope of mountain from we were. I thought to myself, "What kind of a trail was this?"

I told them to stop and come back down but they had reached a small plateau that was just above where the hose had been tied. Mark told me that they were too scared to go back down that way because it was too steep and it was almost perpendicular to the ground. I had two young smaller children in tow which made it harder for me to get a better view of where they were situated. I told them not to climb any farther but to carefully look for a trail going down the other side. I immediately saw them heading directly for a cliff that dropped off 100 feet to the rocks below. I told them to stop and go back up about 20 yards where I could still see them and asked them to sit down while I called the police.

The nearest house was about 100 yards away. I carried Cara and Matt was able to keep up with us on our way to the house. Luckily someone was home and they called the police for me. It was nearly 2:30 p.m. when one Phoenix policeman showed up. He was dressed in his blue street uniform and dress shoes that was not really meant for mountain climbing. He locked his gun belt in his trunk and said he was going to try and reach them. After a half hour he called it quits and called the Phoenix Fire Department. We kept calling up to the kids reassuring them that we would get them down soon. In Arizona the sun goes down at about 5:30 in February and it gets colder as it gets darker.

Two Phoenix fire department trucks showed up a little after 4:00 p.m.. Two of the younger firemen tried to get up there with their big boots on but made little progress. We hadn't noticed that heavy clouds had moved over the mountain and beyond and it started to sprinkle.

A lady from the nearby house came over to me and asked if she could take care of my two kids while the rescue went on. I gladly accepted her offer. The kids on the mountain only had sweat shirts and Levis on and they were huddled together up against a big rock. The temperature continued to drop as the rainfall increased. A fireman gave me a fireman's rain jacket and a helmet to wear. By this time they brought in a truck that had big lights on it that lit up the whole mountain side.

We could clearly see the boys who were now yelling that they were getting really cold. The media showed up, both newspaper and TV. It was extremely frightening for me realizing how much danger the boys were in, how close they were to us and how so many people were able see them in the falling rain but there was no one able to get to them, so far. I asked the police officer to call my wife and give them directions to where we were.

It was very dark and still raining and getting colder when eight members of a volunteer mountain rescue team showed up. We were able to see them in the fireman's flood lights all tethered together using a different route that would eventually take them to the boys who were screaming now.

They reached them at about 8:00 p.m. and took them down the other side of the mountain where the mothers were stationed with a police officer.

It took them about a half hour to get down to their moms and a heated police cruiser where they took their clothes off and then wrapped up in blankets. I was told later by a paramedic that their body temps were in the mid eighties and were very close to being in critical danger. I complained to the policeman, asking him why the mountain rescue team wasn't called in after his first attempts failed. The miserable weather made it very hard for me to continue this conversation as I was now soaking wet and very cold.

I gathered up my two younger children after being told that the rescued boys were fine and headed home. When I got there I found the two boys eating toasted cheese sandwiches and sipping some steaming tomato soup with their mothers and still shivering. Each mother was sitting very close to their sons. The lord was with them and us that day, for sure.

My boys and a couple of our neighbor children got in the news again about two years later when we lived in Scottsdale. We lived about a quarter of a mile from The Arizona Canal located at McDonald Drive just west of Hayden Road. It gets drained once a year for repairs. My boys and their friends went into the empty muddy canal to look for "treasure"..I was home when our youngest came rushing in the front door yelling "You'll never guess what we found?" It was a 50 cal. military machine gun and a lot of 50 caliber bullets in metal belts.

They had a hard time getting these things out of the canal and away from seeing eyes from the nearby vehicle traffic that they feared might bring the cops down on them. My son wanted me to bring the car over on Hayden Road near our home so that they could load the "Treasure" in the trunk of my car.

All the things were very muddy as were the treasure hunters. When we got home they hosed everything off so that I could take some pictures. Then I called the newspaper, the Scottsdale Progress and the Scottsdale Police. The reporter got there first and took pictures of the boys and their find. Just as the reporter was leaving the police showed up. We found out afterward that the machine gun and ordinance was traced to Williams Air Force Base. Someone evidently tossed the stuff off the bridge and into the canal where it was found. My boy(s) made the front page again only this time under much better circumstances.

We continued to be involved in Scouting, Caroline as a Girl Scout leader and I as an assistant Boy Scout leader. I was heavily involved in Little League and coached Pop Warner Football. Now looking back at those times we now realize how much of our spare time was spent being involved in our kids programs.

All four were in Little League, the three boys in football, Kevin with Pueblo School band in the trombone section, Cara with Ballet, Girl Scouts, and playing the flute, and Matt a tuba player with the school marching band. Caroline played the piano and the clarinet and was a great help to her children by influencing their musical artistry.

It would be many years later when our son Matt would tell us that he did not read music very well (me to) and he did not play the Sousa very well because of that. He told us that he would just march along pushing whatever valve he thought might do the trick. I imagine that there might be many other children that did the same thing after hearing some of the middle school concerts I have attended. To be honest the only musical instrument I can play is the radio. I coached on whatever team one or more of my children were on. My daughter Cara was the first girl to play baseball and the first girl to hit a home run, in the East Scottsdale Little League. She had been in ballet since she was three and continued her training at the North Carolina University School of ballet and the Boston School of Ballet in the summers. She finally was hired by the Barry Ashton Dance group at the age of seventeen and finished her high school education while on tour. Her dance group toured throughout Europe and in Germany they got standing ovations when they danced to Beethoven's Fifth. The Germans thought it was wonderful for them to include the masters music in their routine.

Pop Warner Football

Jack Evans and I coached Little League as well as Pop Warner football together. Jack was an amazing coach that led in a laid-back way. Most of his assistant coaches had their children on his teams. The Marauders was truly a great team.

In one league championship football game the ambient temperature was in the eighties and it was pouring rain. Both teams warmed up in this downfall and when the game was about to start the head umpire came over to Jack and said that the game should be canceled.

Jack Above 60. Me Above 30, Son Kevin 72

Where we all came from we played football in all kinds of inclement weather all the time. Jack asked me and the other coaches if we should play and we all agreed that we were ready to play. Then our opponent coaches came over to us and said that the kids would get hurt playing in these conditions. We would not give in and the game began under protest. Well, all the boys on both teams never had so much fun playing football. Everybody was soaking wet including all the many people that were there still watching the game with us. They all stayed throughout because it was so warm. By the way.... we won that one too.

Under Jack's leadership everyone on the team had fun and we were very privileged to have excellent high winning seasons to boot. We had a very talented quarterback that made a big difference. I was in charge of defense, Jack on offense. After almost every game most all the coaches and I would go to Jacks home and talk about the entire game much to the consternation of Jack's wife, Dawn. What a great way for our kids who won under no unneeded pressure. A great concept! This was also true working with Jack's on his very successful Little League teams.

Picking Grapes

One day I noticed an ad in the Arizona Republic newspaper that told about being able to pick your own grapes at Power

Ranch in Queen Creek. I had to look on a map to find out where Queen Creek was. It was Sunday, it was a nice day, so I asked everyone in our family if they would like to go to Queen Creek and pick some seedless table grapes. The ad said they cost thirty cents a pound and it was on a ranch. Wow! Everyone thought that it was a great idea. We were soon on our way and we were all anxious to pick grapes. The ad said that we didn't need to bring anything, everything needed to pick and pack all the grapes would be supplied. We found out very soon you must have a strategy when you do these sort of things but we would find this out the hard way.

We finally got there after about a one and half hour car ride. We were all excited because we had never done this kind of grape thing before. The grapes were in large and beautiful bunches. The man there gave us all grape cutting scissors and a basket and all six of us went in all different directions. Caroline and I soon realized that one person could pick a lot of grapes very quickly and we went off to find our four children who ranged in age from 8 to 14. In less than a half hour we had handpicked nearly fifty pounds of grapes that we now owned! There was a sign there that was pointed out to me, after I discovered that we had way too many grapes, with words to the effect...whatever you pick, you own... after you pay for them, that is.

On the trip back home we had a lot of time to try and figure out a way to use all these grapes before they went bad. Suggestions from the peanut galley included; (1) Eat them every day, (2) Freeze them (now we know that this is an option), (3) Make raisins, (4) Make wine, (5) Make grape jelly, (6) Sell them to Basha's Grocery Stores, or (7) Put them in plastic baggies, go door to door and sell them for twenty-five cents a bag. The vote was unanimous! The kids decided to sell them door to door for twenty-five cents a bag and keep the money. We lived in a patio home complex that had a high density of families in a small area so it did not take them long to sell about forty pounds of those grapes in about two or three hours. They all made about ten dollars each with our eight year old boy selling the most, the oldest selling the least and Cara coming in second place in sales.

One of my attempts at a grand gesture happened in 1982, a few days before Valentine's Day, I bought a Chevy Camero to surprise my wife aka Big Red. She was working for Adrian Arpel Cosmetics in Goldwater's Beauty Salon located in Fiesta Mall in Mesa. I bought the car at Brown & Brown Chevrolet from a female sales person. I asked her to deliver the car to Caroline while she was working at Goldwater's on Valentine's Day.

Kevin "Clowning" Cara & Jimmy

This is the only picture I could find of "Tis Red" because we had so much trouble with it from day one. They had to replace the rear end two times and it had to be completely repainted because the Chevy plant where it was made had a defective paint sprayer the day "Tis Red" was partially painted.

The shop was quite busy when the sales lady walked in. She told Caroline that her husband had bought her a Valentine present and it was parked right outside the front door. Then the woman became very emotional and started to cry, which really piqued the interest of most all the patrons and employees in the salon. With that drama, almost everybody left the shop en mass, with some of woman's hairdos not completely finished and some of the patrons still in their beauty salon capes and aprons. The parade ended just outside the front door where the new Camero was parked.

There was "Tis Red" shinning like a jewel in the Arizona sun and a bunch of women saying "Oh, my God!" and other words of wonderment. By that time the sales lady had composed herself and was able to hand Caroline the keys to her brand new car. It was the only car that I ever bought that people would come up and ask what it was. The only identifying mark on the car was the small name Camero on the lower back trunk area.

Caroline found out very soon that owning and driving a red "sporty" car had it's drawbacks because she was pulled over several times by the various police agencies. Some were because she might have been driving too fast.....yes all were because she was driving too fast. She said that the car made her drive fast.

Work That Paid A Lot But.........

We sold our day care center in 1976 after we found out during the recession of 1973-1975 that the major driver of our Arizona economy was Motorola. During that time period Motorola laid off over 30,000 employees and even that number was in dispute by many Motorola employees as being too low of a number. Our business catered to households with both parents working full time. While we weathered the economic downturn I had to find other work in order to keep the day care center open and food on the table. We lost about two thirds of our customers in a very short time because of the layoffs.

I was still involved with the East Scottsdale Little League when we met a couple whose child was on my team along with one of our children. We became good friends. Joe (still another Joe in our lives) was an electronics engineer for Motorola who secretly owned an electronics assembly company on the side. The person that ran the company for him, John Swatic, was a man that that brought his family from Oklahoma to Arizona who did not have a job set up before moving here. He had worked in an automobile dealership parts department that did not pay enough to support his family. When he came to Arizona he looked for a better job than what was available in Tulsa. He was told that Motorola had many good paying jobs and he should go there to look for work. His story is somewhat amazing in that he not only got work at Motorola but he found ways to do his job that made him the best in his field, even though he had absolutely no previous knowledge in that field.

His wife had found some part time work right after they arrived from Oklahoma but it was not enough for the family to live on, so the pressure was on for John to get a good paying job. He went to Motorola and found out that they were looking for printed circuit board designers. He did not really know what that was but by asking questions from people in the Motorola building he gained enough information about the necessary talking points to approach the head of the PCB (printed circuit board) design department. In those days, before Human Resources Departments existed, in most cases the various department heads did the hiring and the firing of their own personnel. It was so in this particular department. He told the interviewer that he had a lot of experience from working at a PCB design company in Tulsa, using a name he found beforehand that did this type of work. The department head asked John if he would do a test design for him and John said that would be fine, knowing full well he had no idea how he was going to do it. The man said that he would have one hour to do the test. He then took John into a large room with a lot of men working at big art tables using rulers and straight edges and so forth. He had him sit at an empty table right among a bunch of guys that, very fortunately for John, knew how to design printed circuit boards. John proceeded to set up the work on his table the way he saw the others had done. One of the men smiled at John and so he went over to this friendly guy and asked him if he could help him get started. He did this over and over again until it all started to make sense to him. With this man's help John was finished well within the allotted time frame. He took his work back to the department head who told him that he had done a good job and then asked John to fill out an employment application.

Not knowing anything about electronics, John immediately bought a paperback book that showed what all the electronic components were and what function they did. With help from that little book and what little knowledge he had about the job, he was hired and he ultimately went on to be the fastest PCB designer in Motorola. John was not encumbered with all the rules of PCB designing that his new peers had. He just plowed ahead using his own method, getting the job done much faster.

Joe, as a Motorola department head, relied heavily on the PCB design department and soon found out who this new star was. It wasn't long before Joe hired John to be in charge of his outside company and even gave him a piece of it, even though if Motorola ever found out about what was being planned they both would have been fired. Joe would then be in a position to send his own company design work whenever his Motorola designers were overloaded, which happened a lot of times.

One day Joe asked me about what sales and/or marketing experience I had. With that, I gave him a quick verbal resume. In previous conversations I had told Joe that I was not happy at the company where I was working while Caroline was running the Day Care Center. It was not very challenging and I was not making enough money. Joe told me to go see a man he knew that ran an electronics production and manufacturing company by the name of John Swatic. At that time I did not know that Joe owned that company. I told Joe that I did not know very much about electronics and he said that it might not make a difference. The company really needed a salesman and he would pay me much more than I was presently making. I went to see who I thought was the owner with a large degree of trepidation, knowing full well that not knowing that much about what I was expected to sell would be a giant challenge that would be hard to overcome. I was taken to John Swatic's office as soon as I got there and got a warm reception from him. I then felt more comfortable than I thought I would. John began telling me all about the company. I thought before he went too far I might as well tell him how little I knew about the electronics manufacturing world.

He then told me his incredible story about how he got his job at Motorola and then he handed me the same book he had used to understand the basics of electronics. I was hired that day and I started as a electronics manufacturing and fabricating salesman after I gave two weeks' notice at the company I was working for. With that little book I took a crash course on all of the basic things I should know about things electronic.

I also got hold of a book, from where I do not remember, that listed all the companies in the Phoenix metro area that dealt in electronics manufacturing. I never knew that there were so many of these kinds of companies here and all the information that a salesman needed was in my hands. Every buyer that I met seemed to want to provide work for my new company so things started out very well. I did run into two or three jobs that were way over what our company could do but I found places or people that knew how to do the work and I got the jobs any way, and my company made a good profit too.

One of these jobs had to do with fabricating a titanium steel nose cone for a weather gathering information rocket. I knew immediately that this job was something beyond what our company would be able to accomplish. All I did was look through the yellow pages and I found a company on the west side of Phoenix that might just be able to do that type of work. The weather-related rocket company gave me a set their plans. After I left I cut out their names from the plans and drove to the steel fabricating facility. I met with one of their engineers and he assured me that they could build this nose cone which even had a door for discharging a parachute. He gave me a tour of his plant that made me very impressed. I asked him to give me a bid, that included a guarantee, and after a week I was on my way with my bid. It all worked out without a hitch and my company made a three thousand dollar profit.

Another coup that had a great deal of incredible Irish Luck attached to it had to do with a very special camera. When I was looking for companies that might need electronics work to be contracted out, I saw a USGS sign on a building in Tempe and I thought that I would go in there to see what they did because it was not listed in the Metro Phoenix electronics manufacturers book I had. It turned out to be the U.S. Geological Survey Arizona Water Science Center. I asked one of the guys sitting at a desk nearest the front door if they might need our company's services. He told me that there was a USGS guy in the back office from Flagstaff that just might need our help.

The man took me to the back room where there were three men and in the center of the room was a black object on a large table that was about three feet long, 2 feet wide and 2 feet tall. After I was introduced, the man in charge asked me if we could design a printed circuit board based on a PCB that was located in the camera, that was on the table. The man then told me that the USAF gave it to them and it was a camera out of a jet reconnaissance plane that took real time photos of the ground below. He said that it was used in Vietnam. With this camera the pilot could see real time on a screen in front of him what was on the ground. This formally top secret camera saw warm objects even if they were under cover in the jungles allowing him to see troops or vehicles. He then would call in fighter planes that were on station above him to strafe or bomb, depending on what he saw.

The camera had four lenses that would rotate at a speed commensurate with what speed the jet was flying at. All these USGS representatives were laid-back kind of folks and easy to talk with. I told them that our company could do just about everything, as I did with all other prospects, because I knew our people could sort it out back at the plant. The USGS boss told me that he would give us the job of converting the PCB from taking pictures at jet speeds down to propeller driven or helicopter speeds if my price was at or under $5000.00. Otherwise it would have to go out for bid. The USGS wanted this camera to be used around the San Francisco bay area to find violators that were putting illegal waste fluid discharges into the bay area waters.

I took the camera back to our shop and everybody, including John, could not believe their eyes. The USGS guys gave me a giant Texas Instrument Company book that went along with the camera and a sheet showing what they wanted us to do. The book was about 2' X 1' X 3" thick. The word "SECRET" was overwritten with unclassified on its cover. Inside the camera was a PCB that was about 8" square. We had three engineers in our company and they were all there, standing around this thing scratching their heads. The Texas Instrument book was full of schematics, specifications and nomenclature that did not give them a clue as to how to convert the PCB into what was needed.

By this time I knew that the real owner of this company was Joe, my friend that worked for Motorola. I called him at work and asked him if he knew any engineers that had previously worked for Texas Instruments before working with Motorola. He told me that he knew one, a German, and he gave me his name and his work telephone number. Joe told me not to mention his name but to tell him that I got his number from my boss, John. When I called this man he immediately said that he had worked on that very same project and that he was familiar with the PCB. He said he could do the job of designing a new PCB in about one week. All we would have to do was construct the board and install it in the camera.

To the German it was a piece of cake. He told me that he would need $1000.00 after he finished his drawings. We could get the board done in about a week and our people would load it in a half a day. I called the guy at USGS and told him that we could do the job for $5000.00 and we would deliver the camera to Flagstaff as he had requested. He had a man hand deliver the purchase order the next day and we were off to the races. About five weeks later and after we delivered the camera to Flagstaff I got a call from the USGS guy telling me the camera worked fine!

A few months after this everything in our company would change in a very big way. I ran into an entrepreneur that asked me if we could duplicate a video game called Pong and then put this video game into a table that could be used in a bar or restaurant as a table. Of course I told him we could do it but it might take some time to come up with a price. At that time it was not against the law to duplicate a video game as long as the printed circuit board was quite a bit different from the original PCB. I got my hands on an original Pong board and without a contract of any kind we began the process of removing all the integrated circuits from the board in order to re engineer another one to do the job.

Our engineers and John redesigned a new board that was very different from the original. This took about one month of almost around-the-clock tedious work. John and another engineer then designed a table that the game would fit in that had a coin mechanism built in. It was very difficult to make a stylish small table that could hold a TV monitor with all the necessary controls for two people to play the game, the coin mechanism and a speaker but they did it. I was responsible for running down all the parts that would be needed as soon as the table and PCB was designed.

The entrepreneur wanted exclusive rights to the table and our company would still be able to sell another version for the regular upright video game business. We would sell the entrepreneur the machines for about $800.00. He would then sell the machines for about $1600.00 to people that would buy them already placed in locations. The location owner would get 40% of the money that the machine took in and the investor would get the remaining 60%. The people that placed the machines would get $150.00 per location. Everybody made money, including me @10% or $80.00 per machine.

When John hired me I was given a salary, plus 10% of the gross dollars that I generated. When production got rolling I was making more than anybody in the company until all the costs of the supplies needed to make the games was covered. In the beginning I was making up to $2000.00 a week. It was a little freaky for me when John's wife, the bookkeeper, would come out of her office waving my check over her head and telling everybody how much I made that week-- and that I was going to buy drinks for everybody after work.

When the start-up money was paid off, John started making big bucks too. He bought a new truck with a camper on the back. With the money rolling in and him making more than me, even though my check was getting up to nearly $3000.00 a week, John and his wife decided to take a vacation to Yellowstone Park. This little vacation would change our lives yet again.

Joe, the real owner of the company, now had a chance to go over his company's books for the very first time, and he saw that John was paying his wife as much as Joe was making out of the company he founded. He also told me that there were a lot of other discrepancies in the books that he did not like. John had hired a couple of his other relatives when things really got rolling. I guess everybody, including me, was making very big bucks--everyone except my friend Joe, the owner. I got a call from Joe after a few days into John's vacation saying that he was thinking about leaving the company after he got the money back he had invested and a little more.

Wow! What money can do to people? The day John got back, Joe was there and he and John went into John's office. There was a lot of shouting going on for about one hour. Then Joe stormed out with a check in his hand and left the building. Joe was then out of the equation as far as John was concerned.

I continued to receive weekly pay plus my commission on everything that was manufactured as a video game, with a small company that was running at full capacity. Because there were no services or other products to sell, I wound up with nothing to do, receiving some really big bucks every week. I even went out to place these machines for our entrepreneur that was giving us all this manufacturing business. Then I guess John and his wife thought they did not need a sales person anymore and that they could save thousands of dollars a week if they got rid of me. With my next check John told me that they would have to lay me off until further notice.

I told Joe about my layoff and he asked me to join him in a new venture where I would get 22% percent of the profits. I asked him if I could see the books every month and he said no. I told him that the only way I would join him was if I got three per-cent of the gross dollar sales plus a good salary. That would make it easy for me keep track of my pay because I would be the one that would make out all the invoices for the work I sold.

It was then that I realized why the soft drink company that I left was such a great company. Then there were monthly meetings held with all eight managers of the different bottling companies that Carl owned. We all poured over each others profit and loss statements, comparing ours to theirs. We could ask questions of each other. For example, we could ask why was one persons vehicle insurance was so low and who the carrier was etc. This was why Carl's companies were so profitable. He was a great teacher that motivated each manager by giving him or her a portion of their plant's profits. I also realized that while I worked for Joe and Carl I never once had to ask for a raise, because they came consistently for over fourteen years.

Although Joe Y was very wealthy he was quite egocentric and extremely frugal (cheap). He took a leave of absence from Motorola when we began his newest company. I was somewhat alarmed at first because I had never worked with him in the business world. I was used to seeing him only socially up to the time we sat down to start this new company. He told me that his idea of an ideal manufacturing company was big barn with a dirt floor. At first I thought he was kidding but very soon I found out I was wrong.

The first place we started in was a 1000 square foot garage with a very small office. The office had an air-conditioner and the garage area had an evaporative cooler. I believe that as a part of their settlement Joe received a goodly number of Pong type video game printed circuit boards from John.

Before we could start production I was responsible for getting all the supplies and parts needed to put these upright games together. Joe always insisted in the lowest price for anything. He did not think that much about quality, only about the lowest price = highest profit, or so he thought.

There were a couple of times in the hottest part of the summer when Joe, who was in the garage area working with others assembling video game machines, would open the office door and reach in where the air conditioner was and shut it off. In just minutes the office became unbearably hot. I would just turn it on again. After the second time I told him if he wanted me to work there not to do it again. He knew not to do it because I had all my customers names and knew everything about the parts and supplies that would be needed if I left. I thought to myself then that this is not starting off very well.

Right away Joe decided he was going to build some shelving because everything that this very small company owned was in cardboard boxes piled up along the walls in the production area. Joe was about 10 or 12 years older than me and had a degree in electronics engineering. He told me about his idea to build shelves and asked me what I thought he should make the shelves out of. I started out telling him that I would make them out of 5/8" plywood but before I could finish the word plywood he said no way and went on to say that plywood was way too expensive. He told me that he was going to make them out of particle board.

He spent all of a week working with virtually no tools except a hammer, a tape rule and an inexpensive (cheap) hand saw. He bought a pile of 6 foot by 12 inch wide by 5/8" inch thick particle boards. Every day Joe was pounding and swearing, pounding and swearing and going to get more particle board. I just stayed in my little office lining up customers and ordering parts, pretty much ignoring what he was doing. At the end of the week he asked me to come out to see what he had accomplished and to ask me one more question.

What I saw not only alarmed me but almost caused me to laugh right out loud. There were six pieces of particle board lying vertically on the floor nailed together—yes, nailed together with nails—in a 6 foot square box pattern. There was many other 6 foot pieces that had split ends where the nails had not gone in straight that were laying about. The top piece, cut with the hand saw, was really ragged on the ends. This very wealthy man had spent nearly forty hours of his time and purchased more than double the amount of particle board he needed in his ongoing diligent quest in saving money.

The final question he asked me was what he should use for the backing of his shelves. I told him that he should buy an electric drill and get a sheet of peg board and screw it on the top of vertical boards lying before us. He dismissed my idea again to tell me that he was going to use two two inch by one inch pieces of particle board and cross them from corner to corner and over each other at the center. I just walked away saying nothing. To this day I really wonder why he asked me any questions about his now, very expensive project, just in time alone, unless he wanted to know if I was as smart as he was or as cheap as he was or both.

It was nearing quitting time on Friday when he came in my office to ask me to help him stand his "masterpiece" up (my words, not his). This thing was very heavy and it took all our strength to get it upright. After only about one minute the whole thing collapsed in a thunderous pile of broken particle board pieces. I could not help myself and I broke out in more laughter than I had experienced in months. Joe just stared at his mess in utter disbelief. He waited patiently for me to stop laughing before he said, "I guess you are going to tell everybody about this aren't you?" I said, "You can bet your ass I will!"

At work here I had a phone, desk, chair and a fax machine. I came in at six a.m. every morning so that I could make all my Eastern US sales calls. We continued to copy or to buy copies of the best video games and offered kits for video game owners that had games placed out in retail shops, restaurants, bars, bus stations, etc. These kits provided video game people ways to update their old pieces into something right up to date. I sold these kits for $1000.00 each, which was a bargain compared to our customers buying a new machine for three to four times more than that. We were doing very well domestically but not as well as we could have been internationally.

I talked Joe into letting me go to one of the bigger video game shows in the world. It was held each year near London in an old Royal Castle. At that time we had two customers in England, one in Japan and one in France. After attending this show I got many more international customers that included new customers in Japan, New Zealand, Australia, South

Africa, Ireland, Germany, Spain, Sweden, Norway, Canada and France. I then talked Joe into having a teletype machine installed in our office so that we could get orders quickly in print rather that over the phone. The machine also added to our being realized as a larger player in the vast international video game market. By this time we had moved into much larger quarters where there were three offices that had air conditioners and metal shelving. Was Joe changing? Not exactly he was still asking all his employees and me to give him any receipts hey had that he could use as expenses against his income tax report.

I had a customer from Goteborg, Sweden by the name of Jens Jorgenson. He was one of my best customers and became a good friend over time. He was a young man about my age and a little eccentric. He loved to travel and would often come to the States to pick up an order that he sold to someone else in another country. At that time American Airlines offered a lifetime first class ticket that cost about $250,000. With this ticket Jens could go anywhere in the world, anytime he wanted to, and he surely got his money's worth. This was back in the 1980s and there were not too many people that could afford this luxury. Jens told me that he had taken two trips around the world by that time. He also told me that every weekend he would go to exotic places, travel around for the day, and fly back home at night. I knew that he was single but I had no idea how he was able to afford that ticket.

The next time I went to the London show Joe went with me. It was in February and the weather in Arizona was beautiful. Joe never asked me about the weather we could expect in England. I just assumed that he would know. I brought two suits, dress shirts, neckties, two sweaters, a raincoat, and an extra pair of shoes. Joe brought three Hawaiian shirts, one extra sports jacket and little else except underwear and socks. In addition to his lack of any warm clothing he was trying to stop smoking because of his doctor's orders and family pressure. His plan was to keep an unlit cigarette in his mouth for just about all his waking hours. There were a lot of times that the cigarette would have a dark brown stain near his lips from the moisture from his mouth. It wasn't pretty.

We left a fairly warm dry climate in February to land in a country of misty, sometimes drizzling, bone chilling, damp weather. This is normal for London at this time of year. Joe knew that he had made a mistake as soon as we boarded our taxi to go to the Inter-Continental Hotel where we would be staying. We arrived a day early because we were invited to a private cocktail party given by one of my French customers that was to be held the next evening at the nearby Hilton Hotel. Joe knew about this party well before we left Arizona. After seeing what he'd packed I told him that it might be a good idea for him to buy a dress shirt, a tie and a raincoat at one of the nearby clothing stores. In order to go outside to shop he asked me if he could borrow my two sweaters to wear under his sports jacket. We went to three stores and Joe thought everything was terribly expensive so he bought nothing.

The posh cocktail party was given in a suite of rooms at the Hilton. We had to present our invitations at the door, whereupon Joe got rid of his unlit cigarette after seeing some of the attendees in the room, as well as the man that took our reservations who was in formal wear and wearing white gloves. After we had about four drinks and a lot of hors d'oeuvres Joe walked over to the head waiter and shook his white gloved hand and thanked him for allowing us attend his grand party. I could hear the waiter tell Joe that this was not his party but was hosted by a man that he pointed out. He then told Joe that he was just a waiter. Joe slouched back over to me and suggested that we have one more drink and get out of there.

The next day Joe wanted to go to the London Rolls Royce dealer to shop for a new car. It was raining lightly and chilly so I wore my raincoat. Joe wore both my sweaters and two sports jackets and had an unlit cigarette in his mouth when we got to the front door of the London Rolls Royce dealership. We were met by a doorman wearing the regal dress of a redcoat British general. Before he opened the door he asked what we wanted in a polite British way. Joe told him that he wanted to buy a car. The doorman then escorted us into a showroom that was empty except for four very well dressed salesmen that hovered near the back wall at their desks. I think that the doorman must have given the salesmen a signal that he would handle these two chaps and not to bother. Joe went over to one of the cars with the doorman in hot pursuit, asking Joe if he lived in London. Joe told him that he lived in Arizona and he wanted to buy one of the Rolls and ship it to Phoenix where he planned to sell it for a profit. The doorman told Joe that between the cost of shipping and converting the engine over to US air emission standards it would not be worth it. With that information in hand we left.

Some years later Joe wanted to buy a new "American made" Cadillac at a dealership in Scottsdale where he got a similar treatment, except there was no doorman. He was dressed in bib overalls and needed a hair cut. Joe wanted to buy a car that day but not one of the several roaming salesmen came near him while he was inspecting the cars on the showroom floor, so he walked out and went to the local Mercedes dealer. There he was immediately greeted by a young salesman that sold him their most expensive four door sedan for cash and I am sure that Joe got a big discount on his new car. In the video game business all our customers got cash and most all paid us in cash. What everyone in this business reported as income was not what they actually made as income.

The last traveling story that I remember about Joe was when we both went to Japan for their huge electronics show. We met with my customer and found some new sources for new games that would be good to sell in the USA. The show lasted about five days and all the while there Joe had sinus problems. He was relieved when we were about to go home on a Pan American Flight going out of Narita Airport outside Tokyo. It was about 5:00 p.m.. when we boarded the 747. We were getting ready for takeoff when we noticed that mechanics were rolling out a work platform and parked it right under the engine nearest our seats. We were told we had to get off the plane until they replaced the fuel pump on the engine. We all had to wait in a huge room until they told us that they did not have a pump in Japan. We were told we could stay at an airport hotel at no charge inside the customs boundaries or we could take our bags and leave the airport to find a room someplace else.

Me, Dave Nakase & Joe York

The Narita Airport Hotel were we stayed was a building made of plastic prefabricated room cubes. Each room was made someplace else and stacked on top of and alongside each other in a way that formed a ten story hotel.

The rooms were almost completely plastic with the beds, desk, closets, chest of drawers, counters, sink tops, and toilets all built in. All they needed were mattresses, curtains, a TV, towels, bed sheets, wall hangings, etc. They told us that it would be for one night.

Three days later we decided that we had better leave anyway we could. Pan AM. had been telling us every day that we would be able to fly out the next day, all while Joe was suffering from a severe sinus infection. He was in real pain but did not want to see a Japanese doctor. I called other airlines and the only available seats were on Japan Airlines, which had two seats in first class and they would accept Pan Am tickets. Joe would have to pay the difference, which was about $2000. Joe was certainly in a great deal of pain to pay that up-charge to get out of there. The trip was fine and uneventful and Joe was very glad to get home so he could see his own doctor. I would make two more trips to Japan but with a different company.

The Really Big Deal

One day I got a call from Jens Jorgenson, my Swedish customer that would lead me to my single biggest dollar sale in my life. He asked me if I could get him a certain integrated circuit for a customer he had in Spain that made video gambling machines. Jens sold his Spanish customer, Franco video game integrated circuits from other suppliers and Franco needed 10,000 very scarce ICS (integrated circuits) that he could not find anywhere. Joe was supposed to do the buying of ICs and I did the selling to my customers. It didn't take Joe long to find the parts that were made by Motorola. He could get the numbers that Jens wanted and the price was about $30.00 each, which in those days was fairly expensive. I called Jens the next day and told him that I could get what he needed for $78.00 each. He told me to add $24,000.00 onto the price for him. The cost to his customer in Spain would be somewhat over $804,000.00.

I telexed Jens the amount and told him that the payment would have to be in the form of an irrevocable letter of credit to our bank, the "Arizona Bank" and we could only hold the parts for 20 days from the date of the purchase order. I thought that this sale might never take place but I was hopeful. Joe thought it was an impossible dream. He also said that you could never trust Spaniards because they had so much Arab blood in them. Joe put a hold on actually buying the parts just in case. Joe was one of the only people that I knew that seemed to be an Arab racist way back then.

I left for the annual video games show in London the next day. By the time I got to my hotel room I had a message from Joe that he had a purchase order from the company in Spain and he wanted me to go to Madrid to oversee the writing of the letter of credit to avoid any foul ups because of the Spanish to English translation, etc. A letter of credit must be written perfectly or it might not be accepted by the banks involved. I flew to Spain and Jens made sure that his customer waited for me so that I could supervise the writing at Banco de Bilbao in Madrid. The customer, Senior Franco, in Madrid had a young Dutchman that was on his staff that acted as his translator.

I was met at the airport by the translator who spoke perfect English. Before he took me to his boss he told me that Franco had worked on a U.S. airbase under construction at the age of twelve during the Second World War. Mr. Franco was very poor then and gathered rocks near one of the runways that were used as the base for the new runways. It blew his mind when he saw vending machines in the base cafeteria

The factory we drove up to was gigantic. The translator told me that everything that was produced there was all done in-house, from all the printing to the making of all the metal parts and the design and manufacturing of the printed circuit boards.

He took me right into Franco's huge office. I will never forget what I saw. There was a huge desk parked right in front of an enormous safe that was painted in old style cursive writing, yellow over a black surface, with a huge stainless steel dial and handle. Mr. Franco, a handsome, mustached 54-year-old man, stood smiling and shook my hand. He took us on a tour of his plant. It was absolutely amazing how many departments were humming with equipment and people. He thanked me for coming and asked me to make sure that he got his parts as quick as possible because he had a very large order of gambling machines he needed to fill.

The translator set me up in the nearby Princess hotel and off we went to the bank where we had an afternoon appointment. When we got there we went to the manager's office and met the bank's translator and the manager. I had to make sure that all the numbers were correct, our bank and company name was correct, etc. This process only took about one hour.

The next day the translator took me on a tour of Madrid and then to lunch in a small city by the name of Segovia that was about 60 miles north of Madrid. It had an aqueduct built by the Romans that rose about 80 feet above the street and was still in use. The aqueduct was in front of a world renowned restaurant, Meson de Candido, where President Nixon and Premier Gorbachev had dined separately some years before.

The restaurant was probably a very large home at one time, it was about three stories high with a stairs going right up the middle of the house, with each floor having a dining room on both the right and left side of the stairs. Waiters with trays over their heads competed with customers going up and down these stairs all going to their perspective dining rooms. The specialty fare was suckling piglets that were first shown after it was cooked to the diners and then taken to where the little thing was cut up into small pieces, and then served to the waiting diners.

Franco's interpreter then took me to the nearby Queen Isabella and King Ferdinand's castle, The Alcazar (Castle) of Segovia. The castle had a moat in the front and a cliff on the backside. To enter we had to walk across a drawbridge.

All the rooms were immense in size except the chapel which looked like the only warm room in the entire castle because of all the fine colorful tapestries on the walls, the covered altar and all the religious statuary. The ceilings were extremely beautiful throughout the castle as well as the armory where hundreds of shields were hung. Almost every room had a fireplace which I thought might not have been adequate in the winter months to keep a body warm. We were told that Walt Disney sketched this castle and it was used in his movies. That evening he took me to club that was on a cobblestone street in Madrid that was about eight feet wide and in a building that dated back hundreds of years. I will never forget this place because the Gipsy flamenco dancers and guitar players that performed for us and about 50 others, were exceptionally good.

I called my wife to tell her that the deal was complete and the money was on its way. She would tell me later that Joe told her that this deal would not happen. She responded to Joe that "if Ros tells you that the deal is done then it is fact." When I got back to my office I was met with a lot of negativity from Joe. We had about ten days left before the letter of credit would expire. Joe banked with The Arizona Bank, which was not that large in size or stature as far as banks of the world go. I was already getting telexes asking if the parts had been shipped. I then found out that this irrevocable letter of credit would have to go through several banks that did business with each other before it would get to the Valley National Bank and then finally to The Arizona Bank.

On top of all this Joe was still dragging his feet on actually buying the parts. I did not know about this until I got a call from the parts distributor that held the order, a man I knew. He told me that Joe thought that the deal might not go through and he wanted my reassurance or they would have to let the parts go elsewhere. I told him that the money was on the way and that I was at the bank when the letter of credit was written and sent.

We were running out of time, with five days left. By tracking the letter of credit I found out that it was at the Chase Manhattan Bank that was run by David Rockefeller in New York City. I called his office and they transferred me to the head of their telex department. I told him that his bank had held our LOC for five days now. He said that he is in charge of the transactions of fifty telex machines and my measly $800,000 LOC was not all that important. I told him that this measly $800,000 might not mean that much to him but it was worth everything to me and my company. He said that he would personally look for it. The next day he called to say it would be at Valley National Bank that day. I told Joe and he said that he wanted to see the letter of credit himself before he would finally secure the order for the parts.

I called Valley National and asked that they forward the LOC to the Arizona Bank as soon as they got it and they were happy to do so. A couple of hours later the Arizona Bank called and said that they had it in hand. I asked them to stay on the phone and went to Joe to have him hear the lady from the bank read it to him. He refused and said he wanted the LOC in his hand to read it himself. I talked with the Arizona Bank and told them I was on my way to get the documents. It took about one hour before I got back and handed the LOC to Joe, who then went into his office and locked his door to read the LOC. The document was only 2 ½ pages long and I could see him from my office, through the glass, reading the pages over and over again for half an hour or more.

Interpreter & Franco

Finally he ordered the parts with one day left before the LOC was set to expire. Joe asked the parts distributor for ninety days credit, which was good business practice on his part. Back then there was about five percent interest given on savings accounts. Mr. Franco's people were raising hell, the parts distributor was having a heart attack, Motorola wanted to ship the parts to other people and Jens kept telexing me wanting to know if the money was there yet.

When the parts were delivered Joe would not let anyone but him pack them for shipment. He was like a man possessed. I watched him from a distance check out each tube of IC's, making sure that each see-through tube had the right part number on them. He used a used clothes washer machine box to ship the parts because that is what we used to ship some of our cocktail video games in. Joe was the cheapest man I have ever known. It took most of the day for him to the complete the job and after he sealed the box he asked me for the paper work which I had prepared. While he did this he never smiled, he even seemed bitter for some reason. I will never know why.

In the end everybody was happy except Joe and Jens. To this day I cannot think of any reason why he never thanked me for putting this sale together. Joe's profit from this sale wound up being $468,000. My commission was $24,000. Jens was supposed to get $24,000 as his finder's fee. Very little additional expense was incurred by my going to Madrid. My stay at the Princess Hotel for the night was paid for by Franco's company. My plane trip from England to Madrid was only $200.00 extra because I was going to England for the show anyway. This man was a multimillionaire but Joe was paranoid that he might lose even a few cents and I know he didn't like the fact that he had to pay me so much commission for putting this together. He had no imagination at all. What Joe would do next would eventually sever our friendship and business relationship forever.

When Jens was on his way from Sweden to get his fee, Joe began commenting to me that "one telephone call from Jens to me was certainly not worth $24,000". I looked him in the eye and told him that he better pay him what we all agreed upon. I was very upset with his thinking. After all, Jens' fee was added to our bid and was not part of our profits at all. In the end Joe only gave Jens $12,000 behind closed doors instead of the $24,000 that he was promised. Without Jens, Joe would have never made close to a half a million dollars. After all was said and done with this sale I had the feeling of a winning quarterback whose team had won the Super Bowl without getting any praise from the owner of the team. That was the last time I saw Jens. I called him several times but he would not return my calls. It was soon after that experience that I left Joe and opened Greenbrier Marketing International with Nick, another former Motorola employee. I met Nick through Joe Y. Nick had complete knowledge about everything to do with printed circuit boards and their parts. I needed someone to hold the fort down in the USA while I was gallivanting all over the place. Nick and his wife Patty were the very best that I could have found to work with me.

It was a very sad day indeed when copying printed circuit boards that shows the final product made by others was against the law. The FBI was involved in the policing of this new law and that was the end of the line for us and everyone else throughout the world doing copying although some kept right on until they were eventually caught.

It was then when Caroline and I had to fall back on the only company that we had that was still doing business, the Dr. Doo Everything New Construction Cleaning Company LLC.

On July 1, 1988, about two years after he visited our home in Queen Creek, I received this fax from Dave Nakase our customer and supplier from Japan. It read in part the following: *"I am very sorry that I have not written you for a very long time. Business here has been very strict and its movement has been also very rapid and floating."*
"I do not know the situations of the game machine business in the U. S. A. if you are still able to probe the above for the customers there, I would like to offer: P. C. Boards assembled and tested----Jap. Yen 98,000. -FOB- for sample only. I would supply the control switch panel together with the wire connectors harness at Yen 15,000. - to help your quick examination."

"If you do not have any interest in it, please do me special favour to send us several magazines of the GAME MACHINES business in the U. S. A. like PLAY METER or etc." I really hope that you and all your family are quite healthy and are enjoying daily life."*

I replied that we went out of the video game business about 1 1/2 years ago because of the new laws in place and I would send him magazines he requested.

We made a lot of friends around the world when we were in the video game business but that now remains some very good memories.

CHAPTER 3

WHAT A TRIP!

I wrote and formed the Greenbrier International Marketing LLC.. I held all my old customers names and we had new sources where we could buy video game boards from Japan and other far away places. Fairly soon our Greenbrier Marketing business was flourishing to the point that our CPA recommended that we have our annual corporate meeting in Hawaii to spend some of our excess working capital instead of paying 15% tax on the money. So I contacted American Express to set up a trip to Maui for ten days for all management and their families, 17 people total. American Express set us up with two spacious condos on the Kaanapli Beach Golf Course along with three rental cars. It was something that none of us had experienced before. The trip included some briefly agonizing moments after we lost a couple of children at the Los Angeles Airport just before it was time to board our plane to Honolulu. After a lot of disorganized excitement we all made the plane.

About thirty minutes before landing in Honolulu a flight attendant made an announcement over the loud speaker system asking that Alden Rosbrook please put your call button light on. Our group was all seated together in the center of the plane. The attendant came down the aisle and in a loud voice told me that when our group deplaned on the tarmac your group will be greeted by two Hawaiian ladies dressed in traditional grass skirts whereupon your group will be presented with authentic orchid Hawaiian leis. Then she went on to say, still in a loud voice, "Your chauffeurs will be standing by with three limousines and your group will driven to the Rainbow Hilton Hotel."

I immediately realized that this was something American Express did as a surprise to me and the group. There was applause from our group and the other passengers that were able to hear her. Caroline poked me and whispered, "Why didn't you tell us about this?", and I whispered back, "I did not know anything about this!" All the while I was smiling to all our friends that were saying things like "You are great Ros!" and other things like that. I guess that Hawaiian Airlines wanted to make a big deal out of this kind of thing in an effort to get more people to fly with them and hoped the people flying with us would tell others about what happened on the flight. I still never let on that I was as much surprised as our group was. I waited a day or two before I made my confession.

Everyone in our group were hard working, simple folk and were not accustomed to such royal treatment. Then just before landing the attendant made another announcement, asking all the other passengers to wait for our group to de-plane first. When we landed we all had to use the old-fashioned roll-up stairway to get to the ground and, sure enough, at the bottom of the stairs was two wahine u'is waiting with armfuls of fresh orchid leis.

Off to the side were three chauffeurs in black uniforms standing side by side. Behind them on the tarmac were three stretch limos parked one behind the other. After getting my lei I went over to them and one asked me to get all the baggage claims so that they could get all of our luggage. Two of the drivers motioned our group over to the cars, whereupon twelve extremely excited adults and their small children loaded into the first vehicle. Three then got into the second car and that left Caroline and I to get into the last car all by ourselves. Again, I had no plan for the equal distribution of our passengers but it sure was a funny thing to see. When we all pulled up to the Hilton, where we were going to spend one night, we sure did get a lot of attention. American Express even figured in the tips to the drivers but we all tipped them anyway. It was then that our three boys discovered that the two suitcases that they had packed for themselves was still at our home in Scottsdale. They spent a few hours buying some clothes in Honolulu including bathing suits.

The chauffeurs picked us up the next day for our trip to the airport, this time we spread ourselves out in a more comfortable way, where we would travel on to Maui. We split up into the three rental cars that were waiting for us at the airport. And went to our condos on Kaanapli Beach.

Some people told us about a wonderful trip driving to Hana which is only about thirty miles away from where we were staying. Because of the narrow, winding road (Hi-360 has 620 curves and 59 bridges) it took us about three hours to get to the little village of Hana and the base of the mountain that has seven falls and pools that cascade down to its base. The trail to get to the top went through a bamboo forest and up to the highest falls. Then we all went down into each of the pools and through the falls all the way to the bottom.

Mark, Kevin, Jimmy, Matt & Cara

Cara and the guys decided to rent a sailboat and go sailing off the coast of Maui but there was no wind, not a even the slightest breeze. It did make a good picture though. They just motored around in the sailboat until the day was over.

Busted By The Feds?

All the pleasurable things we did in Hawaii were largely due to the video game business and a lucrative contract we had with Tuni Electro, a large printed circuit board manufacturing and assembly company, owned by our marketing client by the name of Jim Tuni. Jim assigned us to acquire some legal PCBs to be used in making their company's own video games. I took the twenty-one year old son of our client, J.T., with me to the Japan electronics show in Tokyo in search of legal video game PCBs.

We had a fabulous time because our supplier, Dave Nakase who was Chief of Export/Import for Kiowa Electronics Co., LTD., Yokohama, Japan took us out every night we were there. Funny thing, he also brought with him three of his very attractive office workers, but not his wife. One night we all went to a Karaoke bar where I sang some Harry Belafonte's songs, not very well as I remember. JT, Jim Tuni's son sang a popular ballad and he was a smash. I thought that most of the Japanese knew English very well because most all were able to sing our most popular songs in English but I soon found out that they only knew the songs lyrics in English. "USA songs number one in Japan," I was told by Dave.

We went to six video game manufacturers in five days who showed us the games that they had for sale. We also found a few new customers and one gave us a sample video PCB called Boatman. It was a game where the player would load and unload his boat playing against another player that did the same. The player that did the job the fastest wins.

At that time there was a very popular new game that was called PAC-Man which was entirely different from the one we had in our possession when we boarded our plane at the Narita Airport in Japan. When we arrived in Seattle Washington I would encounter something I had never experienced before and hope to never again. After we got to customs my client's son took a different counter than I did and he went through without a problem. I on the other hand declared the PCB that I was carrying and its invoice. The customs agent that I declared the PCB Boatman game to must have pressed a hidden buzzer. All of a sudden the custom officer in charge shows up with two other custom officers. They took my luggage and brief case and escorted me to the captain's office which was ironically directly across from the room where full body searches were made, at least that was what the sign over the door said, it was a little disquieting to see how busy they were. The captain told me that their electronics special agent would be there very soon. Soon a short man in civilian clothes came in, walked over to the Captain's desk and very dramatically swiped the desk clean with his arm, sending all of the Captains personal items crashing to the floor. The look on the Captains face was one of total disbelief, but he did not say a word. I'm guessing that this special operations wannabe held a higher rank. He took my suitcase and dumped the contents onto the desk, dirty clothes and all. He then dumped the contents of my briefcase on another table and asked me about what was in it.

With rubber gloves on he commenced to rummage through everything. He asked me to sit in a chair by the window and then suddenly they both walked out the door. I could hear the Captain loudly ask the special electronics technician why he'd made such a production of this inspection. I just sat there knowing I had done nothing wrong and shaking my head at what I had just seen.

I believed that they had me on camera and just wanted me to get something from my clothes or from my briefcase that might incriminate me. After more than an hour, that caused me to miss my connection to Phoenix, I heard two voices outside the window saying "Lets read him his rights right now and cuff him". I did not move and continued to keep a broad smile on my face. Finally the little guy came in and told me to get my things together and leave. He would keep the PCB and send it to the Phoenix Customs Office and agents from that office would bring the board to the Tuni plant so that the agents could view the game and see what it was about.

Two days later a male and female Customs agent showed up at the plant. They were dressed in business clothes and were very apologetic from the outset and acted as if they were just going through the motions. When we showed the video game Boatman on screen to them they both laughed and continued to apologize for what took place in Seattle. Evidently the Captain might have outranked the Special wannabe ops agent after all.

Although the video arcade game business started here in the U.S. with "Pong", resulting with us selling our version to Japanese customers, within a couple of years we were buying video arcade games from the Japanese. We sold these Japanese copied boards all over the world until it became illegal. We even showed our games within fifty feet of the original manufacturers in a Chicago Arcade Trade Show without any problems. Which was before we worked for Tuni Electro.

Tuni Electro

I purchased a custom made display to show off the legal video games at the Chicago video games show for our client Jim Tuni and his Tuni Electro Company. Our large display area was quite spectacular. Jim had some attractive young ladies that worked for him in his large fabricating and manufacturing plant in Phoenix. We brought most of these ladies to the show. They helped us hand out product information and show the games we had on display. I think that we had ten or twelve people with us and we all stayed at the old Blackstone Hotel, which was very close to the hotel where the show was being held.

Upon arrival I was the first one to register at the hotel under the Tuni Electro reservations. I used my American Express card, got my keys and went to the room I was to share with my Tuni Company counterpart, Pat Reed. Little did I know that my card would be used for every other team member that arrived that day. There were no restrictions on expenses for room service, the hotel bar or the restaurant for anyone working with Jim. When I checked out four days later I got a bill for over $13,000! When we all got back to Phoenix I got a check from Jim for the whole amount and within a few days, well before the American Express bill got to me, I paid the bill. From then on, every time I called AMEX I was received with a lot more, shall we say, courteous attention!

We did a lot of partying every night after our show duties. There were a couple of Tuni representatives that were staying on a different floor from Pat and I. At the bar one night we decided to play a joke on the two, who we thought would get a kick out of our antics. We enlisted the help from two other Tuni people which helped our practical joke grow into something we all thought would be something spectacular. We found out that our two targets would be tied up for a long time the next night and that was when we decided to demolish their room. Somehow one of our "agents" got a key to their room.

The plan was to remove almost everything from their room. We put all their personal property in the tub behind the shower curtain Then we put the two beds and mattresses out on the nearby fire escape. Everything else went into a conference room a few doors down the hall. There were only a few hotel guests that saw us moving things and no one reported us, so everything went laughingly well. We found a lot of newspapers and it took us about a half hour to cover their floor with all the crumpled papers.

Then the four of us laughed our way back to the bar and after an hour or two we all went back to our rooms. I got a call at 2:00 a.m. from one of the joke recipients just asking where we put the beds. Lucky for us they were in very good moods at that time and thought the whole thing was hysterical. They had been at the Chicago Playboy Club all evening.

It would be several months later when I was on the receiving end of their practical joke. While I was poolside at a San Diego hotel during a show there, two guys who were at the same show got into my room and did the following, put a lot of toothpaste in my shoes, and removed all the laces, soaked all my socks in water and mouthwash and put them in the bottom of the waste basket, removed all the toilet paper, left only one wash cloth, tied my neckties into knots, hid my underwear behind the window curtains and called the desk to give me a 2:00 a.m. wake up call. What they didn't know was that after getting to my room from the pool I started having some kidney stones pain and after taking a couple of Tylenol pills went right to bed, never even noticing that things were amiss. I was alone in the room and had to catch an 8:00 a.m. plane back to Phoenix the next morning. After my unexpected 2 a.m. wake-up call, the pain started to increase and continued right up to 5:30 a.m. when I got up to get dressed before leaving for the airport. It was then that I dealt with the consequence of my pranks on them. If it wasn't for taking the pool towel to my room I might have had nothing to dry off with except the window curtains.

I never did find my socks, had a tough time getting the toothpaste out of my shoes and had to borrow a pair of laces from the desk clerk. I didn't have to wear a tie and fortunately I did find my underwear! I did feel somewhat uncomfortable not having socks to wear from the hotel, on the plane, off the plane, and in the van to my car. I found I had to laugh at my predicament, even with the pain I was in which helped me ignore the many people that stared at me. At least my feet did smell really good!

This picture shows me on the right sitting across from Pat Reed, my Tuni Company counterpart. The two Englishmen who were selling the rights to their video game to Jim Tuni who are sitting across from Jim. Tuni's plant manager, Mike Capen, is sitting next to me.

Working with Jim Tuni was a blast. He rented three different planes using the same rental pilot in the two years we were his marketing company. I went with him on several trips when he used these planes for short hops to as far away as Seattle. The last plane that he used was a Cessna Jet. In that plane I got to ride in the co-pilot's seat all the way to Seattle and back to Phoenix. I was taught how to fly that jet, and although I really did not fly the plane I enjoyed what the pilot taught me and how everything worked. Flying private aircraft is a real treat, in that you don't have to wait in lines to check in, to board and when you disembark, your cab is waiting for you. First class all the way.

Jim and I went to Tokyo for their electronics show and to meet with two of my England customers that had a new game they wanted to sell exclusive rights for. This show was the biggest I had ever been to. There were so many unusual new things. I had been to Tokyo before with Jim's son J.T. but that was to attend a much smaller video games show. This show covered acres displaying all things electronic and more. There was a young Japanese girl riding around on roller skates. This would not have been unusual except for the fact that one skate had a very small gas engine attached to it. A small wire ran up to her hand that controlled the speed. The size of the little engine was something I had never seen before or after.

We met with the English before the show opened and Jim whispered to me that he wanted their game so badly that he wanted to offer them both $1000.00 cash immediately. He would give a bid to get the exclusive rights after we saw how the game played. I told him we needed to see the game first. The English were the owners of the company but their board of directors would be watching what they did. They would wait to see the very best offer they could get before signing any papers anyway, so we would have to wait.

We kept going back to their booth and played their game each time after going around to other sellers to compare the games that were for sale. Jim kept raising his bid even though we did not know what other bids they had actually been given. At the end of the show they said that they were going to go back to England to decide which bid and which company would be the best one for them to work with. We said that we were open for matching any credible bid plus 10% that we could verify. They mentioned that they were going to stop in Hawaii for a day or two before continuing on to England. Jim told them that he had stayed at a certain hotel on Waikiki Beach and said how nice it was. They said they were booked into the Rainbow Hilton, which was not far from that beach. We then said our goodbyes and left.

After leaving them Jim told me to change our airline reservation to stop in Hawaii and for me to book rooms at the Rainbow Hilton. What a hoot! I had never been to Hawaii! They were very surprised to see us when we showed up two days later. Jim pushed them very hard for the deal but they were hoping for a bid with a larger, more well-known video game company. We didn't get anywhere with them in Hawaii so Jim insisted that they stop in Phoenix, where he would put them in a hotel at his expense for a couple days

Jim wanted them to see his plant in operation, thinking that would better ensure that we got their game. Jim had investors from Holland that he needed to show some immediate progress in the the video game business that Jim promised would be so very profitable. They would later find out about Jim's penchant for renting private airplanes and pilots and were not very happy about it. I was told that the Dutchmen loaned Jim over six million dollars.

Our first show after that was held in Hollywood. Jim had an office in a very prominent office building where many movie directors, producers, etc. also had offices. We camped out one night at the Beverly Hills Hilton Hotel bar where we all had so much outlandish fun strangers were asking us if we were in the movie business. One of the more unusual Tuni guys ate some of the flowers that were on our table and gave the leader of a trio band that was playing there a $100 tip for no apparent reason other than to get attention. He was staying with Jim in a room there and went upstairs afterward feeling ill and threw up in a very expensive pair of his bosses (Jim's) shoes. Was that a Freudian slip or what?

In an amazing coincidence my wife and I met someone who worked for Jim some 33 years ago as a electronic parts buyer. Caroline and I had a eye exam at our insurance company's medical facility recently. When we arrived for our appointment we were met by an attractive lady dressed in medical scrubs that greeted me with a "Hi, Ros! How are you?" She saw our names on their appointment book. She went on to say "Don't you remember me? It's Megg." For the life of me I could not remember her, but she sure remembered me! Megg told us that I made her drink Ouzo at a Chicago Greek restaurant and bar that we must have gone to after one of our video game show evenings. She also told us about my "Greek" dancing solo on the dance floor. We carried on a conversation about our long pastime between her taking care of patients, of which we were two of, and as she passed by me while I was in the waiting room. She told me that she left Tuni a short time before Sheriff's Deputies came in and shut them down for reasons that Megg did not know at that time.

My company, Greenbrier Marketing International, shut down right after the federal government made it illegal to copy or sell copies of video games. Many other companies just kept on until the feds/police showed up at their doors.

A Great Friend

The next time the words Queen Creek came up was when one of my old friends, Mike called me to tell me that he bought three and a third acres of land out in Queen Creek for a little over eight thousand dollars. I told him, "Mike that is way out in the boonies" and he said, "It is beautiful out here, come out and see for yourself". He continued saying he'd built a garage on his property and wanted me and Caroline to come out the next Saturday for a barbecue. We were unable to keep that date.
We finally went there about six months later after Mike invited us again and we both fell in love with the area as we traveled through the desert to get to Mike's place. It was very close to some nearby mountains, the San Tans. The quiet, the open desert views and the price of the land in this beautiful place was very enticing to my wife and I. It was over a year later when Mike called me to tell me about a property up the road from his place, near Goldmine Mountain, that was for sale and that it had some really fantastic views.

Mike fixed his two car garage up and made it into his new home and moved there, bought two horses after fencing off about one third of his three and a third acres. His family had moved from Chicago a few years prior to his buying this land and he was living with his parents before building his new garage home.

He and his father owned a motorcycle repair shop in Mesa where they had a contract with an insurance company that they would buy all the totaled motorcycle wrecks for a set price that included hauling the wreck from the scene of the accident, so no matter what time it was they had to respond in as timely manner to pick up the pieces. Once in the shop they would fix the bike, put it on the market and sell it. Eighty-five percent of the time they were able to make a good profit for what they did.

Now Mike is a Cowboy, or what some call a Coca Cola cowboy, but never the less a cowboy without any cows. As a young lad I'd always had the very same dream that he had and now there was beginning to be a slight glimmer of hope of me being one of those Coca Cola cowboys. Mike wanted to show off his new digs and his new horses that he bought from an auction, so once again we were invited, along with some of his other friends to another barbecue. This was held during a Sunday afternoon that would give us a chance to see the home that was for sale near the base of Goldmine Mountain. My wife and I went a little early so that we could visit the home and find out how much the selling price was, etc.

What we saw we both immediately liked. The property was located in the near middle of a horseshoe of mountains along the south, east and west and was high enough to provide a fantastic unobstructed view to the north showing the Superstition Mountains and all the way to Four Peaks in the distance. The land overlooked Queen Creek, Apache Junction and the then nearby Williams Air Force Base (now Phoenix Gateway Airport) and parts of Mesa. After seeing the place by Goldmine Mountain we went back down to Mike's new home and the barbecue. Everybody was anxious to hear from us about what we thought of the home up by the mountains. Mike mentioned that there was a another piece of land for sale not far from the place we looked at before that might be something my youngest son and wife might be interested buying.

A Big Bump In The Road

At this time I should say that even though Mike had two horses and at that time I had none, our experiences on or around horses was extremely limited. I don't know about Mike but I had ridden maybe eight or ten times since birth, all on rental horses that were pretty much "bomb proof". I relied heavily on the hundreds of cowboy movies that I had seen over the years as the extent of my riding experience.

So, Mike said to me in front of all his urban living friends and my wife "Lets saddle up my horses and ride up the road to see the other land that's for sale". Then I said, without hesitation, words to the affect, "You betcha, Big Fella." These words greatly impressed our friends and their other guests that we had just met.

At this time I should say again that even though Mike had two horses and at this time I had none, our experiences on or around horses was extremely limited.

Mike gave me his mare to ride that he had never ridden, reassuring me by saying, "This horse was a champion roping horse owned by a older person" --at least that was what he had been told by the auction people-- and that "I should not have any trouble with her". After we had mounted, all these very impressed people followed us towards the dirt road in front of Mike's home. In hindsight, the small crowd of people looked somewhat like the pictures I have seen of the Japanese sailors waving goodbye to the pilots of those Kamikaze planes sent out to fly purposely into our ships head first during the later stages of the Second World War. I led the way because, being older, I had seen many more cowboy movies than Mike.

In order to get to the road I had to pass by a pickup truck that had two bales of hay in its bed. Betty, my horse reached out to the hay and started eating it. Being the boss of Betty, I directed her away from the food. When Betty was about ten steps away from the food and fully on that hard dusty road, she must have said to herself, "This jerk is not a real cowboy so I don't think he is a good enough rider to stop me from eating that delicious hay". I think it took at least two bucks, and I don't mean money, when the force of gravity put me face first onto that dusty dirt road. My landing must have forced some saliva from my mouth because my lips and parts of my face were very dirty.

Betty didn't move, just stared at me lying there in a prone position that I often used in the Marine Corps on the rifle range. I must have looked rather ridiculous because I could hear my wife laughing while the others were asking if I was alright. Not one person offered any assistance whatsoever because cowboys never need assistance getting up off the ground or the floor. (You see that in every rodeo video... nobody helps the real cowboy up, even if he's hurt.) Well, this cowboy got up on his own, to the reassuring words of those watching, who by this time were all laughing along with my dear wife.

The general consensus was that, "You've got to get right back on Betty and show her who the hell the boss is." So, I got right up and dusted myself off, wiped my lips and face off with my arm, just like you see in the movies. I think John Wayne must have done it hundreds of times when he was in a fight! Then I headed towards Betty, who had an evil look in her eyes. But a real cowboy must work for his admiring, laughing crowd, right?

I went over to Betty and got right up in the saddle with the small crowd clapping and saying things like "Atta boy, Ros!" but Betty thought the clapping was for her. She did not need their encouragement at all because I could hear her say to herself, "Wait til I launch you this time, Coca Cola Cowboy!" She took only three steps and with all her might she did a viscous triple buck (according to the now totally speechless crowd) and this time I landed flat on my back with my head bouncing on that dirty old road at least twice.

I was really hurting after thirty minutes or so and we decided to skip the barbecue and get home to Scottsdale, which was over an hour drive from the scene of this accident. I am sure Betty did not think it was a accident AT ALL. By the time I drove into my carport in Scottsdale, I found that I could hardly walk. Caroline had to help me to our bed. My back was black and blue from my rump to the middle of my back. She put a lot of Icy Hot on my back (stuff that is cold when it goes on and then warms up nicely). Then she gave me three extra strength Tylenol tablets. It was only about six o'clock when this cowboy went to sleep and he never woke up until about five the next morning.

As I became more lucid that morning I was sure that I would not be able to stand, much less walk. I carefully sat up and put my legs over the side of the bed while my wife was still asleep and to my absolute complete astonishment there was not a bit of pain at all as I stood up. My whole back was now a deep purple. We could not believe it. I showered and went to work eager to tell everyone about my new wonderful cowboy experience.

Another Horse Related Accident...That Hurt Much More Than The Rider

The very same day that Betty the horse gave me her terra firma baptism, our partner in a Beauty Salon business in Mesa had a much more severe horse related incident. The father of the salon's only male employee bought a horse-- you guessed it, from the same auction house that Mike bought Betty from. This horse's problem was when anybody got on her back she would sit down just like a dog would. Sara, our partner in the business, had about the same amount of experience with horses as I had but, never the less, she told her employee's father, Les, that she would help him break the horse of this nasty habit. Yeah, right!

After a margarita or two with Les, they took the saddled horse across the street into a newly plowed field which is about five miles north of Mike's place. Sara's plan was to get on the horse with Les holding the reins. Then, when the horse started to sit down, Les was told to yank hard on the reins in a downward motion but when that happened, instead of sitting down the horse reared up throwing Sara to the ground and fell on top of her, breaking her pelvis.

When Caroline and I were on our way home to Scottsdale after my bad horse adventure, we actually went past the accident scene without knowing what had happened or that our partner Sara was involved. What a coincidence! We remember seeing a helicopter flying in circles above the field but it was too far from us to see what was going on. Caroline did not find out about the accident until I was at work the next morning. The salon was about a half mile away from the hospital where Sara had been taken so right after Caroline opened the shop she left an employee in charge and went immediately to the hospital.

Part of Sara's therapy, because of the extreme trauma involved, included treatment from a psychiatrist who listened intently to her for several hours. She told a story to that doctor that would ultimately cause us to sell beauty salon. Sara and her husband Carl had been trying for twelve years to have a baby. Unexpectedly one day, or most likely one evening, Sara became pregnant and eventually had a baby boy, Paul. After about two years of age the boy began to look surprisingly like Ken, the only male employee in our shop whose father owned the horse that Sara was helping to break from sitting down. When Sara's husband Carl would bring Paul into the shop, which was often, even I had noticed that the child looked more and more like Ken.

Following the accident Sara told her psychiatrist the truth during therapy. Ken was indeed the father of her son, Paul. The psychiatrist told Sara that she should tell her husband the truth ASAP. When Caroline went to visit Sara in the hospital three days later, Sara in a flood of tears, told Caroline the whole story. Right after Sara told her husband that the child they had raised and doted on for almost three years was not his, I got a phone call from Carl. He was very upset and he said that right after he was told the story from his wife, he went into shock and didn't even remember how he got home to his son and the babysitter.

He asked me if he should get a DNA test done, which at the time was a very expensive new procedure. I told him that it was not necessary to put the child through that experience. "After all, you have been his father for all this time and he is your son". I knew that Ken was not interested in raising his son at all! Carl told me that Sara wanted a divorce and that he could have the child. Wow! How weird could this soap opera get? Sara has sex with this man and has his child, not telling her husband until after the horse accident, she wants a divorce and then wants her husband to raise the child-- which I believe Carl is doing to this day!

Sara would wind up having therapy for three months. Unfortunately, Sara produced one third of our business at the salon and Ken did another third of our business or more. He quit after Carl decided to go to the salon and confront him about the possibility that he had sex with his wife.

Carl later called and told me that he had gone there with a gun in his pocket and had asked Ken to talk with him outside the back door of the shop. He said he intended to shoot Ken if he lied to him but Ken admitted it and Carl walked away. I thought to myself, "Thank the Lord Carl did not shoot Ken". Ken told me he didn't want the child and was happy that Carl keep it.

We were just at the point at the Salon that we were just seeing some profits being realized when this happened. The owner of the property where the salon was located had just raised our rent by five-hundred dollars a month. We lost a lot of our regular customers at the same time the bills mounted quickly. Sara and Carl were fifty percent of the corporation and Caroline and I were the other fifty percent and we both would lose about forty thousand dollars each when we sold the business. Thank the lord that Carl and I both were in other businesses or we could have lost our homes over this mess.

Since that time we have seen Ken several times at Christmas Mass and at various restaurants and have tried to approach him, only to have him quickly walk away from us like we were somehow responsible for what happened. We have seen and talked to his parents a few times and they were very cordial although nothing has ever been said about the "situation". I've seen Sara twice over the years and she asked if Caroline would give her a call, I think knowing that Caroline might not want to talk with her, which would be right. I have tried to talk with Carl several times but he evidently does not want to communicate with us. How sad it is that we had such good times together and now that friendship is probably lost forever.

By the way, Mike never rode Betty (the Horse) and took her back to the auction house. She was later sold by Mike to another cowboy who was told that the last owner hardly ever rode this beautiful horse because he was way to busy with his work.

Dr. Doo-Everything Cleaning Company

In all the years since we were married, in 1957, we never had any business failures until we moved to Scottsdale, AZ. Just when we thought that everything was going so well we had the rug pulled out from under us. So again we must adjust, adapt and overcome, here we go.........

In 1983 we owned a new construction cleaning business that was operated by my youngest son, Kevin. Several months before we closed Greenbrier, we had sold the salon at a loss because we lost about two thirds of our customers, our partners did not want to continue in the business and our landlord was raising our rent. All we had to fall back on was the cleaning business. We started with one truck and with one builder and continued in the new home construction business through the several up and downs that the building business delivers in Arizona and the rest of the country from time to time.

We have gone full circle from the day care business that is also affected by the economy to a construction business that suffers in the same kind of way. We went bankrupt twice after the builders we served went bankrupt. We lasted in this business for 25 years. At our highest level we grossed over $202,000 in one year, which occurred a couple of years before the 2008 recession. It was during these years that I wrote a book by the name of New Construction Interior Cleaning Service that was published by The Business Research Division of Entrepreneur Magazine. They sold it as a business guide for over sixty dollars a copy. I received $9.00 per copy royalty which helped us through the many ups and downs we had to live through in the construction business.

Spencer, Mom Lisa, Caroline, Donna &
Ros. The First Dr Doo Crew

Working in the construction trades in Arizona from May through September is very difficult because of the heat. When June rolls around we had to be on site at dawn and finish our work at about 2 p.m. The first clean in new houses we worked in did not have air-conditioning. In about 95% of the time we did three separate cleans on each house.

1) Rough clean (before carpet installation) that included: Cleaning all outside windows and frames, cleaning all tubs and showers using a hose, sanding the concrete in the garage, on the patios, front walkway and driveway. Using a lot of water inside the house and even in the garage with all the doors open raises the humidity level up to some very uncontainable and dangerous levels.
I passed out four times from heat exhaustion and my co-workers suffered from the same thing several times. We drank a lot of Gatorade and water. We had to take a lot of breaks during those hot months.

2) Second clean just before the customer walk-thru that included cleaning all the interior windows frames and window tracks, cleaning the kitchen, bathrooms, closets, carpeting, woodwork, and hosing all the exterior concrete. 50% of the time the air-conditioning would be on, what a treat! 90% of the time the customer would find things that would need repairs, so, we would be called in to clean up after the sub-contractors did their work.

3) Re-clean that included cleaning up after repairs were completed. We charged by the hour and those costs we charged to the builder was passed on to the sub that caused the damage that had to be repaired.

4) Emergency Clean. We were often called to clean up after drastic repairs were made to a home after the homeowners were living in the home. Most were due to slow plumbing leaks that did not show up prior to the move-in but after a few days showed up when the water stain appeared on a wall or ceiling. The plumber is called and he tears a hole in the wall or ceiling creating a big mess. Then the drywall repair guy is called and he adds to the mess. Then we are called when he gets finished and this could be on a Sunday or holiday. We had to rush there to get things cleaned up to the satisfaction of the homeowner. For the service we were able to charge up to forty dollars per man hour.

I am now paying the price of repetitive body movements for almost three decades with having a complete left knee replacement and a complete right ankle replacement. It was very hard work and I still have bad dreams about cleaning outside windows on a thirty foot ladder stretched out to the max.

PART TWO: THE SECOND 28 YEARS

1986-2014 CHAPTER 4

What Were The Trade Offs?

Was there a price to be paid for living in this little piece of heaven called Queen Creek? One of those prices we had to consider was the fact that all the roads out near where we wanted to live were made of good old fashioned dirt. Hunt Highway from Higley road almost all the way to Florence, more that twenty-five miles away, was a dirt road then.

Another price we would have to pay was the inconvenience of not having water service to our home as did all of the homes in our area. You had to subscribe for Fire Department service that cost around five hundred dollars a year, which at the time wasn't so bad. There was no trash pickup so garbage was collected taken to the local landfill or burned. We were fortunate that phone and electrical lines had been installed in the area before we arrived!

Gone would be the convenience of "just running to the store!" The nearest supermarket was about twenty miles away, our church was six miles away, the closest hospital twenty-five miles and the nearest shopping mall was thirty miles from our property.

A factor to consider, though not as much monetary in nature (as long as you weren't bitten by one), was the fact that there were a lot of Western Diamondback Rattlesnakes in the mountains where our future home was located. Add to that many coyotes, the somewhat scarce Gila Monsters and once in a while a wandering mountain lion or two, an even the scarcer bobcat, Javelinas, the Great Horned Owl, Turkey Vulture, various hawks and a thieving Fox. They all traveled on and across/over this mini ranch from time to time. Disregarding all the information that was given to us, what our research told us or the many unknowns that nobody told us about, we bought the mini ranch anyway. It took more than a year after first seeing the property with our friend Mike that we had the necessary money to buy the property.

My youngest son put a trailer on the additional land we bought on the other side of the mountain to the west and raised two of their five children when they lived there.

This is a history of some of the things I remember that took place within the zip code areas called Queen Creek and some things that were told to me by others that lived here before my wife and I and our youngest son and his family moved here from North Scottsdale. This place has given us many memories, some very good, some unfortunately, not so good. We live in a wonderful community that has created a boatload of history for us to write about that includes many memorable enjoyable moments, some very satisfying accomplishments and some about our working, playing and laughing with family and friends.

Do I Live In Queen Creek?

The name Queen Creek means many things to many people and we found out that many do not completely understand just where its boundaries begin or end. According to the United States Zip Codes website, Queen Creek encompasses 176 square miles of land in and around the Town of Queen Creek's boundaries. This land has a population of more than 145,000 and holds almost 51,000 homes. The zip code 85142 covers 71 square miles but the Town of Queen Creek only encompasses about 28 square miles of those 71 square miles.

We now live in the Town of Queen Creek and also live in Pinal County. The Queen Creek Library is located smack dab in the middle of the Town of Queen Creek and is a part of the Maricopa County Library System because the Town of Queen Creek is mostly in Maricopa County.

One day we went into the Queen Creek Library to get our free Queen Creek Library card only to find out that we must pay a hefty fee to get one because we pay Pinal County taxes, not

Maricopa County Taxes. This is just one small sample of the some of the confusion that reigns supreme at times within Queen Creek Arizona.

The Following Was Copied From The Town Of Queen Creek Web Site, with permission from the Town Manager John Kross:

DO I LIVE IN QC?

The current addressing system in the areas surrounding the Town of Queen Creek causes significant confusion among current and potential residents. The Town of Queen Creek often receives requests for information and services from residents and potential home buyers in unincorporated Pinal and Maricopa counties. Residents in these areas often expect to receive Queen Creek municipal services such as water, sewer, trash and recycling, library, police and fire protection; however, the Town does not have jurisdiction to provide these services to residents in unincorporated areas. Because the U.S. Postal Service establishes ZIP codes for efficient mail delivery, Queen Creek ZIP code boundaries do not always match the Town of Queen Creek's incorporated municipal boundaries. Areas outside the incorporated Town limits are often referred to as Queen Creek since the "Queen Creek" name is used in property mailing addresses assigned by the post office. For example, homes in the 85212, 85140 and 85143 ZIP codes have mailing addresses including "Queen Creek, AZ," although these ZIP codes are not within the Town of Queen Creek incorporated boundary limits.

The Town of Queen Creek has authority to provide services only within its incorporated boundaries. In the municipality of Queen Creek, these services are paid for by residents through property taxes, development fees paid with each building permit issued for a new home, and building permit fees for such things as swimming pools and home additions. Local sales taxes and construction sales taxes also help pay for services to residents.

Outside the Town limits, county governments provide some services, water is typically provided by private companies, police protection is provided by the appropriate county sheriff, and fire protection is by subscription with a private provider.

The Town of Queen Creek is glad to help verify property addresses. Please call 480-358-3000 for assistance or click on this link to the ZIP code map.

For additional information about ZIP codes and mailing addresses, please contact the U.S. Postal Service at 1-800-275-8777. For information about county services, contact the county where you live:

Maricopa County General Information: 602-506-3011
Pinal County General Information: 520-866-600

Questions to the Town:

Question: How can anyone who drives around this area believe that Queen Creek is still a small town with rural character? Seems to me that the development along Hunt Highway is out of control and would make a Californian quiver. And the commute along Ironwood to US 60 is all traffic! None of that is "rural" any more.

Answer: None of the areas you ask about are located in the Town of Queen Creek. It's very confusing, but having a Queen Creek ZIP code is not the same as living inside the Town limits. The US Postal service sets up ZIP codes for efficient mail delivery, but the Queen Creek ZIP code boundaries do not match the Town of Queen Creek incorporated boundaries.

The Town has authority to regulate development only within the Town boundaries. Outside the Town limits, the county governments decide all land use and zoning issues and the county governments provides local service. Nearly all of the development occurring in Pinal County is outside the Town limits. The rate of residential growth outside the Town is about twice as fast as inside the Town limits.

Inside the Town limits, the land use and zoning is guided by the Town's voter-approved General Plan which shows half of the geographic area of the Town as low density. Even once the Town is entirely built out, the overall density for the Town of Queen Creek will be only about 1.6 homes per acre. Most communities have four or more homes per acre. In addition, the Town of Queen Creek requires more open space, more trails, more parks, and preservation of the natural desert washes. The standards and design requirements for development inside the Town are distinctly different than those of other jurisdictions.

Please note that the Town now owns the Water Company and has it's own fire department.

This book, the part when we eventually move to Queen Creek in 1986, is about many things that happened within the zip codes 85140, 85142, 85143 and 85212 that are known as Queen Creek, Arizona.

Even some long time residents of the Town of Queen Creek do not fully understand just how big Queen Creek truly is.

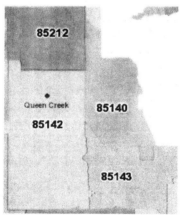

This Is Queen Creek Arizona

Queen Creek Memories

One of the many things that remain vivid in my mind linked to this place we call Queen Creek is the sweet smell of the citrus blossoms in the spring which coincided with allergy season for some. Many water haulers filling up at the water hole (the stand pipe) would swear that the blossoms caused their allergies. I remember there were crop dusters working day & night, the big airplane style blades that towered above many of the orange groves in and around Chandler Heights. The Smudge pots that were used to keep the frost off the citrus trees in the winter months. Only saw them used twice!

We remembered that: The workers harvested tangerines right up to mid-December so that they would be ready for purchase in time for the traditional Christmas stockings. The cotton cage wagons hauled loose cotton to the various gins nearby, leaving the roadsides covered with cotton that resembled snow.

The man that graded our dirt roads came from Florence which is about twenty-five miles from us so he drove the grader that pulled a small pick-up truck behind him. After he was finished for the day he would park the grader in a safe location near a home and drive the truck back to Florence. He would work on our roads every three or four weeks depending on the weather.

There was something special that lived in the road that ran up to the home that we were looking to buy back in 1985. It was a huge saguaro cactus that lived right in the middle of the road. It must have been over twenty feet tall. The owner of the property we were looking at said that the cactus was over a hundred years old and when they put in the road, no one had the heart to destroy it. However, it disappeared before we moved in.

The Pinal County Public Works Department decided to widen our dirt road and took down this beautiful specimen in the process.

Most all our neighbors used "burn barrels" that gave us the not so nice smell of burned garbage every evening depending on which way the wind was blowing. On the other hand, the fantastic good smells of the mesquite and other desert plants after a heavy rainstorm is unforgettable. Large Sonoran toads would suddenly appear after heavy rains. Their skin is toxic which caused two of our dogs to have seizures when they bite them.

The Sonoran Desert Toad

They stay around during the monsoon season and then go bury themselves until the next heavy rain. We used to hear hundreds of these animals croaking when they came out of the ground but that is not happening anymore because most all these toads that visit us now at our house are very small for reasons we do not know. We have not seen any of the much larger toads at our house this year. They are the biggest toad in the USA.

I remember the ranchers and farmers that drove either a white Ford or Chevrolet pickup truck, wore cowboy hats and always waved as they drove by from the opposite direction. There wasn't as much traffic back then. Besides cotton wagons, there were a lot of other farm equipment that traveled the roads in our community. When combines were used for certain crops they would sometimes move in long caravans of six to ten, which really clogged up some of our many two lane roads. There were a couple of early morning accidents that occurred when it was still dark and single tractors were traveling to where they were going to till or plow. People that were coming home from their late shift or from a long night time party did not always expect to come up on slow moving vehicles. One of these accidents occurred on Hunt Highway near Power Road when the driver of a tractor was killed after his tractor was hit by a pick-up truck going at a high rate of speed. After a couple of these accidents the slow moving tractors were then accompanied by another vehicle that had additional flashing lights.

When we moved here in 1986 there were a lot more different kinds of crops being grown in our area, including: table grapes, potatoes, watermelon, cantaloupe, sweet onions, wheat, soybeans, alfalfa, lemons, limes, tangerines, grapefruit, cauliflower, field corn (for cattle), table corn, peaches, pumpkins, pecans and even apples.

Where we came from in upstate New York the apple harvest was in the cool fall moths of September and October. Here we picked apples in July or August. Needless to say apples are not a very big crop around here but my two young granddaughters from Puerto Rico and I did pick apples out near the TRW plant one hot summer day many years ago.

When the potato harvest took place here it seemed like most everyone got some of the bounty. Someone once gave us a fifty-pound sack of these beautiful things. Unfortunately there is only so many potatoes a small family could eat before they went bad. Caroline tried baking these thin skinned gems on several occasions and what we got was pure white mashed potato on the inside. They were great. The Frito-Lay company bought up most of the crop around here for their potato chip division I am told.

The potatoes had to be processed quickly, I think due to the heat when the crop was harvested. I remember the procedure needed to get the potatoes to Frito Lay and other processors, went like this: From the fields the potatoes were trucked to the sorting and dry-cleaning sheds located next to the railroad tracks on Ellsworth north of down town Queen Creek. They could not use water to clean the potatoes because they would start to rot in the trucks that hauled them long distances to the various final processing plants. From the sheds the potatoes were loaded onto tractor-trailers and then sent to the scales that were located at the southeast corner of Ellsworth & Combs Road before they headed to the final processing locations. The drivers would get a pay slip for the weight of the potatoes they were about to transport at the scales.

Driving by those sorting sheds you could see vast brown clouds of dirt particles in the air inside and outside of those sheds. Talk about a very hot, unhealthy and dirty job, that was it. I have been told that those workers were paid very well with local teenagers and immigrant workers working side by side.

The Chandler Heights Trading Post

In the 1930's Chandler Heights was located in the middle of seven square miles of citrus groves. It was the vision of Doctor A.J. Chandler, founder of the Chandler Heights Citrus Tracts and the nearby town of Chandler. The Trading Post has been located in the same spot since 1946, on the southwest corner of Power Road and San Tan Blvd. Jeff Miller owned the Trading Post when we moved near Goldmine Mountain. Chandler Heights at that time was one of the major gateways for immigrants coming from south of our border to find jobs in the states. They temporally settled here first, and then when they had enough money they often would go to other places where there were other crops to be harvested.

A large number of these men traveled back and forth every year and were known by many of Jeff's employees and customers. Between the local harvest times, the immigrants would seek work from home owners, builders, and local businesses. Many of these people slept in the nearby citrus groves, called by some the "Groves Motel" or the "Open Air Hotel".

Many of these workers, mostly men, worked directly for Empire Fruit. They were paid by Empire with checks and every Friday hundreds would line up to get their checks cashed in the Trading Post. Jeff and sometimes a top level employee would hold thousands of dollars in their hands, cashing checks for up to five or six hundred dollars each. Then these people would go to the post office located in the rear of the store to buy and send money orders back home. They would then use some of their money in the Trading Post for food and other things to hold them until the next check was issued.

In the store there were newspapers in Spanish and information telling where farm laborers were needed in California, New Mexico, or even as far away as Georgia. The Trading Post butcher shop was the best for many miles around. For special occasions, and when our budget allowed, I would buy porterhouse steaks there, which were excellent. The butcher was a real character! When he got to know you he would often share the local news, even before it was printed in the newspaper.

I went there often and remember a man who worked as a broker between the people that needed labor and the ones that needed work. When he came into the store he was extremely loud, talking to everyone as he made his way back to the post office to pick up his mail. He reminded me of a large bear that made lots of loud noises and smelled really bad--I guess he never used any deodorant?--but everyone seemed to like him. One day the butcher told me he was found dead in his trailer, most likely from a heart attack.

Whenever we had our community wide clean-ups we would come to Jeff or, when he was not there, to his sister, for bread and cold cuts for the lunches we provided to all our workers. When we said we needed food for the clean-up, they would say: "What do you need?" and "How much do you want?" Over time Jeff gave us hundreds of loaves of bread, many pounds of cold cuts and cheese and anything else we needed. He has since rented his store out to some fine people but I will never forget how important Jeff was in the mix of helping the farmers getting their crops in on time and processed.

One day I walked into the store and back to the post office and found the service door was shut and locked. I saw the lady that ran the post office sitting in a chair and two men talking to her. I asked the butcher what was going on and he said that she was caught sending less money for money orders than was given to her by her most southern across the border customers. She was possibly stealing as much twenty dollars per money order from workers that could not read or write. She was a person that you would never expect would do something like that. It was a federal offense and I cannot find anyone that knows what happened to her after that.

Pancho's Palace

I have a friend that has a green card that lived a short distance from Queen Creek Town Hall for many seasons, when he worked here away from his family in Mexico. The land lord had a beat up old trailer in his back yard that housed six to eight workers who had to pay seventeen dollars a week in advance. There was an electric range, a sink and a ½ bathroom. The palace did not have any air-conditioning. The electric range was used to cook food and as a heater in the winter.

When the trailer was full the landlord would rent space on his back lawn also at seventeen dollars in advance per week. When it rained, the outside tenants were allowed to put up a tarp that could be attached to the house. Poncho sold tarps for ten dollars each. He also sold beer, water, soap and rented out his shower for three dollars for five minutes. Some of these men had green cards but most did not. There were at least two other of these types of housing places for immigrants within two blocks of Poncho's Palace right in the center of the Town of Queen Creek. Pancho's Palace is gone now but others still remain to this day.

Nature At Work In The San Tans

Our area is not prone to the tornadoes of the likes the Midwest has but we do infrequently experience something called microbursts. We had out guest house attacked by microbursts twice in a span of five years.

This is a violent down-draft that creates extreme wind shears at low altitudes and is usually associated with thunderstorms. Microbursts are capable of producing winds up to 100 mph causing significant damage. The life span of a microburst is around five to fifteen minutes. The felling of 30 to 60 power poles on various occasions along Hunt Highway, Empire and Power roads by microbursts has occurred without damaging people or homes in the past. Back in 1986 after we moved here, there were three times that power poles were blown down.

Our area did not have power for almost one week after one batch of power poles were knocked down. I believe that those microbursts came down near the county line parallel with the mountains just south of Empire & Hunt Highway. The person that we bought our home from, collected hundreds of power poles from previous storms before we moved in. I have to wonder what would happen if we had microbursts now with all the new building that has taken place since then.

One summer day my wife and I were in the pool for a swim. There were a lot of dark clouds on the horizon but no sign of lightning when all of a sudden we heard a big noise and the roof on our guest house blew completely off. The winds came from the mountains to the east and brought a lot of dust and some debris. This wind did not do any other damage to the main house or our barn or to any of our neighbors property. This would happen again about five years later.

Another time before we had the barn down back, I had a metal building on a concrete slab that stored horse tack, my saddle on a stand, three wooden shelves on top of concrete blocks that held all the bottles and cans for horse-related things. Caroline and I were both at work and I got home first on that hot DRY July afternoon.

After I got into the house I looked down into the paddock to check on our horse Santanna and saw something my mind had to take a few minutes to comprehend. There was my saddle on its stand and all the bottles and cans on the shelves but there was no ten foot square metal building anywhere to be seen. I had fastened this metal shed with bolts right into the concrete. They were spaced about every 2 feet apart all the way around the bottom edge.

I found the crumpled up shed in a wash about 30 yards away. It must have been a huge dust devil that ripped the shed straight up in the air but it did not tip over anything on any of the shelves.

We have experienced many heavy rains, sometimes with hail and tremendous thunder and lightning. One lightning bolt hit so close to our home that we lost two computers, two answering machines, our washer and dryer, our two wireless phones, our microwave, and our oven. Lucky for us, our homeowners insurance covered it. The telephone wires on the telephone poles were burned so badly that they had to be replaced for about 300 yards down-line from our home.

In recent years we have been getting some extremely heavy rainstorms, with rain amounts much higher than the areas below us on the flat lands to our north. We have one rain gauge on our property, as do our most direct neighbors, the Hunkler's and the Perry's. In 2012 we had three storms that measured four inches of rain or above over a four month period when the official gauge at Schnepfs Farm reported one to two inches.

This year we have had several storms measuring two to three inches when the flat-landers only had one half an inch. It seems like the storms that come over our mountains to the south are more concentrated until they get right over the mountain updrafts that spread the clouds out on their way north of us. Our neighbor directly south of us shares a deep wash that crosses both our properties. We have had several times when we almost lost our roads that lead to the back part of our land.

After the first near washout I asked my cowboy friend Mike if he knew where I could get some loads of rocks to fill in the places that were damaged the most. A few weeks later he called to tell me that I could get two big loads of rock and fill from a nearby road project for $20.00 a load, delivered. About one hour after that a huge dump truck pulled into our driveway. I told the driver where to dump the first load. What hit the ground were medium chunks of asphalt about six inches thick mixed in with the dirt and small stones. After the final load Mike came up with his big farm tractor that was fitted with a blade. He soon had the two loads spread into all the voids and along the edges. Although the stuff that was delivered was not what I expected, after the next big storms came it turned out to be exactly what was needed. It has turned out to be just the thing that has kept our road to the barn from being completely washed out.

Western Diamondback Rattlesnake

More Stories About Shakeysnakes

I have borrowed the word "shakeysnake" from a very dear friend, Donna Blasco, whom we worked with in the new construction cleaning business for several years. She is a wonderful horse woman who also was a member of the "Chandler Heights Twenty" horse group.

For your information, when Mr. Shakysnake starts his rattle a wagging it does sound like a rattle but when he feels in danger his rattling turns into a sound like a boiling tea pot. Most of the ones we have here are in the three to four foot long range. When really provoked they can strike out about the full length of their body. The very first time we saw a Rattlesnake in the wild in Arizona was when we were on a trail ride on the Salt River Indian Reservation east of Scottsdale. The snake was near the trail and did not put up a fuss and just moved out of our way.

Now, for the sake of our local Chamber of Commerce, I should explain that we lived in Scottsdale for seventeen years and would often go looking for Mr. Shakeysnake whenever we went out into the nearby desert for a hike. The first one we saw in seventeen years in Arizona was on that trail ride on the Salt River Indian reservation. The next time was a few years later when we had our horse in a fenced area behind our home near Goldmine Mountain.

I was carrying a flake of hay over to Sanny's feeding station a few yards from our stack of bailed hay. As I was walking a rattler fell out of my clump of hay onto the ground in front of me. I did a difficult hop and jump over it which then put the snake behind me for just a second. I then did another jump forward and then quickly turned around only to come to the realization that the snake was already dead. It must have been baled up along with the alfalfa. This must have looked like a really funny dance commemorating my first real, life and death encounter with a dead shakeysnake.

When we first moved near Goldmine Mountain it became evident that this was the best place to see a shakeysnake because they really like rocky places. I did kill several of them at first but came to realize that we had invaded their land and they do not like humans any more we like them. They are God's creatures after-all and are helpful to us because they like rodents and other things that humans do not like or want.

After a while I bought a snake stick which allowed me to grab the snake by his neck just behind its head. I used a five gallon bucket that has a secure cover to take these fellows about two or three miles away, hoping they will adapt to the lands where I take them.

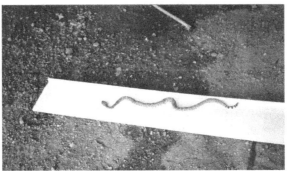

4 Foot Shakeysnake From a Distance

Our fire department provided snake removal service at no extra charge, when I was not home. Caroline had a garden next to our home that has shade in the latter part of the day. She grew a lot of things in her garden and kept it moist when the summer months came along. I got a 999 number on my pager one day at work, which meant there was an emergency. I went to the construction trailer to call Caroline, fearing the very worst. She said that there was a big rattler in her garden and asked me what she should do.

I told her to call the fire department, then Rural Metro. I called her about an hour later to find out what was happening. She said that she was sitting in a lawn chair with our wireless phone, babysitting the rattler until the fire department showed up because she said that was what the fire department operator told her to do.

The next time I called she told me that one of the two firemen that came would not even get out of the truck. The other one said, while smiling broadly, that he was going to have to charge extra because there were two rattlers in the garden, not one, and they were having sex. Caroline told me that the brave fireman put the snakes in a bucket and sealed it but was made to ride on the rear step of the firetruck with the bucket beside him while the other scaredy-cat fireman drove the truck away.

Our Goat Herd

The head of our Pygmy Goat herd was the Matriarch of the herd without a doubt. She would get the entire herd together each day, weather permitting, and from the group with the mothers behind her and their kids behind them. The adult males would be last. They all behaved very well except the adult males who seemed to be mocking the whole procedure by fooling around bucking and play biting each other. The route was the same, up the driveway towards the front of the house, around the house and back down to the barn area. It was about a 20 minute walk with all browsing along the way.

We gave them a covered shelter that was completely fenced in. I would always feed them in the enclosure in the evenings so that they would be safe from the coyotes. After I fed in the morning I would leave the gate open.

One day I heard goats braying away, close by. I went to the door and saw three goats on our ramp that leads to the back door and the rest of the herd was standing nearby. Now this was something special, something we had never seen before. They were all complaining vocally that something was wrong.

When I went down the ramp towards them they all marched ahead of me. My first thought was that one of their relatives might be hurt. They continued braying all the way down the road to the barn and their enclosure. They took me to their gate but no further and all looked inside where there was a very large shakeysnake lying right next to their water station in a small puddle. I had to get my bucket and snake stick up at the house, with the whole herd following me still braying away but when I got what I needed to remove the snake and started back down, they calmed down. I removed the snake and all was well after that.

The next three stories are a little stranger than most and they involve three different cats from the twelve member cat herd we had at the time. I was out in the front driveway servicing my truck one day when I noticed a rattler slithering down the far side of our dirt road. I walked over to get a closer look that was out of striking distance, when the snake started to coil up while rattling away. Out of the corner of my eye I saw Squeaky, one our older cats, run over to the snake while it was still rattling and she sat down right next to it. I immediately started yelling at her to get away from the snake but it looked like the snake was oblivious to her. I even threw some pebbles at her in an effort to get her away from the snake. She eventually walked away and the snake left, heading down the road to who knows where.

About two months later when I was walking down to the barn I heard another rattler near a shade tree beside the road that seemed to be very upset. Once again an entirely different cat, a pure white one we called Snowflake, ran over and sat down right next to this very agitated snake, that did not do anything to her. I really believe that these cats were trying to tell me that the snake was a friend and not to do anything to hurt it. This I will never know but it is something I wonder about.

We had a pool party with a lot of children playing in and around the pool. I went to the laundry room that is close to the pool, and found a shakeysnake lying next to the washer. I felt that I had to shoot this one because I didn't want any of our guests bitten. This was before I had a snake stick. The children did not know what happened, which was my wish, and I cleaned the area thoroughly. The next day I went down to the laundry room and yet another cat, called Tigger, was lying on the very spot where I killed the snake.

One summer night one of our neighbors came out of his home when he heard a hissing sound that sounded to him like his outside faucet pipe had sprung a leak. It was dark but he could still make out the pipe below the faucet. He reached down to feel where he thought that the leak was and was bitten by a rattler that had given him fair warning but he was unable to see it. The man was in intensive care for two weeks and his hand was screwed up for many months.

We live very carefully outdoors here, from May until October, but we keep in mind that Mr. Shakeysnake can be seen in every month of the year, depending on the weather, in

Arizona. One day I dropped my guard somewhat because we had not seen a snake for months. I was going to hook up a hose at our guest house in a place that was just outside a large opening where I keep our garden tools. The pipe is very close to the edge of the concrete floor where the tools were. I started to reach down but stood back up to see if the hose connection was tight. I looked down to where my hand would have been and there was a rattler all coiled up lying next to a shovel. A rattler does not have to rattle before he strikes. If you reach down towards him quickly he will just strike. I was extremity lucky! If I had tried to hook that hose up my hand would have been about twelve inches from his nose. I carefully took him a mile or two away and prayed that I will never see him again.

My grandson was about five years old when he was riding his bicycle on the dirt road in front of his home on Sossaman Road. It was in May and was a bright day when he almost ran over a rattler on the road. He dropped his bike and ran inside his home screaming to his father about what he had almost done. He must have scared the snake, because by the time dad got out there the snake was gone.

Our Visiting Shepherds

There were very few people living along Hunt Highway from Skyline Road to almost all the way to the outskirts of Florence when we moved here. Every year hundreds of sheep camped out on the West side of Hunt near Skyline. The shepherds had a noisemaker that sounded like a shotgun blast which used compressed air and went off about every 30 minutes during the night. It was used to keep the coyotes away from their herds. Some thought the shepherds were shooting at them when they drove on the road that went by the sheep camp. There were many sheep herds that came from up north in the winter and were used to feed on the cut alfalfa fields all over our community and in many of our neighboring communities.

Just a little north of Horseshoe Lake there is Sheep's Crossing Bridge that was built in 1944 by the Flagstaff Sheep Company that would allow a safer Verde River crossing for sheep. The last time we were there, in 1976 we saw some Big Horn Sheep nearby and the remains of a small plane that had crashed there some years ago.

Another thing we found was a bath tub that was surrounded by some tall reeds close by the Verde River. There was water flowing from a spring into this white porcelain bathtub that over flowed and the water then found it's way into the Verde. The amazing thing about this water is that it is warm water and the perfect temperature for a bath. All our family that were with us took turns soaking in that miniature hot tub.

CHAPTER 5

WHAT IS A COMMUNITY?

According to The New Lexicon Webster's Dictionary of the English Language, "a community is a body of people living near one another and in social relationship, a village community, a sharing, a community of interest."

Another concept I found that is a little bit different, was written on August 3, 2007 by James Edwards

A Community!

And what does it take to make one? Is it like-minded people, who share ideals, beliefs or some other common values? Does it take a certain number of people to make a community?

If the people around you encourage and support you, even when you're full of it, are they being a good community? If you aspire to join a clique or elite, and that clique decides to accept you, are you then a part of a community?

I believe that community is nothing but mutual respect. People can form a community without having common beliefs, without having shared identity or defining themselves in terms of each other. Numbers are irrelevant; ideals and desires are irrelevant; even the extent of mutual support and patronage is largely irrelevant. Community is a state of mind. It's a sense of belonging that springs from feeling other people accept you despite, not because, of who you are.

When I came to Australia I did so for personal reasons; I didn't come for my career, or the crowd, or the sense of belonging. I came here because my heart told me to, even though the reasons were wrong. And I never tried to

rationalize that away. I didn't try to convince myself that there were other reasons for coming here, that my career, my social life, or my lifestyle would otherwise improve. Oh wait, no, that's not true. I did try to convince myself of all of those things — and to some extent, I succeeded; because to some extent, those things were true.

But they were never the reason, they were just ad hoc post rationale.

And my reason turned to dust, and here I was, lonely, isolated, unhappy. I only had one real friend here (and everyday I'm thankful for his friendship), and already I'd made a whole bunch of enemies. But you know what — I stayed anyway. Because what I'm looking for is here. What I'm looking for is everywhere.

The world is a community; we can't help ourselves, it just happens." The End!

Whatever a community means to you, I think we have a great one that has a foundation built by people, the pillars, who are caring people, people that care about our lands, that cherish our history, people that truly want the best for their neighbors, people that now live within the Town of Queen Creek, the people that live in the foothills of the San Tan Mountains and within the zip codes that carry the address of Queen Creek. The people that want to preserve and protect the San Tan Mountain Regional Park, knowing full well that the Park is a treasure that needs to be preserved for the generations of people that will come after us.

We are in a state of transition now, where our older pillars are not in as strong a position of governance or in as strong a position when it comes to protecting our community from excessive overbuilding. My fear is that this will eventually take away the rural atmosphere that all our pillars fought so hard for us to keep over the years. It seems that voices of sensibility are becoming weaker with age and the voices that want to cave into the wants of the developer are getting much stronger. Does money buy everything, even our history?

The People Of Our Community

We have lived in several new start-up communities over the years, in several different parts of the country, and all of them that I can remember had pillars, characters, those behind the scenes (the unsung worker bees) & the crazies. This section has to do with a small number of those that live here now or have previously lived here. I leave it to you as to what category you believe they should be in. But it is not necessary.

These are some of the people that I have known and/or worked with in the last twenty-eight years. These are my memories of them--more than some are wonderful ones. Some have submitted there own stories here for which I am very grateful. There are books available about the scores of pioneers that have enriched this land in many ways. They have been diligently recorded by authors like: Francis Pickett, Sue Sossaman, David Salge and Silvia Acuna and others. After reading some of these wonderful historical books I now more fully realize what a treasure this community is because of its truly rich history.

Incorporation

Twenty-four years ago three men, Mark Schnepf, Steve Sossaman and Paul Gardner unselfishly gave many hundreds of hours of their time on a gamble that they could get permission from bordering communities and then approval of the citizens so that they could incorporate the Town Of Queen Creek. These young men are a very important part of the Town's history but to this date they are not even officially recognized or celebrated on the Town's website. The Town of Queen Creek's incorporation process began when Gilbert did a strip annexation that stretched to Power Road, including 600 feet east of Power Road which was a part of farm land owned by Mark Schnepf and Steve Sossaman. They did not like the fact that part of their land was under the governance of the Town of Gilbert. Their complaints to the Town of Gilbert went unheard. They felt that Gilbert's next step would be annexing all the land east and south to Pinal County's boundaries.

They went to their Maricopa County supervisor, Tom Freestone, who heard their story and appointed them the heads of a citizen's advisory group representing Queen Creek, as it was then known. Mark and Steve then talked with Steve's father Jamie Sossaman, who was a high-ranking legislator for the State of Arizona and asked for his help. The Sossaman family enjoys a history of ninety-four years of farming in the area known as Queen Creek. The Schnepf family history goes back for over seventy years of farming here. Neither Mark nor Steve wanted Gilbert to take over the land in name and governance that their families had worked so long and hard to develop.

Jamie Sossaman then crafted a bill that would stop strip annexation. Soon the bill had a lot of support but it was not up for a vote yet. This caused the City of Phoenix, Mesa and Chandler, which were using strip annexation, a lot of consternation. Their future plans involved using annexation to further extend their boundaries they needed for their predicted growth. With this bill looming over the largest populated areas in the state they all put pressure on Gilbert to cede back the 600 feet east of Power Road, which they eventually, very reluctantly, agreed to do.

These two young men, while in their 30's, had now earned the credibility and attention of the movers and shakers from the biggest communities in our State. Their two biggest supporters, Jamie Sossaman and Tom Freestone suggested that they follow up quickly by incorporating.

The Queen Creek advisory group became the incorporation board or council and set up their office in a part of the Queen Creek Water Company's building. At the behest of Tom Freestone his secretary joined the incorporator's because she had years of experience in the Maricopa County's political process and wound up being invaluable in helping the young men achieve their goal. The late Dennis Barney also gave a great deal of his sorely needed help in land division and land development expertise. Then the real work began to incorporate. The Town of Gilbert, the City of Mesa and Pinal County, which bordered the land that was submitted for incorporation, had to give their permission before it could be approved. They wanted everything east of Power Road to be in the new town and had to get the permission from a now slightly unfriendly Gilbert. Gilbert relented and agreed and the Town's west boundary was set. The north boundary was controlled by Mesa.

The council wanted the north boundary to reach all the way to what is now Gateway Airport but the Mesa City Manager did not want to give any concessions to these young upstarts at all. Mark and Steve knew the Mesa Mayor very well and she had a lot of cooperation within her City Council at that time and she stepped in to save the day. The men wound up with Germann Road as the northern boundary as a compromise. Pinal County had no problem with giving permission that the east and south border as a boundary for the new Town.

There were hundreds of papers and forms that had to be completed and permissions granted, some that had to voted on by Councils, water districts and so forth. I believe that they needed 1000 votes from those that lived within the Towns proposed boundaries.

An approval from the State and County was needed after a clear drawing of the Towns proposed bounties was submitted. Paul Gardner was called upon to draw the Towns boundaries which he did very well. No pun intended!

The biggest cost for a new town is the maintenance of the roads within. Knowing this, these men submitted plans that did not include the roads running through the area as a part of the Town. It is a strong guess that whoever had to sign off on the incorporation plans did not see this omission, which resulted in Maricopa County being responsible for the maintenance of the roads within the new Town. After it was later found that these roads were purposely left out of the Town's incorporation plan, a new State law was passed that all roads will be a part of all future incorporation's.

I attended all of the open house meetings that were presented by Mark Schnepf and his cohorts. Most of the naysayers were worried about taxes but the only taxes that the Town could levy were sales taxes. Most people were concerned that their property taxes would rise after the Town was incorporated. The men put that worry down quickly, getting the support from most everybody concerned.

Once the tax issue was cleared up most everybody living within the Towns proposed boundaries were for the incorporation. The Town of Queen Creek was incorporated on September 05, 1989, coincidentally on the same date as the incorporation of another Town with a Q in it's name-- Quartzite. The President of the Council, Mark Schnepf, was appointed Mayor. Vice President Steve Sossaman was appointed Vice Mayor and Paul Gardner was appointed council member. During the interim, until elections could be held Mark appointed Steve Sossaman Mayor. Mark became the first elected Mayor of Queen Creek. All three are still involved in service to the Town Of Queen Creek.

If it were not for these three men and all those that helped them we would likely have been annexed into the Town of Gilbert as their suburb. But we are a Town of about 26,000 people now with amenities that some larger towns do not have. Our citizens, young and the older ones, are encouraged to participate in our government through the the Citizen Leadership Institute program, the Community Town Hall and the Star Student programs.

We have quite a few programs that involve our citizen's children, children that may grow to be our leaders one day. Thank you Steve, Mark, Paul, Jamie and Tom, and all the others that followed their lead some twenty-five years ago.

Mike Lucas

*Mike Working
With Children At
School*

A few years ago Deputy Mike Lucas was scheduled to be reassigned to another community. There was an outcry from the citizens in our community that this not happen. This came from the many that knew all the wonderful work Mike did with many of our school children as well as the superb professional police service that he gave. I heard that this kind of a request from citizens in a community had not happened before in the history of the Maricopa County Sheriff's Department and it went all the way to Sheriff Joe Arpiao, who agreed with the citizens of our community and canceled the order for his reassignment.

Submitted By Mike Lucas

I began my law enforcement career with the Honolulu Police Department and came to Arizona, job related, mid 1970's. I subsequently went to work with the Maricopa County Sheriff's Office. My experience and preference was serving smaller communities and thusly, was assigned to the Queen Creek area shortly before the Town incorporated. I had the opportunity to witness the Community grow over the years to the high level amenities and quality of life the residents are now able to enjoy.

I have seen the Town Management team and staff struggle through the economic downturn, but whose dedicated efforts continued to pursue addressing the needs of the citizens first and foremost. I am very happy that I was able to see the building of more schools enabling the opportunity for better education for all. Medical facilities, infrastructure development and commercial growth are a plus, and more services are on the drawing board. I saw the congested farm roads develop into the smoother flowing roadways that we have today.

I am impressed with the level of Public Safety provided today by the Maricopa County Sheriff's Office and the Queen Creek Fire Department. Both agencies work concertedly to meet the needs of the community. They constantly strive to meet the needs of the future through numerous Citizen safety training programs at no cost to the public. I am. not a resident, but do feel an attachment to the Community.

I have a couple stories that might be of interest. One is a Domestic Violence call I responded to. A dispatch sent me to a residence located in the vicinity of Ocotillo and Sossaman Roads. On my arrival I overheard a man yelling loudly from inside the residence. I knocked and announced myself, then entered to find the man sitting in a chair some distance from his wife who was also sitting while saying nothing. I calmed the man and asked why he had screamed at his wife. The man explained that his wife was calling him bad names and nagging him for the past hour and that he was frustrated with her behavior. I then spoke to the woman who simply stared at me while saying nothing. I discovered that the woman was not able to speak because of recent dental work that prohibited her from talking. The woman then picked up a pen and paper and began writing and then handed it to me. I then noticed several pieces of paper crumbled on the floor around the man's chair. He handed me several pieces that proved to be notes that had been written by the woman and then thrown at him. I read them without repeating the notorious comments and asked him why he didn't simply ignore the notes? The man said, "Well I did have the opportunity to get a word in edgewise, didn't I?"

The second one: I arrived at a residence in the vicinity of Riggs and Hawes Roads where there was a report of people screaming in the residence. Upon entry I met with two portly people who proved to be husband and wife. The husband was sitting in the far corner of the living room and the wife sitting on a couch in the center of the room. The television was blaring and both had their own individual remote controllers. The argument was over which program the other insisted on watching. The husband threatened to smack the wife and visa-verse, but neither seemed to have the energy or means to move. My disposition was to turn off the television, seize both remotes and return them at such time they agreed to compromise.

On another occasion I stopped a man on Rittenhouse Road who had been speeding well above the speed limit. He explained that he and his family were late for church and asked if I could give him a ticket on his way back home.

Once I received a call to the vicinity of Hawes and Hunt Highway in reference to a report of shots fired. On my arrival I met with a young man who was holding a pellet rifle. He explained that he was hired by a lady to shoot birds if they approached her cats' food dish that sat outside her door. I explained to the young man that cats are natural predators of birds, so I don't think his protection was needed. The youth explained, "The lady has the cat inside, in a wheel chair giving it's on an I.V."

Regina Whitman is a community activist that has helped keep our local residential developers in check for many years.

<u>Submitted By Regina Whitman</u>

<u>Where she came from:</u> Born in Brooklyn, NY 2/10/1950. I Lived in N.Y. all my life until moving to Queen Creek in September 1993. A N.Y. State License Veterinary Technician and Wildlife Rehabilitator.

<u>Why she came here:</u> My Love for the desert climate (the OLD dry heat!) and a desire to create a wildlife rescue. The San Tan Mountains had me at first glimpse. The quiet, rural atmosphere

would be a welcome change from the loud traffic and crush of people in NY.

What she has seen in our Community: A lot of good people and a lot of not-so-good people. What used to be an open landscape with folks that waved hello as they passed, some hauling water or livestock, became an overbuilt landscape of tile roofs and block walls with everyone in a hurry! A local government that was once open, communicative and inviting of, listened to your opinions, is now run by special interest politicians with no regard for the pristine Sonoran Desert we live in. It consists of real estate agents, developers and those looking for growth rather than preserving the rural lifestyle many others & I came here for.

Who she is in this Community: First and most importantly, I am a Wildlife Rehabilitator and animal advocate. I have built a facility for the care of injured & orphaned wild animals native to AZ. Founded in 1993, Desert Cry Wildlife rescue & rehabilitation became Desert Cry Wildlife, Inc., a 501c3 in 2005. Over the years thousands of critters have received care here. A great many have been returned to the wild life they were born to live. As a result of my new location, I became very knowledgeable on certain desert species. My greatest success is the Jackrabbit. I have written papers that have been published in the journals of both national and international organizations, as well as presented at symposiums.

I helped collect signatures to outlaw Cock-fighting in AZ, stood in front of a bulldozer and up to politicians & developers to try and save the desert and its creatures. And as the higher powers would have it, I had to become active in the political arena to accomplish this. Many years of attending government meetings, hearings and outreach presentations by developers have brought out the rebel in me. I inspired Pinal County to adopt a new policy of "no animals allowed" after showing up at one board of supervisors meeting with my one-winged Harris' Hawk (who showed his disdain for the proceedings by "soiling" the carpet).

To those that I opposed, confronted and exposed, I became the "troublemaker". In the context it was issued, I was and am still proud that my actions and words were beneficial to whatever cause was being championed. Mine was the first signed petition for the annexation of our area into the town of Queen Creek as a very successful strategy that stopped the development of Box Canyon the first time in 1998. But now in 2013, the politicians that have come to power since then have begun the process to allow this development, thus destroying an incredibly unique ecosystem and Native American Treasures. It has been a series of battles with some defeats, some compromises and some victories. The battles continue, as do I.

Over the twenty-eight years of living in Queen Creek, I have been a part of civic organizations; banding together with like-minded and motivated folks. I was a Charter Member (I still have the framed certificate), Board Member in the San Tan Mountains PRIDE Assoc. for about 7 yrs and Vice Pres/Secretary and President of the Friends of the San Tan Mountains Regional Park from 2005-2007. I have written columns, articles and editorials in The Chandler Heights/San Tan Monthly newspaper and have been the subject of a few in the Tribune, AZ Republic, Ocotillo News, AJ Independent, and the QC Independent.

Our First Full Time Queen Creek Town Manager
Cynthia Seelhammer

Submitted By Cynthia Seelhammer

Here are a few random thoughts and stories for you.

1. Characters -- please do not forget John Stocker, who was my neighbor up the hill from the time I moved to Queen Creek in 1982 until he moved away a few years ago. His wife Prudy told me that John died last spring (2012) after several strokes.

John was an architect who bought a piece of property in San Tan Ranches, located east of Ellsworth and south of Hunt Highway. He himself built a bridge across a wash so that he could park his trailer as far up the hill as possible. He had a pond outside the windows where he and Prudy could watch wildlife, including bobcats, drink.

John was a crotchety old guy with a heart of gold. He volunteered often, and was one of the long-time members of Kiwanis and other community groups. He had a beard and often wore an NRA hat. His political views were nearly the opposite of mine, but I was often glad he was watching my place through the scope of his rifle. He would come down the minute he saw a stranger, or the moment I called. Since I lived alone for several years, he was exactly the kind of neighbor anyone would want. Although he started the foundation of a house, John never did build his dream home. Instead, when Prudy's patience ran out after living many years in a fifth wheel, he and Prudy bought a park-model trailer home and lived there. John always said that when the County paved the roads, it would be time for him to move on. And that is what he and Prudy did.

2. Queen Creek recruited me for its first full-time manager in 1993. I was one of four finalists and flew in from California for the interview. The Town incorporated in 1989 and hired a retired man to be half-time town manager. His name was Mike McNulty and he was something of a legend in Arizona, having helped towns start and serving as interim and part-time manager for many smaller cities and towns.

The pay for the first full-time manager was $34,000 a year, much less than I was earning in California. I'd been working in city government for almost 10 years, had my Master's degree in public administration, and figured this might be my chance to return to my place in Queen Creek and escape living in the shadow of my ex-husband in California.

I remember that two or three of the other candidates brought their wives with them, so when time came for the Interim Manager to give a tour, the City Clerk offered a tour to the wives. It was clear that since I was a woman, people thought I would go with the wives on the tour. Nothing doing -- I was a candidate for the job, so I made the guys in the backseat move over so I could ride in the car with the other candidates.

That City Council included Tom Much and David Johnston and Mark Schnepf, one of the town founders. When I was hired, there was one full-time clerk/treasurer and two part-time secretaries. We had our offices in the old LDS Ward which the Town bought as a Town Hall. We had to run off the Council agenda packet and staff reports on an old copier, and collate the packets by hand. I remember that one of the two secretaries was always in tears as we collated those packets, it was so hard and confusing, and the old copy machine kept breaking down. I remember walking through the empty south wing of the Town Hall, wondering what we would ever do with that empty space. How soon that changed.

At first the Town contracted out many services. We had a contract Building Inspector who came out once a week, but only if we had something to inspect. In those days, we might get only a couple of building permits each year. We had a contract engineer, and a contract grant specialist who helped us remodel some of the old houses in downtown Queen Creek with federal CDBG funds. The tidal wave of growth of the late 1980s had stalled when the savings and loan banks failed, and the RTC came in to take over foreclosed properties. This was a sad time, but it was good for Queen Creek. It meant that the Town had a few years to work with residents to create an excellent General Plan, Parks and Open Space Plan, and Town Center Plan, getting all the hopes and expectations into writing and into the Town Code. Once the growth started up again, we were ready to guide it and to keep some of the things people loved best about living in the Town. If it were not for all those residents putting their hopes into those plans, Queen Creek would not have preserved its washes, created trails and parks, or set the high standards for development that created the character of the Town.

The Council was still learning how to be a real town. I remember there was an old ball field west of Town Hall and it needed to be repaired, shifting the location of home base, re-graded, and a new irrigation system and fencing. The bid for the work was $5,000 and a couple members of the Council thought that was outrageous. Surely everyone in Town could pitch in and make the necessary repairs? So the two of them and friends showed up on weekends to work on it -- but the work far outlasted the volunteers. Eventually, months later, I found an Eagle Scout who arranged for his family and donations to finish that ball field. Queen Creek won a lot of awards for those plans, codes and designs.

For the first couple of years, my personal Ford F150 was the Town's one truck. I was the one who moved chairs back and forth across the street between Town Hall and the Community Center, I was the one who went out and manually turned on and off the irrigation for the lawn, using a long metal key. I was even the one who poisoned the gophers. Every year the State made each city and town fill out a form describing the town's "fleet of vehicles." Other than my personal truck, the "fleet" consisted of a couple of riding lawn mowers.

I remember one strange incident that might have been con men trying to bamboozle a small town. A couple of men contacted the Mayor about a new industry that would create jobs. The Mayor sent them to meet with me. They said that they wanted the Town's help locating a piece of property along the rail line because they were pursuing a federal grant. I think they wanted the Town to give them the land, or lease it to them cheaply. But the more I asked questions, the stranger the proposal became. They said they had a plan to recycle used diapers and turn them into a black block that they hoped could be used to build low-income housing. They had a woman on the phone who said she was their banker. They gave me her business card -- and it was an off-shore bank in the Caribbean. I don't know exactly what they were up to, but since the Town was so small and owned no land, they seemed to lose interest in us. I still wonder if they were planning to apply for the grant, then take the money and run? Or were they hoping to get rights to a piece of land they would later sell? In the end it did not matter -- they vanished.

Queen Creek used to be far enough out in the country that people would dump pets there. Once on a walk in my neighborhood, I found a cardboard box and when I opened it a chicken jumped out. There were several other dead chickens in the box, so I wondered if someone had tired of their fast-growing Easter chicks. My neighbor kept chickens, so the one that survived found a good home.

Another time, someone brought a puppy to Town Hall that was found stuck in an irrigation ditch. We found him a home too. But the incident I best remember was when I found a puppy near my house, lying in the road. I brought it home and put it on the front screen porch. He did not like being alone and yelped and howled. I told my neighbors up the hill, John and Prudy Stocker, about the puppy and not to worry about the noise. Later that day Prudy called me to say that the puppy's cries had brought another puppy out of the desert and to my yard. She wanted me to know that she had added that puppy to my porch so I would not be surprised when I came home.

It was a late night for me, as it often was, since I was the only Town staff person who could attend all the evening Council Meetings and committee meetings. I remember arriving home after dark and seeing a puppy butt scuttle under the daybed on the porch, hiding from me. My fiance Tom was with me and we went inside to get a flashlight. I got down on my hands and knees to peer under the daybed, pulling out the puppy to hand to Tom. One puppy, two puppies - and another, and another and another! There were five by the time I got them all out! I have seldom laughed so hard in my whole life.

Luckily, the folks at Town Hall helped me find homes for all of the puppies. I already had three dogs of my own so I could not keep them. They were cute spotted pups with Queensland Heeler blood. One went to the son of the Town Manager of Gilbert; another went home with a secretary. I remember that we even convinced the copy repair man to take one.

The internet was very new at that time, but before long I was sending my weekly Town Manager Update to all Council, staff, and any resident who wanted it. Every week I sent out info about what was going on at Town Hall and in Queen Creek. Pretty soon people were sending me questions and ideas. I remember late one evening getting email from someone in Rancho Jardines asking me to help because they had found a cow wandering into their yard and did not know who it belonged to. Could I please send an email out to my list and ask if anyone was missing a cow near such-and-such cross streets? I did -- and the next morning received a rather sheepish follow-up email. The "cow" was really more of a calf -- it had seemed so much bigger in the dark.

Speaking of cows, we were finally getting ready to hire our first full-time Town recreation staff person. I had asked a Parks and Rec professional from Mesa to join us on the interview panel. She arrived and said, "Wow, you have cows just behind Town Hall." I said there were several pastures around us, so cows were common. "Don't they damage the irrigation?" she asked. That is when we realized there really WERE cows behind Town Hall, on the ball field and in the parking lot, having escaped from the fenced wash. All of Town staff was soon outside, trying to shoo the cows back to the wash and pasture so they would not wander into the streets and yards in town. That's when I learned that those little red cows with horns are nothing like the gentle Holsteins I grew up with on the dairy farm. Those little tough cows were mean, and one tried her darnedest to use her horns to throw me into a tree. I dodged behind the tree just in time. People in Queen Creek were remarkably kind and supportive of each other. One day we realized that the water in our Town Hall parking lot came from the washtub of the neighbors. These people were washing clothes by hand and emptied the tub water into their yard. I sent a note out to the email list asking if anyone had an old washing machine to donate? Within hours we had several offers of donations.

John Kross Our Second Full Time Town Manager.

Submitted By John Kross

John Kross, Queen Creek Town Manager – Biography John Kross is Town Manager for Queen Creek, Arizona. He has been in planning and community development in both Wisconsin and Arizona since 1989. In Wisconsin, he worked for a private downtown redevelopment firm, and in Arizona he has worked for the Town of Gilbert, the cities of Phoenix and Wickenburg, and Queen Creek, where he has been since 1996. Mr. Kross spent his first eight years in Queen Creek as the Community Development Director, two years as Assistant Town Manager and nine months as Interim Town Manager. On March 26, 2007, the Queen Creek Town Council voted unanimously to appoint Mr. Kross to fill the position of Town Manager.

Mr. Kross has a Bachelor of Arts in Business Management and Leadership Studies/Public Policy from Ripon College in Wisconsin and a Masters of Public Administration from Arizona State University. He is the Immediate Past President of the Arizona City/County Management Association, a member of the International City/County Management Association, an ICMA Credentialed Manager, and a member of the American Institute of Certified Planners, American Planning Association, American Society of Public Administration and the Urban Land Institute.

Mr. Kross serves on the Chandler Gilbert Community College President's Community Advisory Council, and is Chair of the TOPAZ Regional Wireless Cooperative (the Board that oversees the implementation and management of the East Valley's emergency radio response system and is an association of Gilbert, Mesa, Queen Creek, Apache Junction Fire District).

Bob & Mary Clausen

Own and operate Magma Engineering which is an icon within the Town and is known throughout the United States and beyond for their expert work.

They have supported San Tan Mountains PRIDE Association projects that have benefited hundreds of families that live within our great state of Arizona.

Mary was the chairperson for the Town's annual Christmas Parade for several years.

Bob Ingram

San Tan Mountain Regional Park Ranger Bob Ingram is about to receive and award from Pinal County Supervisor Sandie Smith with Queen Creek Council member Bill Heath, Queen Creek Staff member, Maricopa County Supervisor Jeff Groscostt, Bob Ingram, Queen Creek Mayor Mark Schnepf & Maricopa County Supervisor Fulton Brock standing by. This meeting was held at the "Gap" which is one of the most spectacular and beautiful parts of the 10,000 acre park that Bob protected so well.

Bob worked for the Maricopa County Parks and Recreation Department as the San Tan Mountain Regional Parks first and only Park Ranger at that time. He worked tirelessly removing abandoned vehicles, trash and dump-sites from his park. He also blocked the many illegal motorized two wheel and four wheel drive roads that were made in many parts of the Park that were there before he arrived.

He did so much in the early days before there were fences to stop the scaring and trashing of our and his Park. He did not only supervise this preservation but he physically helped do it, much to the consternation of his boss, Bill Scalzo. He was a friend of mine and the San Tan Mountains PRIDE Association.

Bob & Joyce Hildebrandt

Joyce served on the Town Council for many years and helped form our Community into what it is today. Bob owned a vehicle repair garage that was behind our first Post Office and the old Circle K. His garage was located just north of the water stand pipe that served our water haulers for a many years. Bob and Joyce helped at every-one of our community wide cleanups. Bob sorrowfully passed away on September 11, 2011. Both had been in the real estate business for many years

Rudy & Toni Valenzuela

Rudy and Toni Valenzuela not only own and operate a great restaurant in Town but they have given so much to our Community for many years. Toni has served the Town for several years as a hard working council member. One day Caroline and I went into Rudy's Restaurant for lunch at a time of the day when there were few customers there. Rudy came out and sat down with us and we were able to have a good conversation with him. We soon learned that he and Toni were involved in the East Scottsdale Little League when we were. They were working with the younger groups and we were working with the older groups. So our paths never crossed.

We also found out from him that they had lived close to us. Toni found the time to coach Little League in Scottsdale and in Queen Creek and I coached her grandson in the Queen Creek Little League. Albert was our catcher who did an excellent job at that position and had the talent to cover other positions as well if we needed him too.

I had not seen Albert for about eight or nine years. A couple of weeks ago I met him in the restaurant where he works with his grandparents as a waiter. I did not recognize him at first when he came to our table. He thanked me for being his coach and then told me who he was. He has turned into a very handsome young man that knew me but until I knew more about him, my memories of him came rushing back.

Toni has worked tirelessly for many years to the benefit of our community and Town. With her hard work and efforts we can all be proud of the the Town she helped create.

Russell & Jeanie Carlson

Russ and Jeanie started their True Value Hardware store about ten years before we moved to Queen Creek in 1986. The Carlsons have turned their successful business into something they should be very proud. They have been doing business in our Town for about thirty-eight years now. The very first time I went into the Carlson's store I believe that a fellow that helped me was a young man by the name of Dave, who drove to work every day from Maricopa.

The last time I was in their store Dave was still working there and he still drives from Maricopa every day. According to Google Maps he has driven to the Carlson's store that is about 35 miles away and can take up to 45 minutes one way for all those years. He has worked with Russ and Jeanie for 35 years and Barbara another present employee has worked for them for 27 years.

There most likely are others that have worked for these two people for many years too and it does show what fine people Russ and Jeanie Carlson truly are. It is very evident that Russ and Jeanie support their employees but they also work with the many organizations that support our Community. For one the Carlson's have supported the San Tan PRIDE from the year we started our first clean up in 1999 until we disbanded in 2011. These two fine people work very hard in their business and are often there 6 days a week.

Fulton Brock

So far my working with Pinal County, that had only about 110,000 people when the PRIDE was started, who were scattered over 5000 square miles, was done on the phone with little or no formalities involved.

But working with one of the largest county governments in the U.S. that had a population in the millions was something quite a bit different.

Sandie Smith introduced me to Supervisor Brock for the purpose of getting help from Maricopa County on our annual community wide clean-ups. Fulton jumped at the chance to help us and he saw to it for twelve years.

After he got approval from all the other county supervisors he asked me to come to the county building in Phoenix to explain our needs and what the PRIDE wanted to accomplish.

When I showed up at Supervisor Brock's office I was warmly greeted by his Secretary, Peggy. I did not know it then but Peggy and I would work on several other community wide projects together for many years to come, on Fulton's behalf.
She escorted me to a large conference room where I was introduced to about ten or twelve male and female staff members, some in suits and others dressed in work clothes, that represented Public Works and some in the Department of Transportation.

In addition there were a couple of lawyers and about four that were from the Maricopa County Public Relations Department. I was politely asked questions for about 45 minutes pertaining to the role that Maricopa County would be responsible for in our upcoming clean up. I was totally unprepared for this meeting and the only thing I had with me was a pen and some writing paper. I was actually laughing on the inside because I had to make some stuff up as the meeting progressed because it felt like being questioned by a United State Congressional sub-committee about our joint role in inhabiting the moon.

All I had to do after that meeting was to make sure all the things I promised would be in place for the cleanup, which I did. When I finally met Fulton I was amazed on how down to earth he was and how very easy it was to talk with him on almost any subject that I wanted. We became good friends and he helped me by speaking at a couple of functions that I was involved in including one big Arizona Clean and Beautiful seminar.

He and his office helped the PRIDE grow from clean up to clean up. He liked what we did because it was a very good way of keeping trash out of his San Tan Mountain Regional Park that was in his jurisdiction. Fulton joined with us in every clean up we had and he came to work right along with everyone else that helped us. Fulton remains a good friend of mine.

Queen Creek's Good Witch

Yes, we have at least one good witch in our community and based on the fact that I know that several other witch's meet at her house regularly, there could be other good witches among us as well.

Flakey Fred

Fred worked for our local family owned water company. There were about six employees then and I believe Fred was the lead man for all the water line maintenance and for the overseeing of the installation of new water lines. He was a friend to most everybody he met and a very outgoing person. The name Flakey Fred was painted on the tailgate of his pick-up and Rudy's Restaurant even had a chicken recipe on its menu that was named Flakey Fred's Chicken...which by the way, was very good. Fred was truly a loveable character that was a free spirit that passed away at a young age and has been missed for his outgoing personality he displayed everywhere he went within our Community.

The producers of a company called Country Thunder, which had other locations in different parts of our country, picked Mark Schnepfs farm as the place for a venue attracting many major Country Western musical groups that would perform once a year. The original plan, it seemed, was to attract about 100 well-healed fans to stay on site for about a week in their big RV's. The tickets for these folks were quite high because they would have special front row box seats and included the availability of gourmet fare created by on site chefs every day. To kick the whole Country Thunder event off, a steak dinner with all the fixings was offered at no charge to about thirty or so local community leaders and their spouses.

I believe that Flakey Fred was there representing Paul Gardner's water company. Most everyone was dressed up in one form of western wear or another, including representatives from most all the churches that were in and around our community---everybody was dressed up except Fred. He wore a black tee shirt with a large colorful picture of a very cute little kitten on the back with wording that explained what the true meaning of the French phrase "double entendre" meant— words that could have been construed as objectionable.

One very warm day, before the Town had its very first stop light, I saw some barriers in the street around a large square hole that took up the whole width of the turn lane at the southeast corner of Ellsworth and Ocotillo. There wasn't anyone on the street, but in the hole, up to above his waist in very muddy water was bare chested Fred. I called down to him, asking, "What the hell are you doing, Fred?" He had a big smile on his face, probably from all the attention he was getting, and answered, "I am fixing a leak." There were cars behind me so I had to move on. It was so Fred!

I hauled water with my 1954 "cab over" one ton truck with a 1200 gallon water tank on it for twelve years. When we finally got a water line and meter to our land I called Fred and asked him who in Queen Creek could I get to run a pipe from the meter to my buildings. He said that he was doing that on his days off. I asked him to give me a bid and he showed up the next Saturday.

I needed a pipe to my house, guest house and then down to the barn, about 400 feet from our meter. He gave me a price of $850.00. I told him that our business was very slow now and I would call him when I had the money. At that time it looked like I would be hauling for at least two or three months before I could afford to have it done.

Now, again there have been quite a few times in my life that I believe that I have been blessed with different things, like money coming to me from seemingly nowhere, when it was needed the very most.

It happened again when I won $800.00 the very next week in the Arizona Lotto. The Saturday after that Flakey Fred was there with a helper and we had water within about eight hours.

Sandie Smith & Silvia Centoz

Silvia was a charter member, director and a vice-president of the San Tan PRIDE before and after it became a 501 (c) (3) non-profit Association. She has also became our Community's go-to fissure Queen. The fissures in our area are caused by water run-off and collapsed groundwater paths. She has tried to make sure that those land owners who try to fill in their fissure cracks on their properties be noted to protect future owners.

Bill Lally & Fissure Crack

The above picture shows a fissure crack that is anywhere from thirty to fifty feet deep in places and runs for more than 100 yards. Fulton Brock and his Chief of Staff, Bill Lally helped us clean out this mess.

Fissure bet. Sossaman & Hawes/Hunt & Riggs 2007

This fissure crack showed up after a heavy summer rain and was a part of the fissure crack that Bill Lally was in. There were a lot of very upset people who did not know exactly who to be upset with. There were some damages to some homes but overall the damages so far have been minimal.

The Heaths

Bill Heath was a Town Council member for several of the early years who was so important in forming the Town's structure. They both helped us with the Pride's cleanups every year while they lived here. Bernadette is a professional photographer that did work for National Geographic and especially for Arizona Highways. One of her favorite subjects was the San Tan Mountain Regional Park. She did a feature photo story about the Park in the November 1998 issue of Arizona Highways that is outstanding. I have gone on a few hikes with her and others in groups where she has showed us some of her favorite spots inside the Park. Me and other Arizona State site stewards had a hard time keeping up with her during those times on the hikes she led.

Bernadette has had several photo requests from magazines for pictures in the Grand Canyon. On one of her hikes down in the Canyon she injured her ankle near the bottom. A man came upon her and offered to carry her 50 pound pack out. It held a lot of camera and photo equipment. When they got to the top her ankle and leg was badly swollen she had to drive most of the way home using cruise control. Upon reaching her home her husband Bill took one look at her leg and ankle and he immediately took her to the hospital. They found that she had a broken ankle and a broken leg.

Bernadette does this kind of thing to get quality pictures in really out-of-the-way spots that most people have never seen before. With all her hard work she has accumulated around eighty thousand photos over the years. She has given us hundreds of photos of our clean-ups where she included a complete description of what each picture was about. The following submission from her exemplifies what a great community ours has become with her help.

Submitted By Bernadette Heath

A miracle happened here in Queen Creek in 1987. It wasn't one of those "Touched by an Angel" kind of miracles. This miracle happened a little at a time over a long period of time.

The kick off for this miracle happened at the little Catholic Church on Ocotillo Road near the center of town. It was Mothers Day, 1987. It was also First Communion Day and there wasn't enough room inside the church for all the families in attendance. Mass was said outside between the old army barracks and the church. Father Doug Lorig said Mass under the shade of the stage that was built for The Good Friday Passion Play. The rest of the people sat in the sunshine.

It was hot, very hot. Mass was almost over, everyone was sweating, when Father announced "We are going to build ourselves a church. We need a bigger building, more room, and cooler quarters in which to gather for all of our celebrations. We need a church and we will build it ourselves." Some of us thought he had heat stroke, but we soon found out he meant what he said.

At 5 A.M. Wednesday the following week the phone woke me up. "I hope I didn't wake you," the voice said. "I couldn't wait any longer." It was Father Lorig. "Did someone die?" I asked. "No," he said. "I want you to organize the building of our new church." he said. After a lengthy discussion, I found myself in charge of an impossible project.

Our Lady of Guadalupe Mission had a total of $19,000 in the bank. This was accumulated over a period of 30 years. The community was made up of farm workers with just a few recent members who had skilled labor jobs. The average income for a farm workers family was $15,600 a year, if both parents worked. The collection for any Sunday Mass was around $150. Holy Cross Catholic Church, up Power Road 12 miles, collected more in one Sunday than we did for the year.

Putting together a Case Statement to be presented to the Bishop was a challenge in itself. More Spanish was spoken here than English. We had volunteers who could speak both languages but to read and write both was another story.

We were allotted an hour to plead our case with the Bishop. Our hour was wilted down to 45 minutes but we really only needed 30 minutes. That's how long it took the Bishop to list all the reasons why building a church of our own, by people in our community, with only $19,000 in the bank, was out of the question.

The Bishop had good logical reasons why this entire project was absurd. Any realistic, reasoning person would have agreed with him, but that didn't fit the description of who we were. Our people were hard working, determined, humble people that had a great need. That need was a larger church.

That long list of "why not" had to be tackled one at a time. A prayer committee was formed and led by Julie Chavez. It's a long story to tell, but our mission church received 15,000 rosaries. The total population of Queen Creek at that time, including migratory works, was 2,500. I thought a big mistake was made and wanted to return some rosaries to whomever they came from. There was no mistake. All rosaries were passed out with a price tag attached. The tag said. "Please say one prayer for the person that made this rosary and one prayer for our mission" The tag was in both Spanish and English.

A Building Committee was formed. We met outside, in the cool and dark of the evening. Our greatest need was skilled laborers. In our community we gathered four plumbers, 2 electricians, 2 cabinet makers and 1 cement mason. Some of the Catholic Churches in Chandler, Mesa, Phoenix and Tempe allowed us to run an ad in their bulletins. A typical ad read something like this: "Needed: Architect, contractor, surveyor, carpenter, sheet metal man and any other skilled laborer to work on Mission Church. God will pay your salary."

We got help from the diocese of Phoenix in the person of Monsignor McMann. He was the Bishop's right hand man. He made no commitment but he and I got to the point where, when I called, he answered the phone. He needed to know that we could indeed do the impossible and we were determined to build our own church.

After eleven months of working on the "why not's" and gathering materials from donors like Hernandez Electric, who donated $20,000 in electrical material, and Olivas Brothers Plumbing, who donated all labor and materials for a complete plumbing system, a surveyor from St Timothy's Catholic Community stepped forward. An excited Monsignor McMann said."Call your key people together. St Theresa's Parish will pay for your architect. Let us begin." That was April 10, 1988.

The wagon was rolling. We planted a wooden cross on the new church property across the street from the small church on June 15, 1988. That was thirteen months after that famous Mother's Day Sunday announcement. Ground breaking followed in July. Everyone in town was invited and most came. The Bishop came, even though he was sick. He was smiling. He just didn't eat any of our Mexican food.

It took a year and one half to get to the earth moving day of January 21, 1989. The day started at sunrise with teenage boys driving trucks pulling watering tanks, men working backhoes, trenchers, and laying water lines. Women ran for supplies and cooked meals. Between twenty-five and thirty volunteer workers showed up to start this long awaited project. On the day that the cement was poured for the entire building the Baptist Church sent around its bus to gather the workers in the trees so they could help with the project. That day there were fifty workers helping. Setting the cement was a line of four men: One was a lawyer working at the Attorney General's Office, next to him was a retired Air Force Major, followed by a skilled carpenter and last but not least was one of our local firefighters.

The Mormon Church sent over their truck to raise trusses after a crew of strong men brought up the walls made of concrete blocks. Ed Lopez and Peter Boris were the two men leading the group. They were our contractors that held the project together and gave all they had in time, energy and talent right up to the very end.

The roof job was handled by our teens, supervised by a dairy man from Wisconsin. Ed Lopez had four of his classmates from way back doing the sheet metal. They came all the way from Glendale to install our duct system. Our two electricians came every Saturday. Saturday was the work day on the church hall. The women fed everyone lunch. Regardless of how many workers showed up, Mary Camacho and her helpers gave everyone a hardy meal.

Some of the other jobs the women did were sanding the tape on drywall, laying the tile the Knights of Columbus donated in all three of our bathrooms, running for supplies, feeding everyone lunch, creating the outside mosaic of Our Lady of Guadalupe sculpture, praying, cleaning up, calling and reminding volunteers they were needed the next day, and as the project wore on, anything else that needed doing.

Lupe did the stucco job over one long week-end. He was followed closely by Peter Boris with the spray painter. Peter's brother Ray joined us, coming all the way from Glendale at the time. He now lives in Queen Creek.

On June 13, 1988 we received a donation from the Church of St. Joachim and St. Anne in Sun City that doubled our bank account. The Irish priests of Scottsdale and Sun City would send us money from their personal accounts.

Schnepf's Farm donated our landscaping plants and even put them in for us. And so it went, one Saturday after another. By December 1989 we were all dragging but almost there. We had donations of pews from St Anne's in Gilbert. The Frank Miller family donated the cabinet work for the sacristy. John Melfy and family did the doors, gables and other wood work. Pat and Rudy Dvorak built and hand stitched the chairs for the alter. Wood for furniture came from as far away as Minnesota from family members of parishioners.

It was December 23, 1989. We had 24 hours before we needed our new church hall for Christmas Mass. If the county inspector didn't come we would have to use the old church for Christmas. Pete and Ed had been there but had to go back to work. Everyone else went home for supper. It was just Tom Ross and I left to close up.....and into the parking lot came the inspector. A prayer went up. "Lord, help us." Between Tom and me we answered all his questions and as he handed us the use permit for our new church hall he said. "There aren't any other Catholic communities that build their own church." I said. "No, we're only the second one in the diocese of Phoenix and this one IS A MIRACLE.

Lisa Colletto

Sandie, Me, Fulton & Lisa

Lisa is a highly respected young lady in our community that produced an exceptional resume from work done within the Town. Lisa was elected to the Town Council in 2000, at the age of twenty-seven. She remains the youngest member of the council to date. She was appointed Vice Mayor in 2003 and served through June of 2004. Before being elected to the Town Council she served on the Planning and Zoning Commission from 1998 to 1999. Lisa served as chair of the Parks, Trails and Open Space Commission. In that position she chaired the master planned committees for Desert Mountain Park and Horseshoe Park & Equestrian Center. In addition she chaired the Design Standards Task Force and the Youth in Government Committee, where she was instrumental in the formation of the Queen Creek Youth Commission. Colletto served as vice-chair of the Fire Services Study Committee and was a member of the Economic Development Committee, Budget Committee and Financial Review Task Force.

On a regional level, Lisa represented Queen Creek on the Maricopa Association of Governments Animal Control Committee and served on Valley Forward's Environmental Excellence Awards Committee. Colletto is a graduate of the Senior Executives in State and Local Government Program at the JFK School of Government at Harvard University.

In 2003, she was selected by the American Council of Young Political Leaders as a delegate to Indonesia and Malaysia to learn about emerging democracies.

She was named United Volunteer of the Year for Queen Creek in 1998 and was one of the 2002 Phoenix Business Journal's top 40 business leaders under 40 years old. Lisa holds a B.S. in biology from Arizona State University. Her profession is in Hospital administration. She and her husband owned and operated the Queen Creek Veterinary Clinic.

Piggy

Piggy was a biker guy who married a (motorcycle riding) biker lady who semi-retired near the Town of Queen Creek in Pinal County, who lived about two miles from our home. Piggy was a gruff sort of person that wore a full black beard and also wore bib overalls most the time. He had a lot of friends that he knew from his biker days who were from all parts of the country and there were a lot of them that lived in and around Queen Creek.

I guess you could have called Piggy a hoarder of anything mechanical and metallic. After more than a decade he had accumulated scores of vehicles of every kind and hundreds of other things made of metal. The things that he hoarded covered a three and a third acre plot of level desert ground that surrounded the trailer where he and his wife lived. There was no attempt to hide any of the junk he seemed to cherish. There were no trees, bushes or any type of "no see through fences" that you might see surrounding a lot of roadside junkyards.

Piggy also collected a lot of strange friends. A couple of Piggy's buddies were driving south on Ellsworth Road at sunrise one morning when they spotted a huge metal construction tool box that was partially submerged in a "tail" water pond (water left over from irrigation) near the east side of Ellsworth road.

This seemed to be a really big prize that Piggy would surely treasure, they must have thought. It took them a while to get the box out of the mud and water and onto their pick-up truck. It was very heavy and they must have looked somewhat strange by the hundreds of people that drove by them on their way to work that morning.

Piggy didn't have a hard time getting the tool box open and he was hoping that the weight of it meant that there was a lot of tools in there.

Instead there was the body of a man who was quite dead. It was reported that near pandemonium broke out among most of the many onlookers in Piggy's compound who must have been thinking that they might be individually considered a suspect in the man's death. Piggy quickly decided that the police must be called and all those having warrants must leave the property immediately. According to the newspaper, the police discovered that the man was a meth dealer from a nearby community where he had been shot. Piggy and his friends did not get to keep the tool box because it would be used in the murder investigation that would follow.

Our Counties do not have the clout that the Town of Queen Creek or nearby Gilbert or Chandler have to enforce their zoning laws. County laws are written differently than Town or City laws. The only fast avenue for a certain unlawful charges to be filed in Pinal County, is when health and/or criminal laws are violated.

The Pinal County Planning & Zoning Department had been getting complaints about Piggy for nearly twelve years and in that time zoning enforcement officials had served hundreds of notices and letters asking him to comply with the zoning laws. All were ignored. Then the chief Pinal County enforcement officer vowed to get Piggy's property into compliance before her upcoming retirement and found a law in the county's enforcement books that might just give them an avenue to get in there and find a way to "get 'er done."

This law had something to do with allowing Zoning officials to see a property owner's electric bills in person in order to see what their actual electrical usage was, or at least that is what Peggy told me. I have no idea exactly how the law was written, but that is how they were going to legally get inside Piggy's compound and into his home.

For the safety of the zoning enforcement officer's welfare, she took a Pinal County Sheriff's Officer with her. I guess they expected there might be trouble because there were reports that there were over twenty people living on the grounds in broken down vehicles and sheds, and there was a possibility that some of these people had warrants they believed.

I received a phone call from the Queen Creek Town Manager, Cynthia Seelhammer one evening who said that there was going to be a raid on Piggy's property the next day at 9:00 a.m. Piggy's property was not inside the Town's boundaries. Cynthia told me that this should get some press coverage and asked me to please get in touch with the media. She said media coverage would probably help in getting more of the other local junkyards to come into compliance.

I called the news desks of the major newspapers and did the same for all the local TV stations but all the people that I talked with seemed to not be that excited about covering this story, except one. After all, who wanted to see a raid on a junk yard.

Finally a man at one of the TV stations, that had a news helicopter at that time, went bonkers when I told him what was going to happen. He was the only one that asked questions about the history of the individuals that were involved and asked me what I knew about the property itself. It was almost like the TV people at that station had a meeting that day asking all reporters to get stories that could better utilize their new very expensive chopper.

The next day when I went to work with my cleaning crew as I usually did, at about 7:30 a.m. I got a 999 text on my pager about two hours later, which meant call my office/home immediately. I left my crew and went to the nearest pay phone, (remember those, and it was still a dime at that time) called my wife who told me that the PR guy from the Pinal County Sheriff's office, Mike Minter, wanted to talk to me right away.

She said that he sounded pretty upset. I took the number down, knowing full well that I was not going to call him until later in the afternoon, which would give him a chance to calm down. I got two more 999 pages that morning but I ignored them. By the time we were done working, things had indeed calmed down. When I finally called my wife again she said the PR guy was upset because the TV helicopter hovered over the property at about 8:30 that morning, even before the two Pinal County officials had entered the compound.

I think that when the helicopter showed up the Sheriff thought that the big bird would get everybody inside running in all directions when in fact it did just the opposite. The twenty some people just hunkered down just where they were.

The zoning enforcement officer told me that Piggy was not at home when they entered the property and Piggy's wife thought the chopper was with the Sheriff's office. She treated her two visitors very cordially. Piggy's wife was acting very nervous when they entered the trailer and she asked the two to sit down the kitchen table. The female compliance officer with the deputy asked Piggy's wife for her electric bills. While she went to get the papers in her file cabinet the deputy noticed a plastic bag near the back edge of the table next to the wall. He pointed this out to his companion and reached over to check out what was inside the bag. It looked like (you guessed it) pot, and it was.

By this time the news chopper had landed across the road in a vacant lot and let out it's camera crew. They immediately set up near the entrance to Piggy's place, coinciding with a couple of deputies walking into the compound with their hands on their holstered weapons. Very soon many more deputies were called to the scene because of what was initially found there.

It was not long before other media people with their crews started showing up, resulting in a great news story covered by the Arizona Republic, the Mesa Tribune and Channel 12 News.. I waited until after 6:00 p.m. that night to call Mike Minter. I left a message because I did not know if I was still in trouble or not. I finally found out how this turned out from the TV stations that started calling me for comments. Mike, the PR guy never returned my call.

There were Pinal County officials on Piggy's property for several days, the officers were finding all kinds of illegal things including more than fifty guns of all kinds--one (illegal) sawed off shotgun. There were hundreds of health violations found, along with a lot of illegal drugs which included small bags of methamphetamine, marijuana and drug paraphernalia. Pinal County had to call in the Arizona Department of Public Safety to identify six stolen vehicles. They also found a trailer full of stereos, TVs, VCRs and other electronics believed to be stolen. Several swastikas were painted within the compound and one on the mailbox in front of the property. According to stories written in the Mesa Tribune and in the Arizona Republic two children, a 16-year-old girl and a 13-year-old boy, who were believed to be Piggy's children, and four other children were turned over to Arizona CPS. Piggy and his wife were arrested, along with two of their residents that had warrants. Piggy's wife lost one of her legs in a motorcycle accident and was let out of jail later because of the extra cost that the jail system would have to pay for caring for her.

Piggy, on the other hand, was put away for some time and lost his property and most all of his possessions. Most of the junk went to a recycling company but even with the money received from that, the cost to the County to clean this place up was over ten thousand dollars.

Jersey Joe

Joe was a member of the Chandler Heights Twenty. He moved here from New Jersey. Joe called me many times asking me for advice, usually about his demeanor at our meetings, when we had parties or when we had our gymkhanas, which were horse riding competitions held at one our member's huge arena. Joe was aware that his sometimes temper tantrums offended people around him and he asked me for advice on ways to repair damages done.

Jersey Joe had performed with a group of actors that worked at some of our old western towns, riding in productions that reenacted shootouts and armed robberies. JJ's group (acting) did all that the bad guys did in yesteryear. He was the one that got shot and fell off his horse most of the time.

His hero was John Wayne and he had every one of his movies. He claimed to have seen all of John Wayne's movies many times over and bragged to everyone that he knew just about everything about Mr. Wayne. His knowledge of John Wayne seemed to be an obsession with him that he was very proud of. He may have moved here because John Wayne was so much of a part of Arizona.

On one of our private talks he told me that his father was a very prominent detective in Newark, New Jersey. He went on to tell me that his dad got him into the New Jersey State Police. He then told me about how he got in trouble the first time while he was cruising down the interstate in his patrol car.

One afternoon a big bright new Cadillac slowly passed him, occupied by four black gentlemen who had their windows down. They were all dressed very well and Joe could even see some the jewelry they were wearing. He said that they never even looked at him, which made him a little angry.

He pulled them over, telling the driver that the license plate looked fake and he wanted to check out the registration to make sure it was valid. He went back to his car, grabbed the mike through the open window and held it outside the car, pretending to call the dispatcher. But he said he never pushed the control button that opened his calls onto the airwaves. He did this in a way that the men in the car could hear his every word. He told the driver and the other men in the car that that he was going to have to take them to a substation a few miles away to complete the verification process and told them all that he was very sorry for the inconvenience but that it was his duty.

He told them that there were a lot of counterfeit license plates in circulation and that they might have been given one. He also told them that he was doing this so they would never get stopped again for a fake license plate check. It would be in the computer and be recorded as verified. The driver was pleading with him that he had gotten the plate from the State just a few days ago.

The long and short of it of it is that Joe lied to the officer in charge at the substation while holding these guys for over three hours. His commander accused him of being a raciest which he responded, yes I am... STRIKE ONE, he was written up!

He told me that the second time he got in trouble with his father and the NJSP was when, dressed in his civvies, he was in a small "Mom and Pop" Italian grocery store near his home. It seems that when he entered the store there was a young slender Hispanic man berating the elderly check out lady. Joe said that he grabbed the guy by the back of the neck and his trousers and 'marched his screaming arse' down the street to the local police substation. He bounced him through the big oak doors down a couple of steps that led to a marble floor leading to the desk Sergeant's huge imposing desk.

He then tipped the screaming guy forward and threw him face first, sliding him almost up to the front of the desk. The big grouchy-looking desk Sergeant asked him what the hell was going on. The guy continued to lay there, shaking like a leaf, until the Sergeant asked him to stand up. Joe flashed his NJSP badge and told the officer that this man disrespected his elder, an Italian lady, to a very great degree. STRIKE TWO AND he was OUT of the NJSP…Arizona here he comes.

There were two more incidents that happened in Queen Creek he later told me about. He heard about a local resident roper contest being held at a small ranch nearby his home. When he went to see what was going on there he first parked his pick-up in a large, crowded, parking lot. Then he headed towards where all the noise was coming from.

When he got to the roping corral he saw a large man holding the halter of a horse while whipping the horse's face with the the reins. He was cursing and swearing at the struggling horse but no one came to the horse's rescue because, as Joe found out later, he was the host and owner of the ranch.

Joe rushed over to the fence and told the man that if he didn't stop doing that he was going to beat him to a pulp. Joe added a lot more nasty words to that sentence, which infuriated the horse abuser more than he already was. He told Joe, "Let's go out to the parking lot and have at it." Joe immediately said, "Let's go, you #@%$!*&". Then he saw a number of Coca Cola cowboys getting up off their seats, saying they were going to take part in this fight too, saying "Let's show this &% $#*#&@ who he is dealing with." It must have been like Joe taking a long stick and shoving into a hornets' nest and wiggling it all around! Joe never stopped running until he got to his truck and he was lucky that he had a pretty good head start.

He was lucky he made it out of there in one piece and sincerely hoped he would never run into such a disagreeable bunch again.

I certainty agree with Joe telling the man to stop beating the horse, but Joe's extreme passion sometimes got in the way of his good deeds.

Another time Joe told me a story that happened near our home. Jersey Joe found out that there was a wide open cockfighting ring operating just over the mountain from where we now live. Jersey Joe went there with his four-year-old daughter (Can you imagine?) to see the action. When he got there everybody was betting on the bird they thought would win. There was a crowd of about 20 to 30 people.

With his daughter in hand he went into the back area to show his daughter the fighting roosters up close and soon discovered that there was some serious cheating going on. Being from New Jersey and being in unknown territory, he naturally went where the crowd was and shouted out to everyone about the cheating by some guys in the back. He quickly found out that the guys that were doing the cheating were related to the owner of this unlawful establishment.

Joe Talking To A "20" Member

There is a definite pattern going on with Joe, don't you think? He quickly picked up his daughter and dashed to his truck with the child under his arm. This time they almost caught him and as he was backing up in his pick-up, two of "the family" jumped head first onto the hood of the truck, holding on to his wind shield wipers with one hand and bashing on the windshield with the other.

It must have been quite a scene with part of the crowd yelling at the cheaters and the others at Joe and his daughter. With physics and gravity on his side and his daughter crying loudly, the "family members" were soon removed from the hood in a very dramatic fashion. Lucky for Joe no one bothered to follow him and his really upset daughter beyond the parking lot.

The last meeting that Joe attended was a meeting of the Chandler Heights Twenty at my home within a week of our last of the year gymkhana, which involved an incident where Joe's stallion kicked a lady's horse in the cannon (leg/ankle). Joe never apologized for his horse's action and even hinted that it was the lady's fault that was riding behind his much higher pedigreed horse.

The injury was more serious than the lady thought at first and it cost her about three hundred dollars to get the horse repaired. At the meeting of about fifteen of the twenty or so members, the first order of business was about safety around horses. The incident at the gymkhana was talked about and if the majority of members agreed, it would be required that any horse that kicks must wear a red bow on its tail, showing the horse was a kicker to everyone that comes near it.

The chairman asked for all those in favor of the new rule to raise their hands. Joe was quite stoic throughout this whole thing and he did not raise his hand but everyone else did. When the lady headed for Joe with a big red ribbon, Joe went ballistic, screaming, "You want me to put a ribbon on my horse? My horse, that is worth more than all your horses put together?" He went on for about five minutes before he started screaming obscenities. That was when I asked him to leave. He did, saying as he left, "Don't call me! I will call you when hell freezes over!" We didn't see much of Joe after that but we heard that his wife had left him.

The very final thing I heard about Joe was that he had a bad incident with his next-door neighbor, Jake Barnes. Jake is a national champion team roper that had a beautiful home with a handmade wrought iron arch over the entrance to his driveway that heralded his roping prowess. Jake went on to win seven championship titles and was invested in the Pro Rodeo Hall Of

Fame. There was a large horse pasture between Jake's property and Joe's who had a large horse pasture at the front of his home. Joe had "no trespassing" signs up on his fence. I heard that the wife of the roper was out for a walk with her dog. She walked down the lane that passed by Joe's pasture and Joe's home. The lady's dog was not on a leash, when the dog went under the fence into Joe's pasture, Joe came out of his home with a rifle and shot the dog dead. The roper and his wife moved away shortly after this tragic event. Since that time I nor any of my friends have seen Joe and do not know where he went. In the beginning Joe was a person that was fun to be with. Only at times did he show his anger, which sometimes got of control. I must have been a sort of father figure to him and that was why he asked me for counseling about the several other less violent encounters that seemed to follow him everywhere.

The Chandler Heights 20 +

Ron & Karen McCoy

Ron McCoy has served for nearly ten years as a San Tan PRIDE member and board director. He was a tireless worker for our many projects and served as the first President of the Friends of the San Tan Mountain Regional Park.

He was an outstanding treasurer for the Nathan Martens Arizona Memorial. Ron "The Real McCoy" is also a world renowned avid writer.

Submitted by Ron McCoy

Karen & I are products of the Midwest, she being from Cincinnati and me, well I've moved around a lot. Seems the grass is always greener on the other side of the fence. We, along with our eight year old Sar, were living in Batesville, Indiana when one of my older daughters moved to Phoenix. Subsequently, after making several trips over the years to the area and really enjoying the experience, we decided that the summer of 2002 would be a good time to make a change. We bit the bullet and moved to Queen Creek.

Soon we discovered the San Tan Pride under the dynamic leadership of Ros Rosbrook and several others and joined up. The need for groups to voice opinions and take on issues for the general public's benefit are vital in today's society. There are too many single entity people whose only concern is their "what's in it for me?" and monetary profit. Strong volunteer groups are vitally important to keep progress on track for the benefit of the general public. Where are we now? I've been retired for 18 years now and would like to slow down some. I've held key role positions in volunteer groups most of that time, with Karen being a major contributor, supporting my efforts. This Spring I did not run for Chairman of the Board for the Indiana Trail Riders Association, a statewide trail advocacy group consisting of 1,400 members. This was a position I've held on and off for 7 years, in order to move back to Arizona after a three year absence. What's next? I'm on the board of a newly created Midwest Equine Trail Foundation and somehow seem to be included in the Pinal Partnership Open Spaces and Trails meetings. But we are slowing down.

John Boatright

John wore bib overalls when at work and always sported a full white beard. He owned and operated a tire and auto repair shop. The "shop" had a dirt floor with a refrigerator that held beer and not much else, there was a tool closet that was located in the center of the work area. The shop had no doors or windows because it was all roof with no outside walls. I think that there were only two full time employees and a small group of mostly, rough around the edges, individuals that needed some money from time to time that just hung around until needed.

His mechanical area, off to the side, had a rectangular hole in the ground that had two single metal tracks that held the cars up above the hole. I got my '54 Chevy cab-over truck repaired there many times but I got my tires fixed right next door at Reds Tire Repair & Sales.

One day I was driving down the hill on Wagon Wheel Road headed north to the Old Hunt Highway, on my way to get a load of water. The road I was on ended into a T at the bottom of the hill. All the roads in our area then were dirt. Wagon Wheel was not a very steep hill and I was going only about twenty-five MPH when I was nearing the very bottom. I slowly attempted to put on the brakes. Wow! All the way to the floor and the stop sign was now about fifty yards away. I pumped the brakes over & over. There was no emergency brake and I had to make a decision--go straight ahead and maybe plow into somebody on Hunt Highway or make a hard right turn into the desert before I got to the intersection.

Going into the desert would mean that I would have to go over a two foot berm at the edge of the road and then into some thick brush, cacti and bushes. I decided to take the desert route and after jumping the berm and plowing through, I finally drove out slowly onto Hunt Highway heading east for about twenty yards before old '54 rolled to a complete stop. For that short distance, after I found out that I lost my brakes, it felt like I was going about 60 mph. Boy that was some ride! Now I wondered how I was going to get my big ol' truck to Boatwright's repair shop on Power Road.

I marched back up the road to a neighbor's home on Dove Roost Road to call John, hoping that he would be able to tow my truck to his shop. John answered the phone and I told him about my problem with the truck. He said drive it over to his shop and he would fix it right away. I said, "but John I don't have any brakes." He told me to just drive in a low gear and everything would be fine. The journey was about three or four miles, traffic was light and it was not nearly as hard as I had imaged. I very slowly pulled up in front of his shop and just shut the motor off while the truck was still in gear, which caused the truck come to an abrupt and safe stop. John and his crew often worked on vehicles at the roadside in front of or near his business so my parking job turned out to be OK for them.

John had kind of a strange way of keeping track of the work he was doing in his repair shop. When I brought my truck there for repairs he was the one that took down the information. He used a small note pad and a pencil about three inches long. He put the point of the pencil to his tongue at the start and a couple times more as he wrote down the order. Then when I came to pick up the repaired vehicle he could never find the order and would ask me what his shop was supposed to have done. Sometimes there were new parts that had to be used. He would holler out to his crew, asking what was done on the white '54 truck. Then each one that had anything to do with the repair would holler back. John wrote down the information on the "invoice" in the same notebook where this had all started. He then would give me an additional sheet of that small paper with the total. His prices were always more than fair and when I could I would give him a little extra, which would be put into his pocket right away. There should have been a sign hung there that said, "We don't have any stinking paperwork to worry about."

In all the times that I met and talked with John I never heard him say anything in a loud or an angry tone. I knew that John had a beer or two once in a while so I asked him one time what saloon he frequented?

He said that he never went to any bar, stating that he was a "ditch-bank beer drinker". Up until then I never knew that that was a class of beer drinkers.

I think it was the second or third year of Queen Creek's annual Christmas parade when I was asked by the Town, to be in charge of getting a Santa Claus.

Santa John

I knew John and respected him a great deal and when I went to see him about he being Santa his eyes lit up and he was very happy that I asked him.

His job was to ride on an antique fire truck in the parade and then pass out candy at a booth set up behind the community center.

John's wife was a registered nurse and helped John get his beard as white as possible. When I went to his home to give him the Santa outfit a couple of days before the parade he asked me if his beard was white enough. I told him that it was fine. On the day of the parade, there was John up in the passenger seat of the old antique fire truck that did not have a roof waving away while Duane Webb, dressed up as Santa's elf, was throwing wrapped candy to the kids along the parade route. The fire truck dropped Santa and Duane off in front of his booth behind the Town's Community Center and they then passed out some candy bars for about two or three hours.

All of a sudden an older lady came briskly walking over to me with an angry expression on her face. "I have been told that you are responsible for enlisting John Boatwright as Santa," she said. I answered "Yes," and I asked her what was the problem?" She said it was terrible that I had done such a thing because John was a drinker. Before I could respond she briskly turned and walked away. There was only about one hour left before John and Duane would leave.

I never told John, or for that matter anyone else but my wife about what she said. No one from the Town or anyone else ever said anything about John being Santa again, but a lot of people told me he did a really wonderful job.

When I was in charge of the community clean-up in about the third year, there was a lull with people dropping off appliances, tires and other recyclables at the depot site on Sundance Road. Sandie Smith asked me if there were any lots in the neighborhood that needed a large sum of trash picked up. I told Sandie that I would be right back and I went about a 1/2 mile down the road to see John, who just happened to have a huge pile of assorted junk in the middle of his property. When I went there John was standing next to his "burn barrel" talking to "Piggy", the very same very colorful character mentioned earlier who also lived in the neighborhood at that time. John and Piggy looked similar and dressed similarly but Piggy had a black beard and was a gruff sort of a person. I asked John if he would allow some Pinal County trucks and a big front-end loader to come on his property to remove the big pile of junk that was sitting there. Before he answered he introduced me to Piggy, who was going through John's burn barrel looking for anything metal. John said, "Piggy this is Ros, from the PRIDE." Piggy did not even stop grubbing through the burn barrel, he just looked at me for a brief moment and grunted. John told me it would be okay to do the trash removal and said thanks. It only took the County about twenty minutes to haul away more than three big truckloads of John's junk.

A few years later John got involved with cutting up some galvanized pipe with an acetylene torch. Unfortunately the gas fumes given off from cutting galvanized metal was very toxic and caused John to suffer for years and it eventually led to his untimely death. John was a good man and is missed by me and many others.

Lisa A. Barnes

Vince Davis

The above picture is one of a very few of Vince in a suit but he told me that he was really wearing shorts and flip flops for the bottom half of this picture. His former Hawaiian life style is alive and well.

Submitted by Vince Davis

I expected to get a degree from Arizona State University and then leave the state for other, less scorching parts of the world. I added an extra year to his plan by joining Alpha Epsilon Pi Fraternity his freshman year, effectively distracting myself from my goal. During that time I met people and made friends, and ultimately decided to stay in Metro Phoenix a little longer in order to go to graduate school in Glendale. I bought my first house in Arizona right behind Saguaro High School in Scottsdale and lived there for 10 years. While there, I got married, my first daughter was born, and made the decision to stay in Arizona permanently. Staying in Arizona involved finding work, and since my family had always done rentals as a business, I got into real estate.

One day my in-laws decided to get out of Mesa, and move out to the edges of town. There was a place called "Queen Creek" they had heard of to the southeast and it looked pretty good to them, so they called upon their dutiful son-in –law to find them a place to buy there. At the time, there was a newer subdivision called Rancho Jardines, and they bought one of those homes using me as their Realtor. Ultimately, my wife decided that driving from Scottsdale to Queen Creek to visit family was too much of a drive and insisted on moving there.

At the time, Queen Creek still only had about 2500 residents. During the same period the Davis Family was moving to Queen Creek, I was starting a service company that I called Commercial Quality. One of the core services it offered was carpet cleaning. One fine day, I passed out flyers throughout Rancho Jardines, and by sheer luck, a Rainbow vacuum cleaner salesperson happened to be working the neighborhood at the same time. The vacuum cleaner salesman was offering free carpet cleaning, failed to live up to his promise, and an annoyed client found one of my flyers later the same day. Thinking I was in cahoots with the vacuum salesman, they did what any upset person would do; they turned me into the Town Government as an unlicensed shyster. So very soon after that, I got a chance to meet Jennifer over at Town Hall. After clearing everything up, I walked out of Town Hall with one of the earliest Town of Queen Creek Business licenses to hang next to his City of Mesa license, and more importantly, with a few contacts which enabled me to ultimately be Old Town Halls carpet cleaner for a while. Even though the carpet cleaning job was done at break even prices, he thought it was a good way to stay in touch with the leaders of our community..

Clearly keeping in touch with the town government at the time meant being invited to just about everything. Since there was such a need for manpower, over the years I volunteered for or was invited to serve as a Past Chairman, Town of Queen Creek

"Neighborhoods in Bloom" Committee; Past Commissioner, Town of Queen Creek Economic Development Commission; Guest Speaker, Town of Queen Creek Citizen Leadership Class; Past Member, Williams Gateway Airport Passenger Service Task Force; Co-Founder, Northeastern Pinal County Economic Partnership; Committee member, Town of Queen Creek Police Service Committee. Including work at the Chamber, some of these positions led me to be one of the recipients of the Town of Queen Creek Volunteer of the Year Award.

In 2002 the Town Council went on its annual retreat. I attended with Wendy Feldman-Kerr as mayor, Gail Barney, Joyce Hildebrandt, Toni Valenzuela, David Dobbs, Gary Holloway, and Jon Wooten. One of the goals they set for themselves was to bring back a functioning Chamber of Commerce. It would be the area's second Chamber, as the first one was a bit premature for the size of the business community at the time and had ceased to exist a long time before. To launch the new Chamber an invitation for an organizational meeting, to be hosted and mediated by Town staff, was sent out to everyone in the Town of Queen Creek in June of 2002 with a valid business license. At that meeting a new chamber was born. The original Chamber Board, acceding to me was Greg Bond, President; Vince Davis, Vice President; Dru Alberti, Secretary; Doug Adcox, Director of Membership; Peggy Bieniek from TRW as Director of Government Advocacy, Events Director; and Leslie Cochran as Treasurer. That was the board for the first year, and since we had no resources we got everyone to throw in what resources they could. Greg got us a lease on a high-end printer, I put in a postage machine, Dru got us the space at the Historical Society, and everyone gave a lot of time and effort. We met every other Wednesday from late June until November., when things really solidified and we were able to cut the frequency of the meetings back a bit. TRW in particular helped us out tremendously. They donated the money for the incorporation, membership in the East Valley Chamber of Commerce Alliance, all the filing fees, and their graphic designers created our logo, the same one we still use today. The Town was, of course, very generous with their time, advice, and a meeting place complete with refreshments for all who attended. And so the Queen Creek Chamber of Commerce was started on a shoestring. We started with 27 Charter Members by the end of October 2002 when the 501 (c) (3) was formally recognized by the IRS, and we let anyone who joined during the calendar year of 2002 have the status of Charter Member.

As the Chamber actually gained some footing, it became more and more of a time obligation. By February of 2003 Greg and I realized that someone was going to need to be there full time, and that person would likely need to be compensated. They went to Cynthia Seelhammer, Town Manager. Through her guidance, and again through a lot of donated time, research was done on how to properly fund a Chamber of Commerce. A contract for services with the town was drafted, and over a 6 month period, it was negotiated, written and rewritten, submitted to Town Council, tweaked, and ultimately approved. The Chamber had the ability to hire someone, and the Chamber's first paid staff was Lisa Barnes, a freelance photographer who was hired by the board to help with chamber events and ribbon cuttings. More importantly, that meant that the chamber was ready to take its next step forward. During that first year several of our board members had to move on. Dru Alberti, Peggy Bieniek, and Greg Bond all made career changes that not only took them away from Queen Creek during the day, but ultimately took them away from their Chamber Director posts as well.

Greg Bond leaving the Chamber in early 2004 was a scary proposition for most of us on the board at the time. His relationship with the Mayor and several of the town council members had been critical in keeping information and support continuing for the young chamber. It also put Vince in charge, but that was OK since the groundwork had already been laid. The contract with the town had been written, and funding had already begun. The second year into the contract with the town it was possible for the Chamber to expand on it since it had been performing as promised. Vince was able to take a full time role there based on funding, and the chamber in its current form was finally established. Although some of the area's growth was terrific, for example you no longer had to go to Power Road and the US 60 for groceries, (which wasn't too bad back then since Power Road was a two lane racetrack at the time) there does seem to be a headlong rush to be a typical boring community just like all the others. This means a lot more in the way of amenities, but it also means, sadly, that there really is nothing all that unique about the area any more. In the next 10 years, Queen Creek will just be someplace you drive through as you try to get out to the edges of town that it used to represent so well.

Valerie Reed

Huggy Bear Lang

These Two people Teamed Up To Play One Of The Greatest Practical Jokes Ever Played On my wife and I!

Once upon a time Caroline wanted to raise egg-laying chickens. So, as we always usually do, she bought about fifteen Rhode Island Red chicks, but didn't have a place for them to live on our ranch. I had put my foot down about having any more animals, we had a lot of animals here already and the number, by new births, was growing every week but she must have misunderstood me. So it was a complete surprise to me when I went to my office in the guest house one day, when I heard a chirping noise while I was at my computer.

I turned towards the noise and saw a box at the other end of the room with a light attached to it. In the box I found fifteen little yellow chicks. I really raised hell with her for getting these new animals without my permission.

She just smiled and handed me the plans for the chicken coop and the nest boxes needed for our new sure-fire money-making project. At first I was furious but that soon changed. Now I had a job to do and it had to get done before the chickens took over our guest house/office and made a real mess on our brand new carpet.

I bought a ready-made 10 foot square building with a peaked roof. I built the nesting boxes and roosting rails per stringent specifications provided in a bestselling book called "The Very Best for Our Egg Laying Chickens" written by the North American Chicken Council member. My wife even had me build a playground in back of this elite chicken coop for our baby chicks to play in. Then Caroline wanted me to install a small TV in the coop but I refused and compromised by putting in a stereo-radio music system. She set the station to classical music because she wanted the most intelligent eggs possible.

We bought yet another book called "The Dummies Book on Raising Chickens for Maximum Egg Production". It said that these chicks would be able to produce eggs in about 21 weeks. We talked about putting this egg enterprise under a LLC but first decided to see how much our, soon to be, more intelligent chickens would produce.

So far the cost of this endeavor was: Chicks $20.00, coop $350.00, fencing around and overhead with posts $230.00, nesting boxes and roosting rails $18.00, play-ground $26.00, feeders and special high quality feed $26.00, electrical outlets, stereo radio system, lighting and timers $36.00, shading for the yard $35.00, three bales of clean straw $15.00, one case of 100 egg cartons $21.00, lightening rods for the roof and extra insurance covering all this at $12.00 a month. It came to a total of $777.00, not including the insurance. I only hope getting fresh eggs every day is worth all this expense?

Every time we got together with Tom and Val, Caroline would brag about her chickens by telling them what she was feeding them. She gave them milk once a week and fruits and vegetables, in addition to the really fine super-duper chicken feed. At this time I must tell you Tom and I were always playing practical jokes on each other and we always tried to outdo the other.

We were waiting patiently for our chickens to start laying those golden eggs. Then in the seventeenth week, Caroline and I were invited to go bowling with Tom and Val. We were supposed to pick them up at 9:00 a.m. We split the chores up between us that morning; I took on the straightening the house while she went down to the chicken "resort" to care for her extra-specially fed chickens. All of a sudden I heard screaming coming from near the coop. I immediately thought that there was a rattler down there but when I went out on the deck and hollered down to her, she said that her chickens had laid some eggs. She just kept screaming on and on about all the good things she'd given them from the time that they were baby chicks to now, becoming egg laying chickens.

When she came up to the house she had six large white eggs in the first one of the 100 new egg cartons she'd bought. She was so excited she started phoning all her children and friends, including Tom and Val. She even called her daughter in Puerto Rico.

Now it was time to pick up Tom and Val for bowling. Their place is on five acres of land that had two exits. When we got to the front gate Val was there and said that Tom had gone to an ATM machine to get some cash and would be back in a few minutes. All the way to the bowling alley, all we heard from Caroline was about her "Super" chickens. Val kept asking questions about the chickens and their eggs. Val asked why they were so big? Why they were all white? Which Caroline had all the answers for. To me it sounded like Tom and Val didn't believe us. I kept reassuring them that it was true. These chickens laid eggs four weeks earlier than they were supposed to and they laid large eggs to boot.

After bowling I said that I would take them down to the barn on the way home and see if the chickens might have laid some more eggs. When I pulled up there, I really did not think that there could be more, but when I looked through the front screen door I saw a bunch more eggs.

Everybody was still in the car except me. Tom and Val seemed to believe that we were playing a practical joke on them, or so I thought. Caroline on the other hand was ecstatic. She then started to mention getting a contract with one of our local super markets and wondered how we were ever going to handle all these eggs when they really started to produce at full speed.

When I took Tom and Val home they were totally quiet all the way there. When I got back home, Caroline was telephoning all the people she had called a few hours before. Then there was a knock on the door. It was Tom, he handed me an egg with the words written, "The Yolk Is On You!" I took that to mean that they believed that we made a practical joke on them. Tom, who was still outside the doorway, leaned in to say that he had put the eggs in those nesting boxes twice. With that he made a hasty retreat to his waiting getaway car with Val in the driver seat. She drove rapidly out of our driveway producing a shower of flying dust.

Caroline became so upset she said she was going to buy a bunch of those very noisy Guinea hens and put them over their fence and into their yard as payback. I went the other way with what I thought might be getting out of hand by saying that this was the best ever practical joke ever played **on us**, which helped her better grasp the real meaning of what had just happened.

To retaliate for the "best ever joke played on us", I tried to beat them with the following feeble attempt, as it turned out. Tom and Val had just moved into their new beautiful southwestern style home on their five acre property. I decided that it was time to put it up for sale.

Without their knowledge I leaned a four foot by four foot sign up against their fence next to the road, advertising their house for sale. That caused them to get many phone calls. Val thought they were getting so many calls because the house was so beautiful and everybody wanted to buy it because of that. They had no idea why, until one person told them about the sign. This sign caused a lot of people to call Tom and Val but it didn't come close to the joke they played on us.

The sign read: NEW HOUSE FOR SALE, $1000.00 DOWN, OWNER WILL CARRY, Call 480-000-0000 after 10 PM.

Submitted by Tom Lang and Valerie Reed

We moved out here in 1983. We were both working for Shamrock Dairy in Tucson and they were moving to their new dairy on the N/E corner of Chandler Heights and Higley. I was helping to transport some cattle to the new dairy and was told that the best tamales and the coldest beer were available at the Diamond Dot market in Chandler Heights. This market at the time had a great recessed veranda and was surrounded by orchards and, true to its reputation, the best tamales and the coldest beer. After several trips to and from Tucson, the Diamond Dot was a highpoint of the day. One particular day I was sitting out enjoying my repast when I noticed two mongrel dogs squaring off in the intersection of San Tan Boulevard and Power. It looked like it was going to be an epic fight so my attention was riveted. As the dogs circled each other, I became aware of other people exiting the Chandler Heights Trading Post as well as the Diamond Dot to watch this fight. The dogs engaged in battle and it was over in a matter of seconds. I can't remember if it was the golden dog beating the black dog or the other way around, but the people cheered the winner and booed the loser. I sat there and thought to myself, "If this is what passes for excitement around here, I'm in".

We moved in March and enjoyed the cool spring weather but were totally unprepared for the summer. We had no idea how an evaporative cooler worked. Everyone we talked to said, "Well, they're so simple. There is nothing to them." Well, everyone was right.

There was nothing to ours. No pump, no pads, nothing. Our cooler was stripped by the renters who were there before we bought the place. And we had no clue what or how these things worked. When someone finally took pity on us and set the cooler up right, we dutifully shut all the doors and windows and sat in misery wondering why anyone would choose to live in Arizona in the summertime and not have AC. And we were constantly worrying about letting our dogs in and out of the house because the door would practically fly out of our hands when we opened it.

The first year was definitely a year of learning. But we fell in love with the area and the area's residents, all of whom were crazies at this time. I mean, who else would put up with washboard dirt roads, hauling water, and the extreme commute to get groceries.

I started working for TRW in 1992. Prior to that, I was commuting into downtown Phoenix for my employment, so when TRW opened in Queen Creek, I was right there with a smile. It did prove to be an interesting place to earn a living.

The company produced the propellant used to deploy the passenger side airbags, each car manufactured after 1996 was mandated to have passenger side airbags, so the demand for the product was very high.

The facility used sodium azide as the main ingredient, and this compound is extremely reactive and is also subject to special rules regarding it's disposal. The first explosion happened in the new crystallizer that was supposed to recycle any waste azide back into a useable form. I was filling up my car at the Circle K in Queen Creek, when I noticed the large mushroom cloud over the plant to the north. This would be the first of many unplanned plant deployments Due to the demand, TRW operated 24/7, with many shifts lasting 12 hours. This was in the mid 1990's so the unemployment rate was very low.

TRW was out in the middle of nowhere and because the work was dangerous and dirty, many of the people working there had a high school education only. These people were in leadership positions and knew only one thing: Keep the plant producing. Many of the "incidents" occurred in the wee hours of the morning and were, in my opinion, caused by inattention to detail resulting from sleep deprivation. The only way to put out a propellant fire is to deluge the material with a vast amount of water.

This water would then be considered hazardous and subject to federal laws for disposal. With the crystallizer gone, the water pooled everywhere. Any wary animal that drank from these pools was dead, and the dead floated in the containment ponds that were all around the facility. After several incidents, Mesa shut the plant down and threatened to keep the gates locked if TRW was unable to stop the fires.

This essentially forced the company to close the propellant manufacturing process and many good people were laid off. Now the plant is mostly closed, with only assembly work being performed. But for the 1990's, the company supported a great many residents of Queen Creek and for that we should all be grateful.

Dr. Daryl Lamb Of Queen Creek Primary Family Care

Doctor Lamb was the first full-time family care doctor to practice in Queen Creek. There were two part-time doctors that had a practice in the Queen Creek area but they were fully retired when Doctor Lamb moved into his refitted modular home office located across the road and near the present Town Hall. We finally had the full-time physician service we all needed. Caroline and I were patients of Dr. Lamb when he first set up shop.

Dr. Lamb is a fifth generation native of Arizona. He is a graduate of Cornell University, Ithaca, New York. He then went to the University of Arizona Medical School In Tucson. He is trained in both family practice and as a OB/GYN. Doctor Lamb has delivered over 1000 Queen Creek babies. He has received the Volunteer of the Year award from the Town of Queen Creek and awards from local chapters of the Red Cross and United Way. He is married and has seven children. He loves to read, play ball with his children and being in the outdoors. He learned to speak Spanish during his mission to Chile.

When he was delivering a lot of babies and unable to keep some of his family practice appointments, we were turned over to one of his associates. Until I reached my sixties I really thought I was still 21. Then my body all of a sudden started to fall apart. Even though I was Dr. Jason Jones patient, Dr. Lamb kept track of my illnesses. Once when I was in the hall with Dr. Jones, he stopped to tell my doctor that I was an enigma because of all my health problems coming together at one time.

The Guerra's

Kristen, Ed & Reece Guerra

Kristen made her way from Nebraska to Mesa and then to the world renowned home of ASU in Tempe before moving with her husband Ed to Queen Creek.

Ed went from San Antonio to 5000 Forbes Avenue in Pittsburgh (which happens to be the home of the eminent Carnegie Mellon University) and then on to ASU in Tempe.

Ed and Kristen both have engineering degrees and went to work at Garrett Motors before it was transformed, after a merger or two, into Honeywell, which is a Fortune 100 Company that has over 132,000 employees worldwide. Ed and Kristen were among the 22,000 engineers that Honeywell employed. Kristen, who breeds and raises horses, left Honeywell a couple of years ago to be able to spend more quality time with their son Reece and to open a horse related business called Impulse Equine Therapy. It offers acupressure, structural release, aromatherapy, kinesiology, and micro-current therapy for horses. Kristen's equine pride and joy is her Hanoverian stallion Salto, who lives on their Desert Spring Ranch near the Town of Queen Creek.

For those of you like me who do not know what a Hanoverian is, according to Wikipedia it is: a warm blood horse originating from Germany, which is often seen in the Olympic Games and other competitive English riding styles, and has won gold medals in all three equestrian Olympic competitions. It is one of the oldest, most numerous, and most successful of the warm bloods.

One of Ed's main hobbies has been his involvement in a really old Chinese martial arts regimen where he holds a very high ranking.

Their son Reece has spent a lot of time with his parents when they were not working at Honeywell. He worked along with his parents at a very young age when we had PRIDE projects and has attended most all the PRIDE meetings that were held in his home.
Reece also went with his parents when they went to Queen Creek Town Council meetings from time to time. He now attends elementary school at ASU's Preparatory Academy in Mesa not far from their home. I wonder where Reece might be going to College when he finishes high school?

Ed and Kristen love it where they live and believe that change is inevitable but are concerned with what type of change is in store for them and our community. They say that it is in the hands of our elected officials and they just hope that this change is a 'coming does not sacrifice the rural lifestyle that they enjoy but that they can see it slowly slipping away. Ed likes the quote from a Dr. Seuss book, The Lorax; when it comes to our politicians: "Unless someone like you cares a whole awful lot, nothing is going to get better. It's not."

Ed is very active with the Queen Creek School District's scholarship program and was President of the San Tan Mountains PRIDE Association prior to its closing a couple of years ago. The Pride's major projects had to do with community wide clean-ups that were funded by the three governments and were in partnership with the PRIDE: the Town of Queen Creek, Maricopa and Pinal Counties. When our recession began in 2009 all the funding we needed and the use of the counties and Town's equipment and personnel became unavailable to the Pride because of budget constraints. The local landfill became full and closed causing all our trash being sent farther distances and eliminating the free landfill day during our clean-ups. Coupled with the Towns supplying curb side trash and recycling services to all its citizens, the Pride's role as the clean-up organizer became much less necessary.

The twelve years we had to work with the Town, along with Maricopa and Pinal Counties, was a dream come true for us. We were able to do more and more each year, overseeing the collection of thousands of tons of trash and recyclables. On one of our last clean-ups we had about 450 volunteers working with the PRIDE doing roadside cleaning, loading and unloading trash and recyclables in one eight hour day. Ed oversaw our very biggest clean-up as our PRIDE President.

Ralph & Georgia Peterson

These folks have protected the southern edges of our park for many years. They also have coordinated many clean-ups for the foothills citizens. They live in one of the most beautiful parts of our State, just a few miles from where we live at the other end of the park, in an very attractive adobe home. Georgia has been an officer and board member of the Pride for eleven years.

Submitted by Georgia Peterson

"Our families both emigrated to the Pacific NW during the depression from Wyoming and Montana, respectively. (Think vehicles with belongings tied on or packed in back of a truck along with children). Ralph grew up in a small wheat town in the Palouse area outside Spokane, Washington and I grew up on a small truck farm in the Spokane Valley. When Ralph graduated he went to a small nearby teacher's college for a year, and then joined the Navy for two years. By that time I had finished high school and we began at the same teacher's college. This is where we met. Ralph had known my sister. We were married in our junior year and in the following summer we had our first child, a girl. When we graduated we accepted positions in the El Cajon School District in southern California. We taught there for three years, and while there we had a son.

Ralph was interested in a more cultural atmosphere, so he took a job teaching in Palo Alto, CA. There his work was highly prized by students from Stanford to observe. I took jobs substituting so as to be able to be home with the children most of the time.

Then, after three years we decided on a real adventure and took a job in an Athabascan village in Alaska as the only two teachers in the school. We were also responsible for notifying the medical establishment when things went wrong with villagers on a two-way radio. We loved the people and the work, but visits and reviews from Bureau of Indian Affairs officials were a real pain. We did not take to them as an underling should. Soon we were notified our services were no longer needed. We even received a personal letter from Bennett, then director, that he regretted the decision but he had to go with his minions in the field. Within a year the state took over the majority of the schools in Alaska. The La Mesa school district was more than happy to hire Ralph based on what had happened and we knew people in the area so we returned there for awhile.

Again, I did substituting even more often, finally taking a 1/2 year job for a woman who was pregnant. The children were both in school. In another two years or so, Ralph decided he wanted to get a masters and a doctorate and he had contacts at Teacher's College, Colorado. University who were more than happy to have him come. So we were off with some other friends who decided to do similarly. I applied for the masters program and was also accepted. Ralph was given a position at the laboratory school and the children were placed there. I found a nearby job for a while and then also taught at the lab school. When Ralph completed his doctorate he began teaching in the City University of NY at Queens College. He also taught one course at Teacher's College as an adjunct. I worked in two other situations in NY over the years.

In 1975-76, NYC found itself in a financial crisis and was planning to lay off many city employees. Ralph was a likely possibility. He had contacts at Arizona State University and they were eager for him to come there to teach in the Education Department. So, we moved to AZ. I located a job I wanted very much on the Gila Indian Reservation and we both worked in these institutions until retirement. During this time Ralph and some teachers started an organization that operated for several years as a place for teachers to come together with ideas about language learning that gave support to children's ideas and values rather than rote learning. It still stands as an ideal for many. Before we retired we started building an adobe house in the San Tan's with a friend. We had been living in Tempe. Over three years, excluding summers, we built the house and moved there in spring of 1993.

On retirement I started looking for environmental groups I might volunteer with. This had always been an interest. My four and five year old's in NYC had started a recycling program on their own and soon Teacher's College got into the act. That is when I found San Tan Mountains Pride Association. I joined and worked with them for several years.

In that time I also became involved with the State Historical Preservation Office and had a historical site I monitored. Then I worked with Friends of the San Tan Mountain Park for a while. In that time Ralph completed a book on education with a colleague and wrote one of his own. He is now working on another. Life is more in the slow lane now but we still go to our cabin in N. Idaho that we built up over 40 years and spend time with family and friends still in the Spokane and Seattle area. We also still enjoy athletic and theater events at ASU and the Phoenix area.

Community Leaders

Ron & Donnis Hunkler

Ron & Donnis Hunkler are our next door neighbors and very good friends. Ron and I were co-founders of the San Tan Mountains PRIDE LLC and then the San Tan PRIDE Association that was a 501 (c) (3).

We first met the Hunkers in 1986, soon after we moved in (remember the birthday banner story?). On their daily walks both within the nearby San Tan Mountain Regional Park and along our roadways they picked up trash and loaded it into used plastic grocery bags.

When each bag was filled they would leave them along the road to be picked up later.

They are very family oriented and have served the community since moving here in 1976. They were both, of course, very active within the PRIDE, with Ron serving as our vice-president for at least twelve years. They have been involved in many community projects and organizations including: The San Tan Historical Society where they have been very active for many years, the Relay for Life cancer fundraiser, the Chandler Heights Community Church, the Old Timers Monday Morning Breakfast Meeting club, and the "Vixen" Motor Home club that meets at different locations throughout the USA. Relatives Going Fishing Club (their group used to meet twice a year at Big Lake in the White Mountains. Now they meet once a year at Willow lake on the Mogollon Rim. Ron and Donnis moved to Arizona from Barnesville, Ohio to get a fresh start and get away from the rain, wind and snow. Ron initially had a job lined up in Gila Bend, but after pulling in to the town with his five children and a loaded station wagon during a dust storm, he decided that town was not for them! They contacted friends who lived in Chandler and he got a job with Suburban Chevrolet (later to become Chapman), where he worked until getting a job with General Motors. There he started as a test driver, eventually working his way up to heading the air conditioning division at the plant. It was while working at G.M. that Ron began planning to build his dream home—uniquely designed by Ron and then built by him and family members. Because he was commuting to General Motors on Ellsworth Road, living in Queen Creek made a lot of sense. While building the house Ron and Donnis lived in what was to become our home! Its proximity made it possible for Ron to put every spare minute into getting their new home built.

At the time there were no telephone lines in the area and before cell phones, communication was made to a friend in Chandler through a CB radio, who then phoned family members and friends for the Hunkler's. Donnis tells of the early days when Ron would leave for work in the morning and her being "stuck" in the house with no car and no way to contact anyone until he returned in the evening.

Former Mayor Wendy Feldman-Kerr

Wendy was the second elected mayor of the Town of Queen Creek. The first mayor, Mark Schnepf, helped Wendy a great deal with her new challenge of guiding a fledgling town. She also had help from Town Manager Cynthia Seelhammer, who had a great deal of experience in the politics that small towns are involved in on a day-to-day basis.

Wendy came from Cleveland Ohio to get her master's degree in communications at ASU. Her husband, Eric Kerr, is a native of Arizona. They are both worried about how the Town is increasing the density beyond what the Town's Master Plan had prescribed. She was also disappointed with the town voting down the Town's open fences law, which was another law that the citizens voted for in our Master Plan.

In her tenure as a council member and Mayor she felt that the Town's heavy traffic that had to go directly through the center of the Town's two lane highway was a big problem. The increased heavy traffic was caused primarily by the unprecedented large number of new residential building going on just south of the Maricopa County line. It took a long time to build the Town's by-pass route and more time to expand Ellsworth Road to what it is today. Most of that planning took place during Wendy's term as Mayor.

The first ordinance that Wendy had to guide the council through at their regularly scheduled council meeting had to do with bee's. People were getting stung from these creatures in their search for water. The local beekeepers were putting out their hives without providing water for them.

The ordinance would require the beekeepers to put their names on all their hives and require all beekeepers provide water for them. Wendy never knew that a bee ordinance would be something she would be a part of as Mayor of the Town Of Queen Creek. She just thought "So Bee It".

Some months later there was another need for an ordinance that had to do with animals. This time some monkeys got out of their cage and scared a bunch of the Town's citizens. So it was suggested that the Town have an ordinance dealing with exotic animals. The Mayor and council deliberated and so be it again.

In another council meeting a resident brought two horses into the council chambers because the Town Council was going to pass laws dealing with horse stables and their construction parameters. These two horses represented a pony/foal and a full size horse. No one had ever brought one horse into council chambers during a meeting, let alone two horses. Fortunately these horses were made of cardboard.

The woman, a horse owner, wanted to make sure that the size of the stables would be big enough for the steeds to lie down. She laid the horses down on the floor, showing a mare and her foal if they might be together in one stall and how much room that would be needed if they decided to lay down at the same time.

The size needed for the two was very large indeed and the Mayor questioned if all horses lie down with their legs fully extended like the cardboard horses did? The record does not show if this unusual demonstration actually helped in the drawing of the regulations that are in the books today. It is noted that the woman did not take her cardboard horses with her and they had to be "put down" by staff that evening.

The council meetings gave Wendy a lot of satisfaction because the council most always got a lot of good things done. Be it bees, monkeys or cardboard horses, most council meetings were very productive with some more memorable than others.

It is known that Mayor Wendy did keep the Town involved with all the surrounding governments and Town's interests. Her realm of influence spanned far outside the Town of Queen Creek. She was known for her achievements, locally, statewide and nationally, which gave her the opportunity to influence a greater number of people and was a role model to those who wanted to follow in her footsteps.

Very Busy People

Nonda & Gordon
Brown

The Brown's have a passion for the welfare of our community. Gordon is and has been a community activist (on steroids) for many years.

Gordon has served and/or belongs to the following: Triad, GSTAC, Friends of The San Tan Mountain Regional Park, Artisans of The San Tan Mountains, the San Tan Mountains PRIDE Association, the Nathan Martins Arizona Memorial Project, San Tan Historical Society, San Tan Archeology Society, Pan de Vida, O'Connor House Partner, Speak Out Arizona, Better Living Coalition, Pinal Partnership, Pinal County Citizen Advisory Committee, Youth Awareness Think Tank, Pinal County Planning and Zoning Commission, Sizzling Seniors, and Life Point Church Good Life Group.

Nonda has served and/or belongs to the following: Triad, Artisans of the San Tan Mountains, San Tan Mountains PRIDE Association, Nathan Martens Arizona Memorial Project, San Tan Historical Society, San Tan Archaeological Society, Life Point Church Good Life Group and the Queen Creek High School Embrace Club.

Submitted by Nonda Brown

Our Little House In The Country

The December sun gently brightens the desert landscape as we approach the beautiful San Tan Mountains, and home. There is a feeling of expectancy and serenity that appears to waft from the wavering shadows at the base of these desert hills. The mountains seem to be welcoming us home to a place of rest and peace.

As soon as we moved to our desert dwelling in the San Tan Foothills in December of 1998, we knew this was where we hoped to live out the rest of our days on earth. Our home was an old, dilapidated, single-wide trailer on an acre and one-quarter lot. Our dream was to build our retirement home to enjoy in our sunset years. Our rural community was sparsely populated by humans, but was endowed with an abundance of desert plants and wildlife.

The nearest grocery store was twenty miles away, whatever direction one took. Our water was hauled in a water tank attached to a trailer and pulled by our truck, and the nearest stand pipe was ten miles away in the town of Queen Creek. We had a flat tire at least once a month from the rocks that poked up through the dust on the roads, and our truck's windshield needed to be replaced once or twice a year because of the rocks that flew up from trucks and cars that were traveling the same dirt roads. But, when we returned home, and entered our driveway we feasted on the site of baby quails obediently toddling after their parents, with their tiny top knots nodding to and fro. And, in the evenings and early mornings we enjoyed watching the bunnies frolicking in our desert paradise chasing each others fluffy white tails. Nearby, we hear the yip, yip, yip of the coyotes calling to their pups that dinner is on the way. Also, in the early morning when the dew has dusted the creosote bushes the air is filled with a pungent aroma that can soothe the soul.

Some may say that the desert is not a habitable place to live. Some may say that it is crazy to live in the middle of nowhere where there are no malls or theaters. However, to us our desert home is a haven that was gifted to us from our Heavenly Father.

Submitted by Gordon Brown

Nonda and I moved from Mesa in 1998 to an area bounded on the North, South and West by the San Tan Mountain regional Park. The kids were grown, I was retired and looking forward to a reclusive life in the mountain shadows, working with wood and maybe taking up stained glass. 1999 saw a short lived attempt to sell the park land to the North and South of our area, and a parade of rejected urban development proposals, coinciding with the unification of what has come to be recognized and respected as the San Tan Foothills community.

Beyond the Foothills, well, my "hood" has grown. I'm not sure why. I think it is the people I've met. Ancient cartographers defined the limits of the known world with the poetic "Beyond there be dragons". But I've found no dragons in San Tan Valley. There are only Canadians, Californians, Mid-westerners and sundry other migratory pilgrims. What they came for is not as important as what they will find, and what they will build together. There are doers in San Tan valley. They might not always agree, but they tend to know each other. When the bridges between diverse perspectives are built, ideas get polished and become better products than if never challenged. More people always see much more and from more perspectives than any individual can. A lot of very smart folks designed a system of governance that not only recognizes that, it depends on it.

Over a beer, I still enjoy planning my shop, but in the words of Gilda Radner, "There's always something". There is San Tan Valley. There is Pinal County. There is Arizona. Beyond, I suspect there be dragons. How many things a person feels they work on depends a lot on what they see as a thing. One person may recall Saturdays spent pulling weeds, pruning trees, mowing the lawn, having a beer, maybe two, eating chicken and laughing at the neighbor's jokes, while another remembers only having some fun tending the yard.

I moved here looking for a solitary shop. I found a home. I like the people that have moved in with me. I didn't mean to.

Nonda told me, Alden, a really great story about a project that was near and dear to her heart. Nonda served many years as a high school teacher and retired a short time ago from Queen Creek High School. Her psychology class formed a club called "Embrace It" at her behest. She did this because it seems that there are many students that always join together and become different factions within every school....the jocks, the cowboys and the geeks to name a few. Nonda saw these factions not working together sometimes, for the better welfare of the school and she was going to work with her students in the "Embrace It Club" to help change things, hopefully, for the better.

They all decided to try to bring all the factions together as one family unit by getting them to talk and mingle together and then to work together in a more harmonious way. After many trial meetings, a big school assembly in the gym was planned in order to further hear and discuss how we can all be friends with each other as we travel though our school life and on our way to receive our diplomas and then entering the real world. Harmony within the school was a key word for their mission.

The assembly was scheduled just before Christmas and all the appropriate decorations were in place including a 15 foot Christmas tree right in the center of the gym. The stage was set for a wonderful discussion of peace on earth and good will towards mankind or so Nonda thought. When all the bleachers were almost full and the speakers all set to talk a fight broke out near the Christmas tree, between two young men.

It was a combination of a wrestling and boxing match that had all kinds of people trying to break it up. Then the students in the bleachers started cheering the pugilists on and clapping while the tree with its decorations was knocked over, is was pure bedlam until the combatants finally got tired. It didn't look like much damage was done to the fighters as the two males were escorted off the floor to the continuing cheers and clapping of their peers.

When order was finally restored many thought that this was staged to show how fighting was not a god way of settling things and most all the students thought it was the best assembly ever. When the first speaker began speaking about how peace was the best course through life there were was a lot of subdued laughing from those attending and even some from the teachers and administrators as well. Oh yes, the fight was over a young woman.

Pat & Gerhard

Gerhard served the PRIDE extremely well as a director and volunteering for working on each and every one of our many projects. He is a good friend to all the people he interacted with.

Submitted by Gerhard Oberikat

Born and raised in Germany, I immigrated to Canada in my late 20's. After 30 years at Ford Motor Company in Michigan, I retired and together with my wife Pat, started spending long winters in sunny Arizona.

Chief among my involvements in Arizona has been membership in the San Tan Mountains Pride Association in Queen Creek. As a Board member and Site Steward of the Pride Association, I was eager for the opportunity to spend time in the mountains, looking up its history and tradition, enabling me to pass this on to fellow members of my local hiking group. The group always includes the San Tan Mountain on its annual list of trails to enjoy.

The Pride Association's achievements have helped Queen Creek become a better, more desirable community. In past years, the Pride Association has sponsored their annual clean up, relying on the ever-present donation of equipment and refreshments from local area businesses. The Pride Association also sponsored a baseball team in the youth category and a Queen Creek's Cub Scout Troop. A welcome addition to the San Tan Mountains Park was the establishment of a memorial to the fellow soldiers in Afghanistan and Iraq.

Unfortunately, the San Tan Mountain Pride Association has disbanded, but this does not diminish the many contributions to the San Tan Mountains Park.

Carrie, Mark And Their Children

Mark Schnepf and his family have a long and sterling history within our community dating back more than 70 years. Mark and Carrie are both energetic people that produce high quality family fun extravaganza's every year along with the help of their children. Mark was our first elected Mayor and at that time we lived outside the Town of Queen Creek in Pinal County, but we always felt so a part of the Town then. It would be a couple of years after the Town's incorporation that we would be annexed into the Town in an effort to block the "Box Canyon" development which would have been west "over the mountain" from of our property. The Town council believed at that time that this Box Canyon project would overburden the area's meager highways systems and other facilities.

Mayor Mark and most of his council members helped the San Tan Mountain PRIDE Association with our community wide clean-ups from the very first one in 1999. Mark was one of the founding members of the Town's incorporation group. Mark was also the spokesman at the many public gatherings that were used to gain support for the incorporation. Mark, his wife Carrie and their four children remain a very important component of our community's lifestyle.

Steve Sossaman

Steve, the son of a former Arizona State Legislator was another founding member of Queen Creek incorporation. The Sossaman family goes back to when the Indians rode horseback within our community and lived in mud homes. Steve taught agriculture classes at ASU and still farms a lot of land in and around Queen Creek, as his relatives did for many years. He still grows some high quality wheat that he sells to an Italian pasta producer and has reintroduced "Old School" specialty types of cotton and wheat grains back into Arizona's farming community.

Paul Gardner

Paul Gardner was about to enter college when his father passed away. He was in his early 20s when he took control of his families Queen Creek Water Company. Paul sold his company to the Town a few years ago and has a position with the Town in the water department. Paul was one of the founders in the effort to get the Town incorporated. He was responsible for getting quality water service to our homes here on the north slopes of the San Tans in a reasonable time from start to finish. I waited just twelve years for this to happen and some of the original pioneers like Ron and Donnis Hunkler waited for over seventeen years. Paul is definitely an important part of our Town's history and of our great Community. He is a real gentleman with a very large gift for patience and civility.

Joan & Bill Perry

Joan & Bill Perry were very active with the Town of Queen Creek by supporting their various athletic programs. They were also very active within the PRIDE Association and with Friends of the Park (STMRP). They gave their support to many projects and organizations. Bill passed away after a short illness that took him at an early age. His death shocked our community which lost a fine gentleman and a committed hard worker for all he believed in. He and his wife Joan helped build our Community in every sense of the word. Joan continues with her support of Friends of the Park.

Mancel Carter, Man With Goldmine Mountain

Mancel With Maude His Pet Quail

After moving into our new home near Goldmine Mountain in 1986 I rode Santanna up into the park past the little trailer that Mancel lived in then, at least twice a week. After I met him I would stop on the way back to talk with him for a few minutes. He seemed to enjoy our conversations together as I think that he felt the same with all the people that stopped there for a visit. He was very compassionate about his wild animal friends.

One day I drove Caroline and our three year old granddaughter up to see and talk with Mr. Carter before the fences were installed. When we entered his trailer Mansel had "Maude" his Gamble Quail perched on his shoulder but my granddaughter had never seen one of these birds up close before.

When I introduced Tasia to him, she let out a blood curdling scream when see noticed the Quail on Mansel's shoulder, who then flew out the trailer door. Mancel didn't even bat an eye he just reached over and shook Tasia's hand. He was thrilled when Caroline gave him a tin of pipe tobacco and some batteries for his radio.

After he became sick and went to the VA hospital in Phoenix my rides on Santanna into the Park were not quite as pleasurable anymore.

Story Submitted by Ron Hunkler

Mansel Carter was a genuine celebrity of the Queen Creek area. His life-style, friendly nature and Cactus Curios made him a full fledged tourist attraction for both local and visitors alike. The story had spread about "The Old Man of the Mountain" who lived in a little miner's shack with no electricity or water and how birds and animals would eat of his hands and perch on his shoulder "The Hermit," as he called himself on a directions sign on Hunt Highway crafted wood carvings with his pocket knife and old hand saw. The Prospector and Mule was The most famous carving with the $10.00 price staying the same for 25 years.

He began a guest register in the early 60s and the 20 or so of these books list people from all 50 states and over 50 foreign countries. One entourage had over 100 people with 60 some vehicles.

Mansel Carter came to the Queen Creek area in 1948 with a prospecting buddy named Marion Kennedy. Mansel had a photography business and Mr. Kennedy delivered ice in Gilbert during the early 40s. They also worked together for various farmers in that area and that's how they met and eventually decided they wanted to getaway from the "city" and try there hand at prospecting. Mr. Kennedy was a Cherokee Indian from Oklahoma and had attended the Indian school in Carlisle, Pennsylvania with Jim Thorpe, the great native American athlete. He was 28 years older than Mansel and almost blind when they made their move, but he had done some prospecting so he taught Mansel a new skill. They set up camp about five miles south of town in the Goldmine Mountains and spent the first year under a Palo Verde tree as their home. They never struck it rich but they lived the life-style they wanted. Mr. Kennedy passed away in the 1960 and Mansel buried him near their camp. He continued prospecting, but more and more of his time went to his carvings and eventually he could not keep up with the orders for which he never refused a request.

Mansel L. Carter was born to Ellis and Mary Hall Carter in 1902 on a farm near Quaker City, Ohio, the oldest of two brothers and three sisters. He attended the Olney Friends, (Quaker) Boarding School in Barnesville, Ohio for a couple of years and then went to work in his uncle's repair shop in Old Washington, Ohio. He left Ohio in the mid 20s and went to Indiana where he learned the photography profession and piloted a Ford Tri-Motor airplane for a charter airline company. When the depression forced the charter business to go "belly-up" as Mansel called it, he went to New Mexico and worked as a logger on the Zuni Indian Reservation for a few years. In the late 30s he drove to the Salmon River area of Idaho and Montana where he did various farm jobs. On this trip he passed through the Navajo Reservation and was amazed when the people welcomed him by name and knew was coming. There weren't any modern communication systems on the Reservation at that time.

He left Idaho and headed for Arizona December 1941 in his Model "A" Ford pick-up pulling his "home" a little camping trailer with radio antenna mounted on the top. Somewhere in Utah he was stopped and questioned at length as possible foreign agent. The Japanese had just bombed Pearl Harbor and a lone motorist with a antenna on his vehicle was a very suspicious character at that time. Mr. Carter was drafted into the Army a short time later but was discharged after a short tour of duty. It was decided the members of his company who were all over 40 were too old for military duty.

For the people who knew him best, his fresh baked biscuits were marvelous but you had to get there early, because he fed

all to his feathered and four-legged friends every day. He told
one time of having watch out while baking his biscuits in the
Desert for a Desert Turtle family that had hatched their babies
under his stove.

Although he refused Social Security benefits as a matter of of
principle, a small pension from his W.W. II stint and his
"Cactus Curios" income, provided him with everything he
needed. His modern convenience was a little portable radio for
listening to the "Dodgers" baseball games.

Over the years many articles were written and several TV
appearances were done about him, including a segment on
Channel 10 of "On the Arizona Road" with Bill Leverton. The
"Arizona Balladeer," Dolin Ellis, wrote a song about Mr.
Carter and used it in his performances with a slide show
backdrop of Mansel. He was also one of the featured few in
the November 1987 "Phoenix" magazine article about
"Arizona Legends."

Mansel is buried up there on the mountain beside Mr.
Kennedy. His nephew Eugene Bates tells about having a
terrible time trying to engrave the headstone for Mansel's
grave when he got this eerie feeling that someone was
watching him over his shoulder. After that he completed the
task in no time. So he know Mansel is still there on the
mountain watching over his little friends.

Bear

There was a gentleman some years ago that owned an auto
repair shop near the center of the Town of Queen Creek who
organized a motorcycle rally once a year. The town was
inundated with many hundreds of motorcycles and their riders
that came from all over the USA, who would hang out near
and at his shop. It is told that he had to rein in some of Piggy's
motorcycle friends once and a while so they didn't get out of
hand and crazy. When Bear passed away, the motorcycle rally
to Queen Creek stopped.

Mary Gloria

The San Tan PRIDE was very fortunate when Mary and her many friends and relatives joined us when we had our annual clean-ups. General Gloria, my nickname for her, cleaned the roadsides near and around her home and Hunt Highway from the old Hunt Highway to Skyline Drive. The new Hunt Highway always had high amount of vehicle traffic so I made sure that the Pinal County Sheriff's Office provided at least one patrol car with flashing lights along their roadside clean-up route. We also gave them ADOT "workers working" warning signs that they put on both sides of the road. Mary has a foundation called "Pan de Vida" that has become something like the Salvation Army for Queen Creek that gives the bread of life and the other needs of life to the less fortunate 365 days a year. She has received hundreds of awards over the years for her blessed and giving ways.

Son Alex, Mom Diane, Daughter Erin & Grand Daughter Ava

Submitted by Diane Drenk

My three sisters and I are third generation Norwegians that were brought up in Stoughton Wisconsin. I bought my first horse when I was fourteen and I kept it at my grandparent's large dairy farm that was about five miles outside Stoughton. The four of us spent a lot of our time on the farm when we were children. It was a beautiful place and there were a lot of things to do. In addition to the caring for the cows, our grandfather grew corn, tobacco and hay. I spent most every weekend with Doc, my handsome Morab (Morgan Arabian) chestnut in color, with a flaxen mane and tail. At age 16 I bought a 10 day old Tennessee Walking Horse stallion, Doc helped me teach the foal manners. The name of the baby was Prince Merlin.

When I was eighteen I was working, had my own apartment and was going to nursing school. I wasn't really happy with what entailed being a nurse. Then I heard from some of my horse friends that Lasma Arabians in Scottsdale Arizona was looking for apprentices that wanted to learn everything to do with the care and conditioning of horses, purebred Arabian horses. I immediately applied and after a number of telephone interviews I was accepted. I was very excited and knew then that my pathway in life had changed. I gave Doc to a friend, that I knew would take very good care of him as he was getting on in age. I kept track of Doc often and every time I went back to Wisconsin I would see him. He lived until he was 28.

I got a handmade single axle horse trailer and had an older car, packed my duds, said my goodbyes to my parents, siblings and friends and headed for Arizona, just me and Prince Merlin. I took him out at rest stops along the way where we got a lot of attention from those that were walking their dogs. It must have been a sight to see.

This ranch specialized in breeding the top of the line Arab stallions with top of the line Arab mares. Most that they worked with were the crème de la crème and very expensive horses that had to be treated as royalty. Besides the grooming of every horse each day, all of us that were apprentices were taught to feed each horse based on what that horses needs were. Many of the scores of horses we cared for ate different food and supplements that we had to serve them daily. The care we gave was strictly monitored. It was so much fun getting to know each horse and how different each horse's personality was from each other.

Most of the horses, especially the stallions had to be exercised daily in a special horse swimming pool where we would lead the horses by walking around the edge of the pool as the horse swam in circles. It was an excellent way to make sure the horses got the exercise that they needed to keep in the best condition possible.

Within a short period of time I was on the show circuit traveling all over the country to horse shows, we had 2 semis and a 6 horse goose neck trailer, usually around 20 horses in the show ring. Now we get some of those people I worked with together and catch up on our lives during the Annual Scottsdale Arabian Horse Show every February. After I married we wanted to move out into the country where I could house my Arab mares in a better setting. By this time I had two children, a girl and a boy, and the rural setting we moved into in Queen Creek was great for them. Almost as soon as we moved in our neighbors greeted us with pies and a warm welcome to the neighbor hood.

Right after we got settled in I became involved in the East Valley Arabian Horse Association (EVAHA) and soon I was serving as vice-president. By this time I had many years of showing, and breeding Arabians on a national and local basis.

Some of our not so nice neighbors, and there were a few, were doing illegal things that we were concerned with so we joined the San Tan Mountain Pride Association in effort to get the drug dealers out of here. It wasn't long before we were on the board of STMPA and we all helped with the very first clean up in our area. I have enjoyed working with all the characters that made up the board. The San Tan Mountain Regional Park has benefited from the Prides work. I suggested to the board I served on in the East Valley Arabian Association that the our group donate money for the building of a fence, which they did, that is still in place around the graves of Mancel Carter and Marion Kennedy. Before Maricopa County installed their boundary fences a few years ago around the entrance and further toward the east and west shooters would open fire on targets near the base of Goldmine Mountain. I was very worried that some of the bullets would ricochet and come at our children playing outside. I would go get them in when I heard lots of shooting going on up there.

We enjoyed hauling our water as a bi weekly chore for many years, because our kids and I got to meet many more neighbors waiting in line, sometimes for hours at a time, to get their empty water tanks up to the standpipe. Getting our water was also a great way of getting all the local news before it was printed in the Chandler Heights Monthly.

My daughter has recently given us a beautiful granddaughter by the name of Ava. She is our wonderful treasure. Our son, Alex, is in his fourth year as a midshipman at the US Naval Academy in Annapolis, Maryland. We are very proud of Alex for being accepted in the Navy fight-training program where he will be serving right after his graduation in 2014.

I now have five horses, the man of the crew Maxamillion CF, the lady's Talia and Vectra who are full Sisters, and also their daughter Drenkara and Monave.

I have been in the RV industry since 1985....Love it....assisting people to be able to enjoy their lives. Living the dream... I look forward to doing it someday myself...more than short trips. I never tired of looking outside into the mountains to the South, or the view to the North of the entire valley from the Superstition mountains to the far west valley. The drive home every day from work, coming up the hill, I am amazed after 20 years. How lucky I feel to be living here.

Alex Wilson

When Alex applied to the Naval Academy he was among 20,000 other men and women that applied that year. Along with his application he would need recommendations from his high schools and his congressman. He had to pass his college board exams and pass stringent medical and physicals exams.

After that; To become a Midshipman at the United States Naval Academy in Annapolis Maryland he had to pass the scrutiny of their admissions board that consists of about a dozen members, including the Dean of the Academy. They debate and discuss the characteristics of each of candidate's application that reaches their huge table.

Ensign Alex Wilson
USN

To even be a part of their discussion, each candidate must complete several steps, steps that are above and beyond what the ordinary applicant must complete as a part of the college admissions process at our nations finest colleges and universities. But the Naval Academy is no ordinary place, in fact it is extraordinary, and so are the men and women who earn the high honor and privilege of being accepted each year. In contrast to paying for college, the young men and women who enter the Naval Academy get paid while they are enrolled, and they serve a five year commitment as paid officers in the United States Navy or Marine Corps. If they choose to leave the Navy or Marines and pursue a career outside the military, the world is waiting, graduates from all of our service academies are in high demand.

Submitted by Alex Wilson

I had lived in Queen Creek for nearly 15 years going to Queen Creek schools except for my senior year in high school. I have seen QC being transformed from having mostly dirt roads near where I lived and where there were no stop lights, where the Town is now to a more modernized community. The western lifestyle has dulled down quite a bit from what it was when I was going to the Queen Creek Elementary School but we still have horses, pick-up trucks and "wanna-be" cowboys. I know a lot of us moved here to get away from that city life style and it seems that Queen Creek is slowly creeping towards what a lot of us were escaping from. Yes we now have most everything we need close by and convenient to us and we don't have haul water anymore. Our roads are paved now where I used to live. I know our Queen Creek school system is developing and has a better reputation and image than they did when I was growing up. Their facilities are new and the sports teams are notoriously good and academic achievement is higher now than in the earlier years. From where I lived up on the mountain my friends and I were able to hike, ride our mountain bikes and that still remains today. Where I used to live we can see how things have changed right in front of us. It is getting crowded down there!

Alex's Class USNA

The Nathan Martens Arizona Memorial

Robert Nathaniel Martens was a credit to everything he was involved with in Queen Creek. He lettered in baseball and football and was President of the Queen Creek 4H club. Nathan liked to horseback ride, hike and mountain bike ride in the area that is now the San Tan Mountain Regional Park. Nathan was married to Erin and they had a daughter, Riley Jo.

Nathan joined the United States Navy to become a Corpsman because he wanted to enter medical school after his tour of duty to then study to become a pediatrician. In the Navy he opted to become a United States Marine Corps Corpsman, whereby he would have to go to the Marine Corpsman Boot

Camp at Camp Lejeune North Carolina. Once he completed the course he was considered a Marine as well as a Navy Hospitalman.

Immediately after the Marine Corps graduation he was shipped out to Anbar Province in Iraq. Just 10 days after his arrival there he was killed in a HUMVEE rollover accident while on a midnight patrol. He had just traded places from the front seat to a rear seat because a Marine sitting in the back was getting sick from not being able to see the road ahead. Nathan was the only person killed in this accident and probably would not have been killed if he had not chosen to trade places with the other Marine.

Within weeks of his burial many members of our community wanted some local organization to spearhead a funding for a memorial in his name. Being a Marine from the 1956 era I asked our San Tan Mountains PRIDE Association Board to let me be chairman for the funding and building of a memorial honoring all those Arizonans that gave their lives in Operation Iraqi Freedom.

Craig Barnes, who was the Commander of the Queen Creek American Legion then, suggested that we add Operation Enduring Freedom casualties to the memorial at our very first Memorial meeting, which was accepted. I stepped down as President of the PRIDE so I could spend full time on the Memorial fund raising and construction. The STMPA Board appointed Vice-president Ed Guerra to President to fill out my term. I remained on as a board member and chairman of the Nathan Martens Arizona Memorial.

One of the very first things that I did as chairman was to call Senator John McCain's office to ask what the guidelines were to build a Memorial. I was told that as far as they knew there were not any and had me call the U.S. Department of Veterans Affair's National Cemetery Administration. When I called them no one knew if there were any written specifications for the building of one or if there was any rules pertaining to a memorial, per se.

The first person I thought of to oversee the construction phase was Gordon Brown who had many years of commercial construction experience. Gordon soon became my partner in all things Memorial and was an invaluable asset to the success of our dream.

Gordon introduced me to Liz Guy, a local artist and photographer, to help us design a sketch of what we thought would be an appropriate memorial. We all thought that a memorial in the San Tan Mountain Regional Park would be a wonderful place, in view of the fact that Nathan spent so much time within its grounds before he went into the Navy. I went through the STMRP supervisor and through our Maricopa County Supervisor then, Fulton Brock to obtain approval for us to build on park land.

The Maricopa County Parks and Recreation Director and the County Supervisors gave permission to give us the land but turned down our original concept, which included a wooden flagpole. They told me that a wooden telephone pole flagpole would have be replaced too often. At this time I sat on the board of a state wide non-profit organization called Arizona Clean & Beautiful.

There were two very instrumental board members that sat with me at our monthly meetings. One member worked for SRP, one of our local power & light companies, and the other one worked for a company that designed golf courses and other outdoor projects. During a break in our ACB meeting, within a month of the inception of the Memorial, I asked the SRP lady if we could get a metal power pole for our flag pole from her company. She said that she would find out.

Right after the meeting, as we were all heading out to our cars, I asked Mike Buschbacher, the golf course designer if his company might be able to design our Memorial. Within about two minutes after he made a call to his company he replied that he thought his company might be able to do it all, at no charge. WOW! I was on top of the world.

These people were so very important in getting this project going and it only took about ten minutes total to put the plan in motion. The next day, Mike Buschbacher called and said that he would do all the designing personally and emphasized that it would be done free. Two days later I got a call from the SRP lady and she told me to call an engineer in charge of power poles who had a pole available for us, also at no charge. I called the man at SRP and he said that he had an eighty foot, large power pole made of special steel that rusted to look like a wooden power pole. He told me that all we had to do was get the pole off the lot within one month. I asked him how long the pole would last and he said at least 100 years or more and he would put that in writing.

Kathy Denton, "The Tornado Lady"

Gordon asked me what our budget was and I said that the PRIDE had some money but we would have to get most of what we needed in "In Kind" contributions. Gordon told me that this was quite a challenge but he was up to it and that that was the way he liked to work anyway.

For those that do not know, the San Tan Regional Park lies wholly within Pinal County but is managed by Maricopa County. This meant we had to work with both counties in order to get this project completed. While this was going on I was also busy running a new construction cleaning company, and business was extremely good.

I then enlisted a lady that was on our board to get the details worked out for us and to find ways to get contributions. Her name is Kathy Denton, aka the Tornado Lady. Without her help we might not have gotten as far as we did in the record-breaking time that it took us. In less than one year, using very little money, we had the Memorial ready for its dedication. **K**

THE TORNADO LADY

John F. Ellis

Our project got on the front page in a few newspapers including the Arizona Republic. They published the times and location of our weekly Memorial building meetings. Our meeting were at 7:00 p.m. at the park where the Memorial was going to be built. We were about to start one of our meetings when this man came in the door and asked if he could sit in the meeting with us. I told him is was an open meeting and he was welcome to join us. He said that his name was John Ellis. We all thought that he was a local resident and just was interested in what we were doing.

At one point of the meeting when we were discussing how we were going to build the circular concrete benches to the specifications of our drawings, Gordon Brown started to say that we could rent a concrete mixer from Russ's Hardware but he was politely interrupted by Mr. Ellis. He calmly said that he owned a concrete construction company and he would like help by building whatever we needed to be done in concrete for the memorial.

The seventy foot pole had to have 5000 psi concrete poured around it in the ground. I think that the benches had to have 1000 psi concrete poured over rebar cages in colored concrete. John gave us a crew of about 6 to 8 men that worked for about three weeks before the pour was scheduled to happen. Gordon arranged for the pole to be set the same day as the benches were to be poured. This meant that the whole pour would have be 5000 psi colored cement for the pole base and the benches.

The cost for this type cement was very expensive and John Ellis paid for it and all the time his crews took to build our circular benches and for everything else that was needed.

Regrettably John was involved in a major motorcycle accident that happened close to the time that our dedication was planned. Ed and I visited him in the hospital and he wanted so much to be there for the dedication but his doctors were against him doing this because of his many injuries.

After watching what his crews had to do we really realized that John was the most important person in the building of this Memorial. Those benches should last as long as the pole or maybe even longer than 100 years. What a wonderful man John Ellis is!

Major Bryan Martyn USAF

We were very fortunate indeed to have Major Martyn act as our chairman of the Memorial Dedication. This man has served his country as a special ops helicopter pilot who is the recipient of the Silver Cross which is the second highest award our military gives to it's heroes. Bryan has received many other awards over the near two decades he served.

As our master of ceremonies he arranged a fly over by the USAF and had the US Army Band from Fort Huachuca march in our parade and play for us during the ceremony. In his last tour of duty he was sent to Afghanistan to teach some of their Air Force personnel how to fly the big Russian Attack helicopter. It seems that that the Russians left a few behind in their hasty retreat out of there. Bryan also served his community very as a Pinal County Supervisor and is presently serving the State of Arizona as their Executive Director of Arizona State Parks.

Ed Guerra, Me, USMC, USN & USCC,
SRP Calender

The Nathan Martens Arizona Memorial flag is 18' X 12'

Nathan Martins, US NAVY & Marine Corpsman A Honored Queen Creek Friend & Neighbor.

Nathan Hugging Riley Jo

CHAPTER 6

Sandie Smith

Our Former Pinal County Supervisor

Sandie Smith, a 43 year resident in Pinal County, is president and CEO of the Pinal Partnership. She has served in that position since January of 2009. Pinal Partnership was created with a mission "to improve research, planning and coordination of private and public efforts related to infrastructure, natural resources and community development in Pinal County". Pinal Partnership is a coalition of community, business, educational, and governmental leaders whose goal is to provide leadership and support in specific areas of focus that include; Transportation and Infrastructure, Government Relations, Economic Development, Parks, Trail, Open Space and Public Lands, Education, and Health and Human Services.

Sandie was elected to the Pinal County Board of Supervisors and served from 1993 to December 2008 and was the first woman in Pinal County to be elected to the Board of Supervisors. During her distinguished 15 years as a Pinal County Supervisor, Smith's dedication to forming partnerships between public and private sector businesses is well known throughout the State of Arizona. Sandie served on many local and state committees and commissions while serving as the District 2 Supervisor. Sandie's first public service office was in 1986 when she was elected to serve as a member of the Governing Board of the Apache Junction Unified School District and served as President of that board from 1988 to

1993. She is a current member of the Apache Junction Boys and Girls Club.

Sandie owned a business in Apache Junction from 1970 to 1995 and served on the Apache Junction Chamber of Commerce Board for 6 years and was president for 2 of those years. She and her husband, Tom Smith, have been married for 50 years and have three children: Sheryl, David, and Kenneth and six grandchildren, Ashley, Kirsten, Davis, Abbott, Cassandra and Nicole.

This lady is truly an extraordinary woman whose father passed away when she was very young. The family that was left, her mother and two brothers, moved so often before she was a teenager that she often thought that it must be a normal circumstance. When her children became older Sandie became more and more involved in her community. After a few more short years she became involved in politics, further serving the Pinal County community she lived in. Sandie recently told me that she had never lost an election.

I complained to Sandie when she was our County Supervisor many times about the many zoning violations that were left unenforced in our area and she always returned my calls and faxes. I also told her of many other things about the criminal activities that were going on in our community as well. As a result of our conversations, a meeting was set up between our PRIDE members, interested local citizens and the chief Pinal County zoning inspector on May 2, 1998 at the Town of Queen Creek's Community Center.

At the meeting, the Pinal County chief zoning inspector, Peggy, was very surprised to see the director of Pinal County Planning and Zoning and the Pinal County Manager there in the audience. Whispering to me, she asked if I had invited them and I said no, I had never even met them before. I had a list of the legal addresses of the properties we thought were the most flagrant abusers of Pinal's zoning laws. I also had large pictures of most of these properties, including two that had outhouses on their land, along with many others that had extra trailers, more that had several broken down old vehicles, and two with 50 gallon barrels being used as septic tanks. Everything that I showed them was in total violation of the Pinal County zoning regulations and some were in total violation of the County's Health Laws.

Peggy the Pinal County chief zoning inspector was about to respond to my presentation when the Pinal County Planning & Zoning Director got up and introduced himself and the Pinal County Manager. In response to my presentation the Director said that outhouses were legal in Pinal County. He went on to say that the Pinal County Zoning Department had the legal authority to have land owners arrested for any flagrant violations and he directly told me that his department would not use any selected list that we gave him to check on whether or not they were in compliance.

The director said that his department would conduct a sweep of the entire region on the north side of the San Tan Mountains in Pinal County, which consisted of about three hundred properties. He also said that all parcels that were not in compliance of the County's regulations will be cited. The Director seemed to be quite upset that his department was being called to question.

There was a gentleman there who lives next to a rented parcel that that had one thirty foot trailer, a couple of small camper trailers, a couple of old broken down school buses, about three sheds and several old cars and trucks. The school buses were parked right up next to the gentleman's property line. On the property line adjacent to the buses was a wash which ran through both properties. In this wash, which was a part of the gentleman's property, there were hundreds of piles of human feces and wads of toilet paper.

We discovered that the rented property was being used as a staging area for human smuggling of immigrant farm laborers. These folks would be brought there from different areas and then put on medium sized trucks or vans and delivered to big farms that had crops that needed to be harvested. Some as far as Georgia.

The man that owned the adjacent property asked the P&Z Director if his neighbor was causing a huge health hazard by allowing people to use his land as a toilet and, if he was, then should he be responsible for cleaning it up. The Director said if that was the case then the gentleman is responsible for cleaning up his own land and if you do not, then you will cited. OUCH! The gentleman became very upset and immediately left the meeting.

After the meeting was over and all the questions somewhat answered, the Zoning Director and the County Manager left without saying anything to their chief zoning inspector. She told me that she was never informed that her zoning department had the power to have zoning violators arrested and she had been in the Planning & Zoning Department as long as the Director, which was about twelve years. She also told me that she was sorry for the now impending "sweep" and what issues it would cause us.

The next workday I called the Director of Pinal County's Health and Human Services regarding outhouses. I really believed what the Director of Zoning said in the meeting was true. I asked her if I could get a set of regulations of how an outhouse should be built. Before I completely finished my question, she began to laugh. "Sir," she said, using a very authoritarian tone in her voice, "outhouses are not legal in Pinal County,!" I retorted, "It might be a good idea for you to tell the Director of Zoning that, because he said that outhouses were legal in Pinal County at a meeting in our community center two days ago!" Our conversation ended shortly after that and she did not comment about anything that the Director said.

The Sweep Begins

The telephone calls began slowly with complaints about my being responsible for causing the callers receiving citations from Pinal County. I even had a call from one woman that said her husband was a police officer in a neighboring city-- I was not sure what she was implying by that comment. She then went on to say that my causing the removal of one of the trailers from the land she and her husband owned would cause them a financial loss of monthly rental fees. One man told me that he knew where I lived (Gulp!) and the removal of an extra trailer on his property would cause his disabled father to have to move into a home in neighboring town. I told him that the county had provisions for allowing a trailer on their property for a disabled relative and all they had to do was fill out the application and then get it to the PC planning and Zoning Department.

Some callers told me that I was doing this because I was in the cleaning business and would profit from everybody getting these citations. I had to explain to those people that had been cited for having too much trash around their place that I did not have the equipment or manpower to do that kind of clean-up because we only did new construction interior cleaning. The bulk of the calls were from people being cited for having too much trash and junk around their homes.

I was told that my name was given by the Pinal County inspectors as the one that caused them to being cited. I called Sandie Smith to complain about the calls I was receiving and she asked me if she could meet with me and the PRIDE board at my home and try to get this resolved.

We met with her about two weeks later in the fall of 1998 and together we scheduled our first clean-up for March 1999. She asked if we wanted the Town of Queen Creek and Maricopa County to join in by making this a community-wide project, which would include all of the Town and the parts of Maricopa County that surrounded the Town, as well as all the land surrounding the San Tan Mountain Regional Park which is in Pinal County and the park is under the Jurisdiction of the Maricopa County Parks And Recreation Department. We agreed and she created the union between two counties, the Town and the PRIDE.

Whether Friend Or Foe We Did Not Know

The unsettling scares that many of us lived through in the eighties, here in this part of our community, consisted of being around criminal activities which we were cautious of disturbing because a lot of us newbie's were unsure who was a criminal and who was not. There was rampant shooting at night and/or occasional explosions after dark. I would call County officials, reporting about what we observed or heard and being criminal, but not sure, but rarely got any answers before Sandie Smith came along. When we "Water Haulers" would get together at the standpipe, we would discuss these concerns with other people, sometimes strangers that we hoped would be sympathetic with us and not one of the guys or gals that strongly believed in the status quo in the community we now lived in.

The San Tan Mountains PRIDE Association Is Formed

In 1997, after the Town of Queen Creek was incorporated, I called on 12 families to ask them if I could use their names under the title of San Tan Mountains PRIDE. Ron & Donnis Hunkler were the first to join. We had our first meeting in a small beauty salon that was attached to a nearby home. We all agreed to work together to help provide a safer community for our families. We did not live within the Town' limits then so the Town could not help us. It was Pinal County's problem.

By talking with our neighbors we all realized that our immediate area was rampant with drug dealers, drug manufacturers, chop shops, and at least one house of prostitution that also dealt in selling drugs. In addition to this was the fact that there was a lot of drug users that lived in our area that traded locally stolen goods for drugs. Some of our local people were stealing cars outside our area and bringing these cars into our neighborhoods to be chopped up for parts. On top of that we found out our area was called the "tweaker" (methamphetamine user) capitol of Arizona at that time.

There must have been a lot of trading and selling of guns related to these criminal enterprises because on many nights, and especially during the weekends, there was lots of gunfire that could be heard after dark--sometimes even machine gun fire. We would all call the police to report shots fired but by the time they got out here the shooting had stopped and they were unable to locate the shooter.

In addition to the gunfire in the neighborhoods around the San Tans there was an extreme amount of gunfire during the day from "visiting" gun owners that lived in nearby towns or cities every weekend throughout the San Tan Mountain Regional Park before it was fenced in and before it was patrolled.

It was very dangerous for horseback riders, hikers and others that used the park at that time. Our property and our closest neighbor back right up to the Park's boundary. Sometimes the target shooters would spend an hour or more shooting out of our sight but still close to us. Even living in a place surrounded by such beautiful views has a price to pay because these shooters were not breaking the law at that time as long as they didn't shoot in our direction. It was hard to know which direction the the bullets were headed.

It is important to know that back in 1999 Pinal County consisted of an area of over 5,000 square miles, larger than the size of Jamaica and a little smaller than Northern Ireland with only a population of around 100,000 people. Pinal was a relatively poor county with services stretched thin and to the maximum. In comparison, we had moved here from the City of Scottsdale, which was about 15 square miles in size and with a similar population as Pinal County.

Our First Clean-Up, March 27, 1999

None of government entities, Pinal, Maricopa Counties, the Town or the PRIDE, had funds set aside for this kind of project at that time but Sandie got equipment and manpower from Pinal County's Department of Transportation and manpower and vehicles from the Pinal County Planning and Zoning Department. For our first clean-up Pinal provided one dump truck, one front end loader and four pickup trucks with drivers, ten inmates from the Pinal County Sheriff's Department Corrections Center (with supervision) and five inmates from the Arizona State Corrections Center (with supervision) from Florence.

Maricopa provided fifteen inmates from the woman's chain gang (with supervision), one dump truck and one front end loader with drivers, two forty foot trash roll offs and a smaller truck with a driver. The new fledgling Town offered their council members, elected officials and staff using their own vehicles, including John Litchenburger's truck that almost always held his dog Willy. I think that the only vehicle that the Town owned then was their two riding lawnmowers.

Our first clean-up advertising consisted of: hand made signs, free newspaper blurbs, hand made flyers that were posted in all the nearby businesses, and a special mailer, paid for by the Town, that went out to all the areas that would be covered, even out of the Town's boundary limits.

A few borrowed tables and chairs that were used as the command center sitting along side of Sundance Road and next to the depot site. The Town offered free use of their landfill for Pinal and Maricopa Counties trucks and to all homeowners in the areas covered.

The PRIDE'S mission was to: (1) provide lunches and ice water for all workers involved, (2) generate support for additional manpower, getting other equipment that could be used like vehicles from local farmers, ranchers, new home developers, and churches, and getting PRIDE members and their vehicles, (3) producing media support, making road signs, and posters to be put in local businesses, (4) provide pop up tents, tables and chairs for the command center and (5) coordinating a plan for all the factions involved.

We went to local merchants for supplies needed for the signs and posters and for the food for lunches and the water and ice. (Whew!) Every place we went to and every person we called willingly gave their help and support to this clean-up... and all the other eleven clean-ups that followed for that matter.

In the first clean-up we asked that all homeowners bring their trash to the edge of their road and we would pick it up. This turned out to be a nightmare because all the trash and junk was intermingled, which meant that everything went into the landfill because we had no way of sorting out the recyclables from the trash and we had no way of rejecting any of the things that were left on the roadside. There was one homeowner that left all the broken pieces of concrete from his torn-out in-ground pool next to the road. There were hazardous materials and tires that wound up in the landfill that day that should not have gone there, but we had no choice. We had to get the roads cleaned up and we were overwhelmed at times.

We made one hundred and fifty sandwiches the night before and ran out of sandwiches and water during lunch time. Diane Drenk and her son Alex went out to get more water, ice, sandwich meat, bread, cheese and bags, etc. When they got back we made more sandwiches under the pop up tents at the command center along side the road and were able to feed all the rest that helped us that day.

This day was a huge lesson for all of us, a lot of what we did was not exactly done by the book. The next year and all those that followed were done by the book as to all the health and safety rules that were in place and we never sent anything into the landfill that should not have gone there. At the end of that very long first day we were all dusty, dirty, sweaty and very tired.

Sandie Smith stayed until every person, truck, and piece of equipment was sent home to its proper place. We learned very quickly from this experience. The clean-ups that followed had a depot center where the people would bring their discards even some things that were not allowed in the landfill like hazardous materials. We had a special truck that handled those things, allowing us to sort out everything so that everything would go to its final proper resting place and where it belonged.

It Took A Few Long Years And....

As far as squashing the criminal activities that prospered in our very rural area of our community this is finally what happened: With the help of Sandie Smith, Pinal County Sheriff's Roger Vanderpool and Chris Vasquez, Maricopa County Supervisor Fulton Brock, Maricopa County Sheriff Joe Arpiao, the Chandler Police Department, the Pinal County & Maricopa County Health Departments and the Counties respective Zoning Departments we are now about 99.9 % free of all the criminal activities that had flourished here in the past. I know that Sandie was directly responsible for all the good things that transpired here. In working with Sandie I found out that she was the hardest working full time elected official I have ever met. I do not know how she juggled so many of her government duties and still had the time to show up at so many of our meetings and projects.

The Clean-up Depot Site

Vacant land on Sundance Road between Wagon Wheel Road & Wildhorse Road was our site for all drop off discards. Our citizens were able to drop off, in addition to Haz Mat things, appliances, tires, cardboard & paper, glass, tin & aluminum cans, electronics, including: computers, cell phone, printers, fax machines, phone answering machines etc.

Roadside Clean by Maricopa County Inmates

THE HAZ MAT DEPOT SITE

Recyclable Depot On Sundance

2002 Clean-up

Bill Scalzo, Sandie Smith, Fulton Brock, Treasurer Diane Drenk, Me, Wendy Feldman-Kerr, Mark Rosbrook, Regina Whitman, Silvia Centoz and Sylvia Acuna

Trash Depot Site On Sundance

Canyon State Roadside Clean-up Crew

Project Challenge Roadside Clean-up Crew

I Am Very Sorry To Say that the National Guard Program For Challenged Youth Was Closed Due To State Budget Constraints. We Made A Lot Of Friends With Many Of These Wonderful Young Men & Women That Helped Us Every Year With Our Clean-ups. Their expert Honor Guard was present at several of our memorial events.

The Maricopa County "Grabber" Machine Was The Best Piece Of Equipment We Ever Used

For all the years that we did the clean-ups Mr. White from Maricopa County Public Works was at the helm of this machine and he unloaded and loaded the recyclables very fast with it. He even demolished old house trailers in minutes. Every year we worked with the same people from Pinal and Maricopa Counties and the Town of Queen Creek. Each year we were able to do more in less time. Our hats are off to all the excellent people, that included all the inmates from Pinal and Maricopa Counties and those from the state prisons that were trained in the proper handling of hazardous materials.

The Chandler Heights 20

Donna Blasco Leading the "20" Choir

We had a group of horse owners that got together for gymkhanas, trail rides and horse related camping events. We called ourselves the Chandler Heights twenty. One of our camping trips took us out by the gap near the Gila Indian Reservation access road to Olberg.

We had a great time. On one ride nearby we found a old stage-coach road that must have led to Olberg way back when. Late that night, after sitting by a big campfire shooting the bull, Donna Blasco said she was turning in. She went to go to sleep in the bed of her pickup truck, which her non-riding husband Tom had brought to where we were camping.

About an hour or two later, there suddenly came loud howls from a big pack of coyotes. I would guess there were 10 or more. It was very intimidating, even though there hadn't been a recorded attack on man by a coyote in Arizona history, everyone around the campfire went silent. I noticed several with their mouths wide open as in a sign of concern. Then we heard a vehicle engine start up and saw taillights nearby. It was a very frightened Donna, backing her truck up to within twenty feet of our camp-fire. She became slightly upset when everybody started laughing at her but she never said a word and just hopped back in the pickup bed. We didn't hear from the coyotes the rest of that night, nor from Donna.

Caroline & Huggy Bear at Coyote Campsite

Our Fabulous Gymkhanas

The Chandler Heights Twenty were very active for several years with trail rides, moonlight local dirt road rides and lots of gymkhanas. The contests at the gymkhanas always varied, with a lot of time and effort put into each one. We have never been involved with a group where so many members participated in each and every event. Many of our little contests had hysterical outcomes!

Jersey Joe always won the contest which involved tying a balloon onto a person's rear belt area. When the signal was given ten riders, using only folded newspapers, rode around each other trying to break each others balloons with the newspaper. Some horses, like mine, spooked easily which was dangerous, so I never entered that one. The last one to have a full balloon still tied to them, won.

There was a dessert (desert)-eating contest, involving ten small pies piled high with whipped cream which were set up on benches. Ten riders started near the finish where the pies were set up. They raced down to a standing barrel about thirty yards away, then raced back towards the pies, dismounted, ran over to their pie, knelt down and with hands behind their backs, then they had to eat their pie. We only did this once because this race, like all the others, generated tons of dust.

No one could see the riders attempting to eat their now very dirty whipped cream covered pie, which must have tasted awful and, most likely, was not very good for them. Loud laughter was heard when the contestants could finally be seen with all that very dirty whipped cream on their faces.

Then there was one contest that tested your steed's ability to hold perfectly still (called ground tying) when the reins were dropped to the ground after dismounting. One robust lady always swore that her mare was trained to be rock-solid still when the reins from her horse hit the ground.

One rider at a time would race about thirty yards down to a barrel round it and then race halfway towards the finish line, dismount dropping the reins to the ground next to where there was a open ended barrel on it's side. The rider would then crawl through the barrel mount their horse who should be (hopefully) standing very close to where the reins were dropped and then race to the finish line. The rider with the best time won. The bragging lady was a little too big to crawl through the barrel and got stuck. Her exceptionally well trained horse just kept wandering all over the place while at the same time the horse's owner kept struggling to get out of the barrel. The lady in the barrel who could see her horse slowly moving, kept hollering Whoa, Whoa, dammit WHOA!!, It was hysterical!

The phone book race had one rider at a time race down to a table with a Phoenix phone book on it. Each rider was given a page number, had to dismount, hold onto the horses reins, find the page, tear it out and bring the page back to the finish line.

The rider with the best time won. One excited lady by the name of Valerie Reed, raced down, got off her horse and ripped out the page. With the page held in her mouth and in a very excited state leaped onto her horse so hard she went right over the saddle and fell safely in a big heap to the soft ground below. She had a little trouble getting her horse after that, laughing all the while she kept the page in her now very dirty mouth.

The egg race involved each rider balancing a raw egg on a spoon with the handle held in the rider's mouth. Five riders are sent through a rather easy obstacle course with the winner arriving at the end with their egg still on the spoon. Hands could not be used to help with the balance or positioning of the egg. This was not a very exciting completion because it was a very slow race and so many never finished. On one occasion Jersey Joe went so quickly through the course that he set a new record. Before he was declared the winner he produced his Super-glued egg on a spoon, showing it to everyone with a laugh when he held it upside down.

Then there was the trail obstacle course that had a wooden bridge, logs in the trail, a plastic tarp to walk over, a small puddle to walk through, a gate to open, go through and close while mounted, and balloons waving in the wind with long strings attached on some posts very close to the trail. My horse did very well with everything except when he came to the water puddle. Sanny and I stopped just in front of the very small man made puddle, he hunched down and jumped over it before I knew what was going on. Very exciting indeed!

We had a couple of Honeywell engineers that were in our group that really made a big difference with our gymkhanas by their rigging up automatic timers that recorded the times on all our races. They also set up a super sound system for us. In addition to that most all the shows were videotaped.

Riding Blind!

Most of our moonlight rides were great. On some we had a horse-drawn hay wagon that was made available for those family members that did not ride or that did not have a horse, and for smaller children with supervision. Each member could sign up to take charge of any event they wanted. I am not picking on the woman of our group that signed up to run a moonlight ride where the moon never showed up, but? The calendar showed the date she choose had a full moon scheduled, something we always needed. but on this night the moon didn't rise until 4:00 a.m..

Let it be known that no one knew what time the moon was going to rise that night and after a while on the trail we were all wondering if it was going to rise at all. Needless to say, it rose long after our ride was over. The route she chose for us included a ride through a large orange grove. With no moon it was much darker there than even being in the open desert, but onward we rode very quietly, not able to see anything. Nobody really complained. We did not know if we were going up or down or when we were going in a hole or about to go uphill. It was very surreal and almost everything was left up to our horses, who must have surely been able to see much better in the dark that we could.

At the end of the ride we rode through the streets of Chandler Heights to a member's home, we all parked our steeds under a street light for a break while remaining on our horses except for Tom Lang who got off his horse, who then tripped and fell down, breaking his ankle. It was ironic that we rode for over an hour in complete darkness and finally when we got under a light, one of us has an accident. Go figure!

Fancy Party In The Boondocks

One late afternoon, while coming back from a long four-hour ride, we happened upon something very unusual way out in the desert near an unimproved dirt road, that most of us that were there will never forget. There were twelve of us taking a short cut, carefully weaving our way through a large Jumping Cholla cactus patch. Someone said that they could hear violin music in the distance. No one responded to what sounded not possible.

When our group broke into the open we were totally amazed. Here we were about three miles away from any homes or paved roads, and in front of us was a whole bunch of people in evening wear standing around, drinking cocktails. There were long tables set up with white table cloths and candelabras setting on them. There was a bar set up and waiters in tails & white gloves serving drinks and hors d'oeuvres.

In the background there were violinists and a harp player playing. They had a long barbecue grill with three chefs all dressed in white. The person in charge came up to the lead rider and asked us to get off our horses and join the crowd for a couple of drinks. These easterners at first thought that we were part of their dinner experience! They all came over and asked questions about our horses and where we worked and so on.

They were with a big Ohio company that had brought all their sales people to the San Marcos Resort in Chandler for a big week long sales meeting. They told us that to get here they came in a big bus on a really bumpy road. We were very glad that we were a part of their Arizona experience.

I think that the reason the "20" dissolved was probably due to the eight month recession we had from July 1990 to March 1991. I know there were a lot of people in our group that were laid off and some even had to sell their horses. My Dr. Doo Everything company suffered because new home sales fell rapidly. That is why I went to work temporally for our government while Caroline took charge of our cleaning company that had very few jobs scheduled on the books.

Team One, 1990 Census

I was a supervisor for the 1990 Census, coordinating up to fourteen people for canvasing northern Pinal County. I think that the rule for our census takers was to stop at every seventeenth house they counted, to ask the homeowner to take a survey. In the back country there are some who would refuse to answer any questions at all or wanted to scare those that wanted to ask Census questions.

I had two ladies quit because of what they saw at the homes of two different "out back desert" folks. One of my ladies was invited into a man's home who had a big smile on his face, he was very polite and was answering her questions.

About 10 minutes into the survey, she spotted something slowly moving towards her. His smile got broader when she realized that a very large snake was inching towards her left leg. It happened to be an eight foot Python. It frightened her so much that she drove directly to my office in the Florence Town Hall and quit. She was sure that the man was laughing very hard by the time she ran and reached her car and that made her even more furious.

Another lady had her twelve year old daughter, who was on school break, with her while she was working and everything was good until they entered a drive way where a trailer was back off the road about fifty yards or so. She swung the car around in towards the front door and little porch with the daughter in the passenger seat closest to the trailer.

When she got out and was in front of the car and about to step up to the door, it suddenly opened and out walked an older man, wearing cowboy boots and a straw cowboy hat and nothing else. His lack of clothes was bad enough but he was also carrying a shotgun.

She screamed at her daughter to get down and as she made a dash for her car door. She heard a woman yelling, "Dammit, George! Get your ass back in this house NOW!", as my census worker fumbled to get the keys into the ignition she could hear the bare naked man laughing out loud. She then drove directly to my office in Florence to turn in her reports and time sheet and told me what happened and then quit. She said that even if her daughter were not there she would have quit anyway. She felt that the job was too dangerous.

Our Animals, Our Friends

Sanny & Me With a Wet Face

Before we even moved to our new mini ranch by Goldmine Mountain we bought a horse, a beautiful Morgan Arabian or Morab, not at an auction by the way, but from a respected horse trainer. Please always remember to never buy any animal larger than a goldfish before you have a proper place for it on your property. But thanks to my good friend Mike for allowing us to keep Santanna at his property for us! His place was close to mine and Mike had two other horses that Santanna could be friends with until I got something built on my property.

Santanna was three-years-old at that time and it wasn't long before he and Mike's other two horses broke down Mike's fence and took off to another, much nicer ranch a couple of miles away. This trip meant that the three of them had to cross a few busy paved roads to get there. Somehow Mike found out where they were. Mike called me and we went to the ranch where the horses had been put in a corral. We loaded them up in a borrowed horse trailer and took them back to Mike's home. This would be the start of many new exciting experiences with horses that we both would have for some time to come.

The man I bought Santanna from said the he was "green broke" and that someone with a lot of experience should be the only one allowed to ride him. I did not know what green broke meant then and I didn't really care because I just liked Santanna so much. After realizing how little we knew about horses my wife and I decided to go to the Chandler-Gilbert Community College and take courses in Equine Science.

Santanna de El Rancho de Santanna

We traveled to many horse breeding and horse training ranches, something which was included in the courses. This taught us a lot but we found that to know horses well you must work with them and read many books, see many training videos, and continue a never ending learning of how these fine animals tick. One thing I learned is that all horses are different. Duh!

Ride'em Mike!

One Saturday when I was not around, my youngest son Kevin, who was married with one child at that time, decided he wanted to ride Santanna. Luckily, for Kevin, Mike was home and said that he would ride Santanna first because he had seen many more cowboy movies than my son had ever dreamed of seeing. Mike had a very large fenced-in area to ride in but it wasn't all cleared of the desert fauna yet. Kevin was inside the fence when Mike got on my horse and almost immediately Sanny took off in a full gallop.

When Mike found out he could not control Santanna, he started screaming to Kevin to help him stop this S.O.B.. Santanna kept running up to the fence in different places, acting like he was going to jump it, and then put on the breaks and then headed in another direction. Mike kept screaming for Kevin to grab the reins as they went flying by. All Kevin could do was to dive under the fence as they came roaring towards him.

After about 30 very frightening minutes Santanna ran out of gas, luckily just before Mike had decided to jump off and into the many cacti that was all around them.

Mike had white knuckles for about two weeks after that from holding on to the saddle horn. When I finally showed up, later that day, Mike would not even talk about what had happened! And as time went on I realized how traumatized he must have been and that it would probably leave an indelible imprint in his mind forever.

Animal Parade In The Park

Before Santanna went to horse school I wanted to get him used to walking on the park trails and have some exercise at the same time. The first time I led Sanny up into the park our three dogs and Squeaky, one our cats, came along with us. This was when there was not many daily park visitors using the trails then. The next time Caroline led our very first goat, Bunker, as I led Santanna, along with us, our cat Squeaky, our dogs Blackie, Goldie, and Peachy, tagged along. What a scene this must have been. We did this for another four or five times until Sanny went away to "horse training school" for two months at Lawrence Sparrows nearby ranch.

Lawrence Sparrow, is a very fine gentleman that raised and trained Arabian horses. Lawrence did a great job training my California bred horse, that now, I would be to be able to trail ride through our thorny deserts without too many problems, I thought.

After Sanny graduated, I rode Santanna all through the San Tan Mountains before the Park fences were installed and where we have crossed the path of a great many diamondbacks. In these instances Mr. Sparrow's training really paid off. When we found one on a road or a trail, Santanna would stop about ten feet or more away from the snake and then do a side pass in a complete semi circle, keeping his eye always on the rattler until he was out of range before turning and continuing our walk down the trail.

The only time it became edgy was when we were off-trail. One time I was coming down a steep slope when we came across a big one right in front of us. Santanna started his side pass to the left but it was steep and there were bushes in the way. He adjusted his side pass so that he never got closer to the snake than ten feet but he missed the bushes as well, all the while the snake was coiled ready to strike and making one hell of a racket. Santanna did this instinctively, without my help or any command.

On one long ride by ourselves and after Sanny was quite sweaty we came to a big mound of dirt and small rocks. To get around this obstacle I had to ride Sanny on a steep slope horizontally which I never did before. All of a sudden my saddle started slipping down to my right so fast I could not or did not have time to use my left foot try and correct the slide. I fell in a big heap on the slope leaving the saddle hanging almost under Sanny's belly. If Sanny had spooked there was no telling what might have happened with that saddle hitting all four of his legs if he had run away. Instead, thank the Lord he just stood there looking down at me with a big smile on his face or so I thought. I had to carefully get the saddle off him, set it down on the slope and lead him to a nearby tree so that I could tie him up and re-saddle him again. It was then I realized that the you can go vertically up or down a steep slope but never try going horizontally along a slope because of gravity working against you and my big overgrown body. When riding horses or with most everything you do in life you should always try to use common sense. It is free and given to you by our God almighty. After that experience I have vowed to use in as often as I possibly can.

Bunker

Santanna's first pet was a large goat named Bunker. He was the size of a heavy set Great Dane. Bunker had free roam of the place during the day then we locked up safely at night. One day after I gave Santanna a bath by the house, Bunker was nearby keeping track of his friend Santanna. Bunker wore a cow bell on his neck so that we could keep track of him because sometimes he used to wander away.

When we went back down the road to the barn, Bunker was about 30 feet behind us. I was leading directly in front of Santanna, which you should never do (common sense tells you to always stay off to the horses side), when Bunker started jumping and running and towards us from behind. The sound of the cow bell startled Sanny and he ran right over me sending me crashing to the ground, which smashed the cordless telephone I was carrying in my front pocket. Sanny was loose and ran right into the open gate to his corral with Bunker following and me, huffing and puffing following even farther behind.

Bunker

One hot afternoon when I got home from work before Caroline. I heard Bunker bleating down in the corral near Santanna. I went down there and found Bunker with his long horns stuck in the crotch of a tree.

His two back feet were just touching the ground and poor Bunker was stretched out all the way up to V in the tree.

To get him out I had to cut one of the limbs which added about 15 minutes more to his suffering. He was bleating all the while until I got him down. He was alright and went over to get a long drink of water right away at the horse tank. I have no idea how long he was hanging there but everything turned out OK. Unfortunately Bunker passed away from colic several months later.

Soon Santanna had his much smaller second pet. His name was Jingles, and he was a Pygmy Billy Goat. We had a lot of free range goats, but Jingles stayed close by Santanna most of the time. They played together quite a bit. Once Santanna pulled his horn off, which left a stem of flesh about five inches long. The vet told me to cover it with a medical type tar, which I had to do every day until the horn grew back again. Jingles would buck Santanna in his front knees and he also would eat Santanna's tail, to the extent that his tail went from five feet long to only about three feet long.

Jingles Father to 30
Kids

One day I was out on our back porch which overlooked the corral where these two friends were playing. I watched intently until I saw something I had never seen before, Sanny picked Jingles up buy the top middle of his back with his teeth, he lifted him high off the ground and slowly swung him around in a complete circle and gently set him back on the ground almost exactly were Jingles had stood before. The absolutely amazing thing was that Jingles never struggled or cried out all the while he was in the air.

I ran to get my camera, in hopes that I might be able to get a picture of him doing that again. While I waited, I told Caroline what had happened. I watched for about one and a half hours, but had no luck.

The next day I decided to get up on the barn roof and lay there with my video camera in hopes of photographing them doing the trick again. I wanted to send the video to a then new TV show called "America's Funniest Videos". I been had waiting for about two hours when three of my horse buddies came riding down my road towards the barn as I was laying up on the roof.

They all had very mystified looks on their faces when they finally got within talking range. After I got down from my perch, I explained exactly what I was doing, then they left and wished me good luck. It was at that time that Santanna picked Jingles up again, only turning about ¼ of the way around, and put him down—of course, before I could get my camera ready. I never saw Santanna do that again.

The last time I "tried" to ride Santanna, I was about to lead a group of about fifteen riders that were with the East Valley Arabian Association, of which I was a director. We were going to go into the mountains and up some steep trails just south of my home. I had a very bad left knee and was scheduled for a knee replacement within a few weeks. With the bad knee I knew that I would not be able to get off my horse to re-cinch the saddle on the trail because I knew I would never be able to get back on him.

So, cowboy that I was, I thought that I would cinch up my horse extremely tight and with the help of a five gallon bucket I started to get on Santanna. When I put the weight of my body into the stirrup he jumped away from me in pain. I fell down backwards, with my punkin' head hitting a large rock. I was out cold until the paramedics arrived. When they asked me who the president was before Bill Clinton, I answered Ulysses S. Grant! When I could not answer what my address was or even the correct name of the road it was on. It was then that the EMT asked the hovering medical helicopter to land, but not before all the group moved far enough away so their horses wouldn't get spooked. I was hauled off to the Scottsdale Osborn Hospital for emergency treatment. Caroline would follow by car but by the time she got there I was found to be alright, except for my remaining really low IQ, which they could not fix at that time.

We had a four inch rainfall one night, which we slept through. I was busy on a project that morning so Caroline went down to feed Sanny at about 8:00 a.m. I heard her holler that Sanny was upside down in the wash. Now, there was no wash before the heavy downpour in the paddock area where Sanny lived, so I thought that maybe he had somehow gotten outside the fence and into the very deep wash that was closer to our house. I ran down to that wash but I could not see him there nor could not see Caroline. I called to her, asking where she was. She called back saying that she was inside the paddock area, which is 50 feet wide by 100 feet long. The rain had gouged out a four foot deep by about five foot wide cut in Sanny's paddock! When I got closer all I could see was four feet straight up in the air but I could not see Sanny's body at all. When I got closer I could see him struggling on his back. We had no idea how long he had been there.

I asked Caroline to go to the house and get some blankets that I could use to use for his head and sides. Then I called our new Queen Creek Fire Department. A truck and their Captain showed up in about fifteen minutes. I then asked Caroline to call a vet we knew that was close by so that she could give him a shot to calm him down and stop him from struggling. I was sure this was hurting his back because there were so many rocks in and on the soil where he lived.

Soon there were about eight fireman there, along with my friend Mike Ciotti, all were talking as men will do, about getting a machine in there to lift Santanna out of that ditch. The rain had come and gone, as it does here in the desert, so my horse was not bothered by any water at all.

The lady vet showed up right away and quickly gave Sanny a shot that made him unconscious. We men had all decided that we must get a front end loader with chains and straps and use it to lift Santanna out of the hole. My friend Mike then went to get a front end loader. After Mike left the vet took charge and told the fireman to shovel and rake a path up to the nearby ramada. When that was all smoothed out she told everybody to grab a hold of Sanny's legs and asked that one fireman care for

Sanny's head. She counted, and we all pulled together, and again, and then again pulled and to our amazement it was clear that we could pull this 1000 pound horse up the bank and into the shade of the ramada in short order.

Is it possible that women have more common sense than men do? Nah! That's impossible! Cannot be! Not a chance! No way!

The vet told Caroline and I to halter Sanny with a lead rope to keep him from going back to where he had fallen in.

It was about one hour before Sanny started to wake up. He had not eaten breakfast that morning and now it was past noon. We had his feeder set up with his breakfast. His head rose up slowly at first and all of a sudden he got up on his feet. He shook his head and body and with the lead rope in hand I followed him to his feeder where he ate as if nothing had happened. I tied him to the rail by the feeder and everything was back to normal, or so I thought.

The vet and the firemen had left right after we got Sanny up to the ramada. Now Mike showed up with the front end loader and was surprised that we had gotten him out of that ditch using manpower only. Mike went to work with the loader filling in the hole and leveling all the ground around it. After Sanny had eaten and the tractor had left I let Sanny loose. It was sort of amazing that he immediately went over to where the ditch had been and sniffed all around the area where he had been struggling in pain just a short time before. At about that time the Fire Chief drove up and asked how Sanny was doing. I thought that this was a great gesture on his part and I thanked him for all that he and all his men had done.

It was a few days later that I realized that Sanny was not eating as much as he was before the accident. Our vet got us a prescription for pain medicine that I gave him every day. All was well for a few months but we had to help him get up after he laid down more often.

I had to ask our vet to put Santanna down in July of 2011 when he was Twenty seven years old. He laid down early that day and we tried for hours to get him up before calling Doctor Olsen, our regular vet. After he got there he did some of the same things we'd tried until he said it was time to put the old guy down. It was a very sad departure but we all felt that it was necessary. I think of him a lot and remember all the good times we had exploring all the new trails that we found in the San Tans together. He had to go down his trail alone that final day. I had lost a very dear friend, a pet, that I had spent some very considerable time with for over twenty-seven years on a day to day basis. I will never be able to forget him.

Rascal

Caroline had a horse called Rascal that most have been part Dutch, as my wife is. He was gelding, half Arabian and half Quarter Horse. He was a very handsome "devil". If Rascal did not want to certain things while in saddle he would buck Caroline off. Rascal was given to us by a friend of Caroline's and the horse's history that was given to us was very vague. We now know why. Caroline kept defending Rascal by saying that she fell off the horse when it was clear to, me that Rascal bucked her off.

Rascal & Caroline. Both are very stubborn.

I found out much more about Rascal when I started lunging him. Lunging a horse gives the horse exercise and allows the owner to train the horse to do certain voice commands. The horse is on an about thirty foot lunge line and the owner usually carries a short whip. A large level open space is necessary and a round pen is desirable but not necessary.

I used to lunge Santanna before almost every ride in order to cut down on wanting to run right after being put in saddle. It did not take long before he was working with me on voice command such as: trot, walk, gallop, stop, reverse direction etc. But with rascal is was totally different. He would go along for most everything for about thirty minutes but after that he thought that that was enough for him. It finally got to the point that one time he started for me and was showing me his front hooves. Lucky for me I had the whip. I did not hit him with it, that is something I would never do to any horse, but I popped a couple of times right in front of him when he came towards me.

When Grandma Caroline went down to Puerto Rico for a visit, I put an ad in the Arizona Republic hoping to sell Rascal before she got back. The ad read: My wife left me and I need to sell our fine Arabian/Quarter-horse so that I can have a big celebration party. CALL 480-000-0000.

I got a call soon after the ad appeared from a young lady with a very sexy voice that said her name was Veronica and she was calling about my ad in the newspaper. I answered saying, "Are you interested in buying my horse?" She answered, "I am not interested in the horse at all, but I am interested in you." WOOPS! I almost could not answer her because that was not what I wanted to hear. I had to tell her that "my wife left me for just two weeks and I'm trying to sell her horse before it kills her and I love her very much!" She said, "OK and hung up.

The next call I got was from Edythe Jensen, a reporter for the Arizona Republic that I knew. She told me that someone from the paper gave her the ad and she wanted to know if it was true. I told her the complete story about Caroline and her horse and about my call from Veronica. She asked me a few more questions and the next day the story appeared in her paper! It said, "Man puts ad in our paper and it backfires!"

A few days later a Phoenix fireman came out to ride Rascal and ended up buying him. I told him on the phone before he came out that Rascal was prone to bucking riders off and he said that he was a good enough horseman and it would not be a problem. Rascal was a very handsome horse and that is what impressed him more than anything else. When Caroline returned she was not upset at all about the horse being sold but she was a little upset about Veronica calling!

Our Animal Entourage

My first pet was Max, a brindle boxer--my first canine friend. Caroline's first pet was Tony, a horse, that she got when she was ten or eleven. We both had a few other pets over the years but after we moved to Queen Creek we had an explosion of many different animals.

The picture shows Max in my mom's driveway on 3 Columbia Drive, East Greenbush, N.Y. That white stuff I am trying to move was just one of many "white stuffs" that we got back east in the 1950s. Our local radio weather man lived next door to us and Max is looking for him in this photo because he never forecast this storm that dumped on us during the night. Max was my first pet dog.

Since moving to our mountain property we have had a great number of animals living with us on El Rancho de Santanna. They included: 9 horses, 35 pigmy goats, 50 Holland Lop rabbits, 23 cats, 20 dogs, 6 ducks, 15 chickens, and 1 Mexican Black snake, in a span of Twenty-eight years.

More About Our Friends

We owned only three of the nine horses, the rest were boarders. Caroline sold about 40 goats to people from all over the state all the while more were born. Caroline sold more than 50 rabbits to people all over the Phoenix Metro area all the while more were born. All the male cats were neutered after the first six or so female cats had litters. Most died of old age with a few living up to 20 years old. We think at least three were caught by coyotes. All the dogs were orphans--one dog died of allergies the rest died of old age. For a few years we had six dogs at one time.

Two ducks were killed by coyotes and two by a thieving fox and two by a Great Horned Owl. The ducks killed by a fox were about 12 years old. 13 chickens were killed by a fox when they were about four years old. 2 were killed by a fox when they were about 6 years old. When the fox killed the 13, 12 died of fright and only one was actually mauled by the fox (the roster).

We currently have two cats, Lauren and Luna, and one dog by the name of Ellie who is blind and a diabetic. Sable the snake is about 12 years old and was purchased by one of our grandsons, who bought the snake with the help of his grandmother but he was never allowed to bring the snake home.

Max & His Bunny Friends

Maximilian, an Arabian Saddle-bred cross & a National Champion, sharing his sweet feed with some cottontails, was a boarder and my good friend. Once when I came down to feed, he was at the far corner of his large paddock area, where he always greeted me. I was wearing a loud Hawaiian shirt and when I got close enough to pet him, as I always had, he grabbed the shirt and tried to tear it off me. It seems that his former owner that had passed away, always wore Hawaiian shirts and it may have been that Max didn't believe that I should be wearing the same kind of shirt that Jeff wore. It was so unlike Max who is a huge gentle giant.

Bootsie

One evening our black and white cat, Bootsie was lying on top of the telephone pole fence that surrounds our pool while I was working nearby. I saw a great horned owl swoop down and grab her by her head. After seeing this I hollered very loudly and the owl dropped her to the ground about five feet away from Bootsie's perch. I ran over to her, finding her lying there with blood all over her head. We patched her up and she never went up on that fence again.

She was an inside/outside cat that tolerated her other cat friends but when we brought another young female cat into our home, Bootsie took off and decided to go down to our barn to live.

The barn is located on the back of our 3.5 acre property. I brought her up to the house three times but Bootsie would go right back down there. She seemed content to stay there and everything was fine until it got hot.

Our grandson brought her up to the house one day when it was about 105 degrees inside the barn and this time she stayed in the house until she died at the age of fifteen.

Michael A Very Special Goat

Michael was abandoned by his mom so Caroline had to hand feed him until he got old enough to eat solid food. When that happened he was no longer accepted in the herd. He really didn't want to be with the herd. Michael was more like a dog, not a herd animal. He used our pet door and often we would find him up on the counter in our kitchen. He wanted to be with his mom, Caroline.

The Three Musketeers

Ellie was a foster dog that was given to us by our son's family. When Ellie was a pup she lived in Cave Creek, where there are a lot of coyotes. Two days before Christmas she was attacked by a large coyote while the family was unloading Christmas things at their front door. The coyote jumped over a five foot block wall near the front gate and jumped back over the wall with Ellie in it's mouth. The Coyote dropped Ellie about the time the family heard her cries for help. The coyote then grabbed Ellie again and headed for the family's back yard. Our son Kevin was in chase and hollered very loudly, whereupon "Wily" Coyote dropped the dog for the last time.

Ellie seemed fine but was certainly in a lot of pain so I took her to an urgent care emergency animal care facility on Christmas Eve day. Little Ellie had damage to several internal organs including her lungs and liver. When I took my grand kids to see Ellie she looked so dejected with her head drooping down as the doctor brought her out in her arms. As soon as she heard the kids voices she was so excited she jumped right out of the doctors arms to the floor. Luckily she landed on her feet and no additional harm was done.

Ellie, on the right, is the only one that is left of the three Musketeers. The picture is rather eerie in that it was shot through our screen door and the only one alive shows up in color in the color picture.

Goldie and Peachy were twin Queensland Heelers with two entirely different personalities. Goldie was the dominate sister, although she joined us about three months after Peachy was already part of our family. Peachy was more an introvert than her outgoing, friendlier sister.

I guess in the dog world pecking order the introvert sister Peachy was the boss of our dog home because she was at our home first. Peachy's role as the top dog in our home would show when Goldie and Teddy, our little Pomeranian male, would play together in the living room. Peachy, who didn't play with any dog, would just lie close by until she thought they were having too much fun. Then she would get up and go next to them and in dog language tell them to stop—now!-- which they did.

Goldie was not afraid of any animal but was very careful around rattlers. She was a natural born hunter. She loved to chase coyotes, sometimes right up and over our little mountain down back. I was always worried about her getting ambushed by several coyotes in a group, but in the 16 years we had her it never happened, as far as I know. Both sisters passed away within months of each other. Teddy was our only dog school graduate. He graduated from PETsMART University with honors. Teddy always met me at the gate and would lick my hand once, then he would run into the house. In the nineteen years Teddy was with us my wife never had to greet me at the gate when I got home. I think that he would always worry about Caroline when she drove away alone because he always kept watch out the window or would wait by the gate for her until she returned.

Screech Owl

These are great pets to have, you don't have feed them and they will work for you for free, ridding your outside property of unwanted (Small) pests.

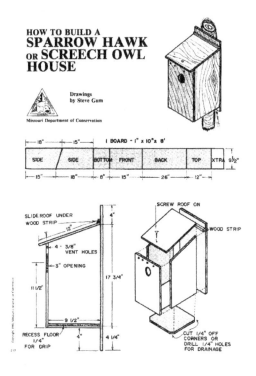

These little Owls live in most all of the USA and in parts of Canada and Mexico. They can help keep your outdoor rodent population down. Why not build a home for them, they do not need water or food. The nest box needs to be up about 10 feet in a tree. Or on a shady part of a barn or any out building

CHAPTER 7

The Water Haulers

Almost everyone living south of Hunt/Empire hauled water from a standpipe located behind the now "old" water company building and directly behind the "old" Town of Queen Creek post office. I hauled water for twelve years but many others hauled it for Twenty or more years before we got water piped to our homes. People used everything from 55 gallon drums up to 1200 gallon tanks on trucks. My water hauling truck held 1200 gallons which was one of the larger ones.

One time when I was at the "water hole" a "newcomer" got in line with a five thousand gallon, old shell gas tanker semi-truck. The day was very hot and the line was long, snaking south along the shoulder of Ellsworth past what is now the present Post Office. When this man finally got up to the stand pipe, a small group of old timers approached him, one with a his hand on a holstered gun, and they all strongly suggested that he take only one thousand gallons at a time and then go to the end of the line four more times until his tank was full. He left and must have called the sheriff's office because a deputy showed up about 45 minutes later. The deputy never did find out who threatened the man with a firearm, so he went on his way.

When filling my water truck at the pump, which took about forty-five minutes, I would watch the daily training flights out of Williams Air Force Base where the young pilots would fly right over downtown Queen Creek at about an altitude of 3000 feet in a giant circle, the same circle every time. About half or more made jerky turns, the rest did the turns very smoothly.

In the summer during the very hottest days of the year the waiting times at the water hole could take up to two or more hours.

Most of the men would get out of their vehicles and gossip like a bunch of old women. I rarely saw any women haul water except Diane Drenk and Regina Whitman. A few haulers would bring a cooler full of beer with them and once, two 30-something male yokels were so smashed that they could hardly stand when they finally made it up to the pump. A few of us went over to talk with them to keep them from driving. Another person who knew these people and was in line went to the old Circle K, which is an auto parts store now, to call one of their relatives. After a while a couple of people showed up to drive the drinker's vehicle to his home.

A Big Box Of Water

Sometimes during the long wait some really funny things happened. Once I was about three vehicles behind a big old van, one that had a sliding door on the passenger side. I wondered what he had in the van that could carry water. When the man got up to the pump he opened the side door and there was a big plywood box where the rear seats usually were. Inside the box there was a bright blue plastic tarp. I guess that the box might have been able to hold up to 300 gallons of water. A group of us just kept talking while the man filled up his "box tank" from the slow filling pump. When it was finally full the man shut the side door, then hopped into the driver's seat, he started the engine and got ready to drive off the pad that went down gradually about six feet to the road.

As soon as he moved the water started sloshing over the side of the box towards the driver. About half way down the slope he hit the brakes and the whole box broke apart. I never saw so much water come from the inside of a vehicle before. Everyone was laughing hysterically until we realized that the man might be trapped in his seat. But no, he had already opened his door and got out to run around to the passenger door to open it, whereupon he got knocked to the ground from the rush of water that came out. He was already soaking wet when he got out of the driver's seat then got soaked again. I am sure that we all felt extremely sorry for this guy and I am sure he was very embarrassed. He quickly got to his feet without saying a word and got into his driver's seat, leaving the side door open. The van was still running, and we all wondered how that could be because some of the water must have gone up and under the dash. Nevertheless, he took off with water flowing out the doors all the way to Ellsworth Road.

During the summer months, the hotter it got the longer the lines at the water hole were and the shorter the tempers got. One time I went to get my water at about 5:00 am to avoid the long lines in the afternoon and also because it was somewhat cooler--only about 90 degrees. There were about five water haulers in line when I pulled in. I knew something was wrong when I saw all the drivers standing by the coin slot at the pump.

One guy was banging away on the heavy steel plate that protected the coin unit with a ball-peen hammer. I went over and asked one of the men what the trouble was and was told that the coin chute was jammed. There was a lot of swearing going on and one older man said he was going to go over to Paul Gardner's house and wake the SOB up. That is when I found out that Paul and his brother lived right across the street on Ellsworth in plain sight of the stand pipe.

Two of the men went marching over there and one started loudly beating on the door of the house while yelling out obscenities at the same time. Wow! I thought, "These guys are crazy!" Paul's brother opened the door and asked "what was the trouble?" When Paul's brother crossed the street they followed him, still yelling at him that "the @#$%@&&#@ coin chute was jammed again". I was amazed at how calm Paul's brother remained during this outrageous verbal assault. He still remained calm while he opened the coin box and removed the slug that stopped the coins from activating the pump. He gave one of the still angry men the slug and some of the coins that were in the blocked chute without saying one word, locked the box and slowly walked back to the house across the street.

Eventually the rusty old steel tank on my old '54 started leaking at the rear bottom. I was asked a few times if I knew that the tank was leaking all over the dirt roads that went towards my home. I simply told them that I had a contract with the county to water the roads and that seemed to satisfy their curiosity. In fact we were in one of those down turns that affected the building business and the work we did as new construction cleaning business. I just did not have the money to replace the tank and it was in such poor condition that it could not be welded.

Then out of the blue, I got a phone call from a old dear friend, Mike Markis, whose wife Lois worked for us at Mary Moppets in Scottsdale, and whom we had not seen for a couple of years. He said that he had a new 1000 gallon fiberglass water tank that had been damaged and he wondered if I could use it. I told him that I sure could use it and I asked how much he wanted for it. He said that it was free and he would deliver to my home. He just wanted to get it off his driveway.

Here was another wondrous thing that we have enjoyed so many times before and the timing was fantastic. My good neighbor friend, also named Mike, hauled the old tank away to the scrap yard and got a few bucks for it. The same friend helped me patch the leak in the new tank with a roll of fiberglass mat and some resin and "voila", I had a brand new, lighter tank that would not rust. Wow! Was I ever thankful! With the help from two different Mikes I was back in the water hauling business.

Pink Panther/Cara Lee

My wife and I along with our daughter In-law celebrated our birthdays together with friends in a private room at a posh restaurant in North Scottsdale one year. Caroline and I were born on the same day and Cindy was born on the next day.

When all a sudden, before the twelve of us were served, one of the waitresses came in with a video camera in her hand. Then someone in a Pink Panther costume came in from another door. I thought this was something that the restaurant was doing as a gift to all of us or something like that. The Pink Panther put a small tape recorder on our table and danced to the music and after that was over our daughter took the Panther head off and I could not believe my eyes.

I said out loud "that looks like Cara Lee" but it couldn't be, Cara, our daughter, was over 3000 miles away in Puerto Rico, or so I thought. I could not believe what I saw until Jimmy, her husband, came into the room. They could only stay until the a couple of days because of their company business.

It was a real shock to most of the people in that room, especially for Caroline and I. It literally took our breaths away! In order for our daughter and our son in-law to pull this prank off, in complete secrecy, they had to fly for over eight hours to get here, rent a car, get a costume and then fly another eight hours back to their home in Puerto Rico in a couple of days. Best prank ever.

Good Jenny on Bo

More Of Our Neighbors

We had two neighbors with the name of Jenny, but that is as far as the similarity went! The two Jenny's were entirely different but lived across the road from each other. Jenny (the good one) lived on Wagon Wheel Road) who used to be a U.S. Army truck mechanic that, after her discharge from the Army, moved to a trailer across the road from us on her three and a third acre property. She had two horses and a pot belly pig that was house broken. Ms. Pig went in and out of her home via a big pet door. My wife and I asked a local cowboy to give us lessons on horsemanship once a week. Jenny and her boyfriend attended the lessons with us until the day that our cowboy teacher did something that caused us to cancel any more lessons from him.

After week four he was trying to explain to us how important it was to show our horses who was boss (sound familiar?), when he hauled off and booted Jenny's horse right in the stomach while the unsaddled horse was just standing there with Jenny holding the lead rope. That class was over!

One day Jenny called me over to remove a shakeysnake that had camped on her door mat at her front door. With my trusty snake stick and an empty five gallon plastic pail I went over and removed the snake and took it about a mile from any homes and let it go.

On another day when we were getting ready to go shopping I caught a glimpse of a horse running on our road from the barn. It seems that I did not chain snap one of the gates down back were Sanny stayed. I had just "open" hooked the gate, allowing one of our playful goats to push the hook off with it's nose until it dropped. The wind, or Sanny, must have pushed the unlocked gate open.

In utter disbelief I realized it was him, our steed, leaving our hallowed grounds really fast. I rushed outside to see him heading across to Jenny's desert property to where her horses were housed in a large circle corral. I walked over there slowly so as not to further spook Sanny, who was following her horses around the circle. I kept thinking of how far he'd gotten from Mike's place the previous two times he'd escaped and I sure didn't want that to happen again.

Now there was a lot more traffic on the roads north of us. Sanny went around that corral a couple of times with me following. Then all of a sudden he took off again, heading due south towards the Hunkler residence. I saw him stop suddenly in the Hunkler's rear driveway. He was looking up at the Hunkler's balcony at their dog "Darth Vader". This dog was a very large Newfoundland Shepard that weighed over 175 pounds. Santanna seemed to be mesmerized by this huge barking animal that had long hair that would flop fluidly up and down as he barked.

I was just about where Sanny was standing, who was still looking at Darth Vader, probably not really knowing if it was a predator that would attack him any minute or not. Whoops! All of a sudden Sanny started running again, out of the Hunkler's driveway, hung a right and headed north on the road in the direction of my home. I could just imagine him going all the way to Mesa or some other far away place. But without any hesitation he hung a left into my driveway, went right down to the open gate near the barn, ran inside his corral and came to a complete stop. Now I began to run, hoping that he would not change his mind and run back out again. He didn't, thank the lord! Now years later I double check to make sure that every livestock gate I enter or leave is always locked properly.

Then The Texans Moved Into Jenny's Place

When Jenny moved out a couple of years later a very unique couple moved into her place. We met them prior to their moving in and they told us that they were from Texas. They dressed like they were Roy Rogers children, although they were clearly not children.

One day when my wife was at work I went over to their new home and presented them with a "Wilcox" apple pie. These were special pies made in Wilcox Arizona and brought to the Mesa area for sale for a couple of weeks every year. These were tall pies, baked to perfection and very delicious. They asked me to come into their new home, where I gave them the pie.

I started off my conversation by telling them that the last time I was there it was to remove a three foot rattler that was laying on the mat at the front door. Seeing that they looked like they were country folk from Texas I did not think for a moment that this would disturb either of them, especially from a lady that hung small fishing lures from her ears.

But NO, I had made a very bad mistake! The Mrs. went ballistic right after I told them about the rattler. Her husband glared at me and she was so upset I had to excuse myself and leave for safer ground. That was the last time I saw them because they moved out within weeks and I think that they may have gone to a motel or hotel soon after I left that day. They never did thank me for the pie and for all I know she may have thrown it at her husband right after my hasty departure.

The Meth Merchants

The other Jenny was the wife of a methamphetamine dealer/manufacturer and the mother of two children. Bob, Jenny's husband, was not only a drug dealer and manufacturer but also a "fence' for stolen property. He had dug a big cavern away from his trailer and built a shed over it. The hole had shelves built into the side walls for his drug storage; the rest of the tomb-like area was used for the storage of chemicals used in the making of meth.

Their children were often neglected and sometimes would go next door seeking food. That neighbor would always give them something, not really knowing exactly what was going on a hundred yards from her home. She and her husband would become directors of the San Tan Mountains PRIDE, the group of local citizens that joined together to help rid our neighborhood of all the criminal activities that were so prevalent at that time.

Van & Van & The Circus Clown

Coincidentally, in addition to having two neighbors named Jenny, we also had two people named Van, all living within three hundred yards of each other. The clown, by the way, also also lived near us. Van (#1) was a black man who lived by himself, given space for his trailer on a property just 50 yards north from the kind lady that lived next to the meth dealer. This Van had many regular clients that had him do handyman work for them. He had a friend, a man called Terry, who was a rough and tumble chewing tobacco kind of guy that had mining experience and some (UN)valuable horse training knowledge. .

On my way to the trading post one day I noticed a lot of flare residue in the roadway at the corner of Sossaman and Hunt, which usually meant that there was an accident there very recently. Judging from the amount of flares that had been used and the oil stains that remained it must have been a very bad auto accident. Van was coming out of the Trading Post when I pulled up and I asked him if he knew what had happened there. He got a strange look on his face and said that he knew exactly what had happened because one of his friends was involved. I asked him who it was and he said it was Terry. He told me, the previous night Terry went over to his place and got very drunk. When he was going to leave for home Van implored him to drive the back roads to his home rather that going by way of the main road.

Terry never took his suggestion and hit this young man head on with his pick-up truck. Van said he only knew that the young man, who had just become a father a couple of months before, died, but Terry only got some non-life threatening injuries. He said that beyond that he didn't know anything else.

There was not anything in the news that I saw about this accident. In those days we had to wait for the Chandler Heights Monthly to come out with our news because we are beyond any coverage in the major newspapers that covered the Metro Phoenix area.

Several months before this happened I was horseback riding with a small group that included a local pastor. We were finishing up a ride that would take us by Terry's property. He was working out by his horse corral when we approached. The pastor was having some trouble with the horse that was loaned to him for the ride. Terry saw that and motioned for us to come over by him and he immediately told us that you must show the horse who is the boss, where have I heard this before?

He went on to tell us that when he breaks a horse he takes a bottle of Jim Beam with him and every time he gets thrown off he takes a swig of the booze, then gets back on. He would then repeat the process until the horse gave in or he ran out of the JB, at least that was the plan. He went on to say, "See that stallion over there? When I was breaking him in, after I got thrown for the third time, he reared up at me as if to strike me with his front feet. Well, I ran out of there and got a piece of a two by four and went back in there and hit him smack on his fore-head." There was complete silence within the group; even the horses were astonished. I figured it was time to leave, so I said, "How about joining us sometime when we ride again", knowing full well that the invitation might never be accepted. Terry then said, "I don't have a horse to ride." I answered, "What about your stallion over there?" He quickly answered, "I won't ever ride the SOB because he has a great memory" I answered, "Then we will see you later," and we all continued riding down the road, hopefully towards a place where more sanity existed.

The other Van (#2) lived on the next three and a third acre property from Van (#1) and was a United States Air Force retiree. He served with a group of specialists that supported the Air Force Thunderbird's Flight Demonstration Team, being a part of their ground crew.

When we moved into our new home this Van came by to tell me how the prior owner of our property, Charlie, had built a dirt dam across the deep wash that crossed our land. Van had not found out about it until a very heavy rain washed it away, bringing many thousands of gallons of water rushing down onto Van's property that was about 300 yards downstream from the breached dam.

This happened a few years ago and I could see that Van was still very upset with the damage that it caused. He warned me not to ever build a dam across my wash or there would be trouble. I promised him that I would never do anything like that.

Van (#2) was very proud of being in the USAF and spoke often about his time a being a part of the Thunderbird ground crew. He had a small 1970's bright green truck that had a small water tank mounted on the back. He had to make almost two trips a day to get water in the summer because he had a lot of plants that he cared for and two full grown, loud, he-hawing mules that he cherished. His wonderful wife was nearly totally blind and the tending of her plants was priority one for Van.

One evening my wife and I were looking out of our home enjoying our fantastic view when we saw a car pass our property about three times and go into the Hunkler's driveway. We knew that our neighbors were away on a trip. Well, my John Wayne instincts kicked in!

I grabbed my unloaded Winchester model 94 lever action 30-30 rifle, the same kind as John often used in his movies, and rushed down near the road, waiting for these thieves that were clearly stealing stuff from our neighbors to come back again.

After a wait of about thirty minutes or so I saw the headlights of the thief's car slowly coming up the road. I did not know how many thieves were in that car but, no matter, I was going to do what John would have done. Just as they got about fifteen feet away from where my mail box stood I jumped out from behind a big Saguaro cactus onto the road, holding my unloaded rifle at port arms. My wife was yelling "be careful, be careful" and I yelled, "Stop! What is your business here?" (I really don't think I said that, but it sounds like what someone would say back in the eighteen hundreds!)

Anyway, Van jumped out of his car and yelled, "Ros, I am so proud of you! You are one fantastic guy risking your life like that and protecting our neighborhood." He came over and shook my very embarrassed hand. I could hear his wife laughing while she remained in the car.

It turned out that Van and his wife were transporting sand from a nearby wash in their trunk. They were taking this sand to the Hunkler's place for a sand box they had made for the Hunkler's grandchildren. The sand box was going to be a surprise. It was summer and they did this transporting of sand in the evening because it was cooler. This incident happened before I knew Van and his wife that well, but it was just like them to do something nice for a neighbor.

We were good friends from then on and would have good talks down at the stand pipe while waiting in line for our water. Van had the second telephone number in this area. Their last number being 2 and the Hunklers who had the first phone with their last number being 1.

Now...about the circus clown! I think that everyone living for a long period of time within the zip codes encompassing Queen Creek in their address will agree that there might be a few clowns living here, but the clown I am referring to actually worked for Ringling Brothers Barnum and Bailey Circus. This clown by the name of Rick, and his girl friend lived in the conclave that one of or drug dealers and his wife would move into after they got out of jail. We could see this commune from our front deck, the Bigton's place, and Van's (#2) place is right across the road from it.

One New Years Eve Caroline and I were watching TV, waiting for the ball to drop in Times Square, when I saw a flickering light, out of the corner of my eye, in the dark sky from our our Arcadia door and couldn't figure what it was. It didn't seem to be imposing a threat to anyone so I didn't even mention it to my wife, who was still watching TV.

Then all of a sudden we saw a brilliant flash in the sky. The explosion shook our house and our dogs began shaking and whining. This was before we had 911 and contacting the sheriff's office was a hassle so I didn't call. I expected people nearer the explosion to call, which they did.

Come to find out Rick had built a miniature hot air balloon made mostly out of large garbage bags. Inside a large garbage bag was another sealed bag that was full of an explosive gas, probably gas used for welding purposes. Hanging from the bottom of the bag was a container that held fire used to lift this thing up into the air. Back then on New Year's and the Fourth of July there were always a lot of people shooting firearms up in the air, using shotguns, rifles and pistols to signal their support of these celebrations. Some had illegal fireworks they shot off that really scared many dogs whenever the noise got too loud. But this one topped them all.....BOOM!

At about four-thirty that morning the phone rang and it was a very irate Van #2, telling me that something had blown up almost directly over his house. It scared his mules so badly that they knocked down their fence and they ran down the road. Van said it took him three hours to find the mules so he called the sheriff to tell them that he thought that the explosion was caused by someone from the Bigton's place. The operator told him that all deputies were out on other similar calls and it would be a while before they could get one of them to respond.

A few hours later Van called again to tell me that a sheriff's deputy was on his way to see him and he asked me if I would be a witness. I told him that I would tell the deputy what I saw and heard. It was a couple of hours later when the deputy came up to my home to ask me about what I'd seen and heard. Through the grapevine I found out later what had actually happened--it was the clown who did it.

The Alaska Dodges

The Dodges live directly South of us with a three and a third acre empty property between our home and theirs. They owned a boat livery in Alaska and they wintered in Arizona almost every year. George, his wife Joanne, and their son John were real pioneers in two different states. George worked for Alaska Airlines until he retired and son John still works for the airline. This has given them an airline employee advantage traveling between the two states. George is a very hardy person and was always working on his place as I would, either fixing or improving when the weather was kind to us.

One day I was home alone and decided to finish the roofing on my small barn located about 200 yards west of our home. The winds that day were gusty. My wife would not be home from work for six more hours and our neighbors to the southeast were gone on a trip. Working on the barn roof without gusty winds was hard enough, especially when installing roll roofing, and with winds gusting it could become very dangerous, as I found out.

I had tacked down one edge of the 30 by four foot section and was about to tack down the other end when the wind whipped the loose roofing and it knocked down my ladder. This left me stranded on that roof without any water on a bright sunny Arizona 'dry heat" day, where temperatures would reach about 106 degrees by the mid afternoon. There was no safe way for me to get off that roof. At its lowest point I was twenty feet above the ground.

The only people home were George and his wife Joanne. The main road was too far from where I was and traffic on the road then was very sparse, so my only hope of getting down was the Dodge's that were about two football fields away from me, with some short bushes in the way. The gusting winds did not

258

help my voice to carry very far. It was nearly two hours before I saw movement outside the Dodge's home. It was George. He was hammering on something I could not see. I must have hollered for another thirty minutes before George began to hear me. Then he did what any good neighbor would do and waved back at me as I screamed his name. He went back to his hammering, then waved back again, until I used the words HELP! I was getting somewhat dehydrated by the time he drove over and saved my butt. It was a very embarrassing situation for me but George realized that and did not laugh once, at least in front of me.

Possible Vehicle Insurance Fraud?

Another time George Dodge and I were working outside when I heard a terrible crash and saw a van tumbling down the side of Goldmine Mountain from a road that Mancel Carter and George Kennedy had built with a bulldozer. The road was intended to go to their mine. I dropped what I was doing and was running for my truck even before the van stopped rolling. I thought sure there was one or more people in that thing. George called the Sheriff's office and then followed after me to where the totally destroyed vehicle came to rest.

Strangely, I passed a car parked on the road as I headed up toward the accident. Even more surprising was that there was a woman just sitting in the car, her face expressionless. Her vehicle was facing away for the wreckage so I just kept going to get as near as possible to the crumpled up van. What was left of the vehicle was about 300 yards away from the road. The side of the mountain was now covered with glass, trim, parts, a spare tire, pop cans and all kinds of other metal things. George was right behind me then, when we heard a man yelling from the road where the van came from. He said that there was no one in the van and it had just rolled down the side of the mountain on its own after he got out of it to go to the mine.

A Sheriff's deputy showed up and George and I briefly reported what we saw, then went back to our homes scratching our heads and wondering about what we had witnessed. There was an article in the Monthly Newspaper that said that the people involved were directly responsible for removing all the wreckage and that the insurance company was investigating the accident.

The Not So Mysterious Explosion

Every once in a while everybody makes a mistake, even policemen. One fall evening a few years ago, I was driving by the north entrance of the San Tan Regional Park which is about 150 yards from our home. In the small parking lot I saw a fire truck with its flashing lights on and about five police cars. I noticed that the cars were from different jurisdictions. My window was down and I wondered what was going on. When I heard laughter from some of the officers, I knew that whatever had happened was not an emergency, so I continued on home. I told Caroline about what I'd seen and didn't think any more about it until about a half hour later when we heard a huge explosion, followed by a lot of glass breaking in our home. At first I thought something broke through our Arcadia glass door. We had no idea what had happened. After investigating further I found two large glass covered pictures had been knocked of our walls with glass shards all around them. While I was calling 911 Caroline went out on the deck and saw a procession of vehicles heading down the far road. She could see the fire truck in the middle of the parade lit up by the headlights from the other cars.

The 911 operator told me that she would send a deputy out to check it out. I told her that there was a whole bunch of deputies leaving the Park then. She sounded confused and repeated what she had just said. I started calling the few neighbors we have up here and they had all called 911 too. There are two neighbors closer to the Park than we were, so the sound of it must have been much louder for them. After cleaning up the glass we went to bed. In the morning I got a call from the newspaper asking me about "the mysterious explosion" in our area.

The reporter told me that a Town of Gilbert bomb squad had disposed of a hand grenade that one of their policeman had found in a suspects possession. I told them about the pictures being knocked off the walls and about all the police cars in the Park's parking lot. My version of the story came out in the next edition of the paper. Case closed, over and done, right?

No! I have a good friend that I will not name that called me after he read the story and he, being one to explore the wrong doings of any one in authority, wanted to take things further. So after talking to me he called a friend that works for the Town of Gilbert to get the whole story. This friend told my friend that the bomb squad from Gilbert called the Pinal County Sheriff's office to find out where was a good place to blow this BOMB up.

The whole thing became some kind of "bomb party". The fire department was called because they had a key to the gate at the park entrance. This would allow the bomb squad to drive up to a deep wash where the explosion could take place. The Park is on Pinal County land but governed by Maricopa County which is why there were so many vehicles up there--as many as eight or more deputies and three firemen.

My friend wanted to press the issue, questioning why the immediate neighbors were not notified and why it took so many deputies to carry this out. While he was having so much fun raising hell with the superiors of the agencies involved, he got a call from a good friend of his that held a high ranking position in a local government. He asked my friend to please stop investigating this embarrassing inter-agency "bomb party thingy", which he did. Case finally closed. But we were out about twenty bucks for the new picture glass and Caroline and I both wound up with a mild case of PTSD.

In Case Of Fire......

Wildfire on Goldmine Mountain

I was about 35 miles from our home when I first saw a big plume of black smoke in the direction of the mountains that surround our mini ranch. I was coming down Power Road, which is near a straight line to the area where we live. At first I thought that it might have been a house fire because of the black smoke. I immediately went to the nearest pay phone to call and my extremely agitated wife answered. She asked me to get home as fast as I could because there was a wildfire in progress about ¼ of a mile south of us up near where Mancel Carter used to live. She said that she was loading up her car with as many pictures as she could and that the very few animals that we had then would be last. She said that she had called the fire department three times already and they were not there yet.

The Lord was with us again, that day because the wind started blowing the fire towards the nearby mountains to our east. By the time I got home Caroline had called the fire department 11 times. She said she was screaming at them because only one fire truck had shown up so far and the fire was getting much bigger.

Within two hours a large helicopter was hovering just off the ground across the street from our home over empty desert land. About 10 or more hotshot crew members hopped down with shovels and other equipment in their hands. They were Native American Indians, dressed in yellow wildfire fighting garb with packs on their backs. They landed within twenty yards of our house. I could see every man's face clearly. It was something I never dreamed that I would ever see so close to our home.

The fire was still quite a distance from our place and there were many places much closer to the fire that they could have landed. I wondered if maybe they had to land away from the fire on purpose because the whirling helicopter blades that could cause the fire to scatter in all different directions if it came to too close.

The winds did not blow the fire any nearer our property and the hotshot crew saw to that, just in case. It went due east to the mountains very quickly and then went then due north all along the face of those mountains. By this time a local crop duster with his bright yellow plane showed up dropping water on the flames. It was then that I realized Queen Creek had its own volunteer fire fighting air force--our local crop duster!

Later it would be found that a few children were playing by "the hermit of the mountain's" now empty place in the Park and admitted to starting the fire according to the Bob Ingram our Park Ranger. The Gilbert Tribune reported that one Rural Metro fire truck with two men was first on the scene that day but had to call for more help right away.

Soon the Bureau of Land Management, with hot-shot teams from Globe, Pleasant Valley and Tonto National Forest, used nearly twenty pieces of equipment, including fire and brush trucks and water tankers that were set up around our mountain area. We could see that the fire was headed right for a house that was at the north end of the mountain. The flames got near the home but the firemen there saved it and about ten others that were right around the point where the fire was heading.

I drove over to Tom Lang's place that had a good view to where the fire was spreading. A big fire-retardant air tanker preceded by a much smaller twin engine lead plane flew over our heads headed for the fire. The big plane suddenly dropped about 50 feet, probably from an air pocket, before it could pull up but made it OK. From then on the passes by both planes were not as close to the ground.

There were other wildfires in and around the park that were set on purpose that year. My son Kevin was riding his trail bike out on the road that went from Bell Road south into the Park area when he saw a man lighting a large fire with a propellant, like kerosene or charcoal lighter.

The fire was too big for my son to put out but he was able to get the man's license plate number. He was on the way to his house to call the fire department when he saw the vehicle pass. He followed it to the Trading Post in Chandler Heights and my son used the pay phone outside to call the sheriff's department. He gave his name but never heard from anyone about whether the man was caught or not.

During this time there were also wildfires being set in the Fountain Hills area which is about forty miles from our home in Queen Creek. **Way Too Many Crazies Out There!**

CHAPTER 8

Cancer

In August 2011 I went to my primary doctor for my free yearly Medicare physical. Part of this examination was an extensive blood panel that showed I had a high PSA count. Doctor Mitchell Gadow our Cigna Health Care Advantage Plan doctor referred me to Doctor Pratik Patel a young man who is a major part of the Arizona State Urological Institute.

He did a biopsy on me within a couple of weeks from my first visit. It took a couple of weeks more after the samples were sent to a Lab in Texas and then on to another lab in Indiana for a DNA sample for match testing to make absolutely sure that these twelve samples were mine. On October 13th 2011 my wife and I were given the results by Doctor Patel who told us that I did have high risk prostate cancer. At this time Doctor Patel told me that I would have to go for many tests to see if the cancer had spread to any other regions in my body. At that time we realized that we did not have the money to cover the more expensive co-payments for the many procedures that I would have to go through to make the finding necessary to continue on a path to eliminate my cancer.

My wife mentioned my diagnosis to our friend and neighbor, Diane Drenk, as well as our difficulty in paying for the necessary co-pays. Diane's husband John happened to be recovering from his fight with bladder cancer. Diane was fully aware of the costs that come with fighting this disease. She then spearheaded a fund drive on my behalf by soliciting her friends and relatives on my behalf.

I needed three procedures that cost $125.00 each in co-pays and many doctor visits from specialists that cost $45.00 per visit. In 2011 many people were hurting financially so getting donations from many people that I did not know that well should have been difficult but Diane a Seal Team 13 Norwegian Angel and her close relative angels did get us the money we needed just the same.

John Drenk remains cancer free to this day and is receiving dialysis treatments twice a week. What this man had to go through was a lot more harrowing in many more ways that what I was served up.

Our relatives that did not do as well are: My younger brother Fred who died from cancer at 46, my father at 44, my uncle Seth at 33, my uncle George at 83, Caroline's brothers David at 52 and Edmond at 64.

Please support the Cancer Society!

CHAPTER 9

Family Album

NYS Trooper Alden Eugene Rosbrook, My Father

Pauline Fitzsimmons Rosbrook
Bergren, My Mom

Party Greeting Fred In
Scottsdale 1971

In May 1987, Fred's son, Frederick Terrance Rosbrook II married Leta Cox in Guelph Ontario Canada. Fred had just built a new home there and most of the Rosbrook's gathered there for the big celebration and reunion. It truly was a fantastic time that we will always remember. A few months later, on September 13 1987 Fred was tragically taken from us at the age of 46 due to extensive cancer. It is hard to believe, seeing these pictures that this disease could take his life in such a short time.

Maureen, Mr. Cox, Lita, Terry, Stella Cox & Fred

Patti Ann, Kathy, Terry, Kerri, Tim & Fred

*Michael, Fred &
Candice Rosbrook*

*Fred &
Marilyn*

A " Rich Hold Up" In Kinderhook

Kathy, Kelly, Rudy, Shannon & Colleen

Our Aunt Marjorie, Brother Richard & Mom's Best Friend Hilda Burton.
99 S. Pearl St., Albany NY, Summer 1993

Marjorie, Cornelia, Seth, Alden w/Jerry & George Rosbrook 1920 on the
farm where everybody, except papa, worked almost every day. They lived
on farms near Watertown, Newark & Nassau NY. My dad, in this picture,
drove a tractor from the age of eleven.

3 Columbia Drive, East Greenbush NY. Our home had a second floor made by a huge dormer built by my father and his friend Johnny Maynes. One very big bedroom was the result, with two built in bunk beds and one single bed for me and my two brothers with lots of room left over. Much to the dismay of our parents we held "sock wars" (stuff many socks into one sock until it is as hard as a rock) up there mostly at night while mom and dad were trying to watch the new TV, circa 1950.

My Brother Richard Piping Along The Hudson.

*Rich is Not Wearing
Underpants!*

The Scottsdale & Phoenix Family

Marion & Mark Rosbrook

Mark & Marion live in Scottsdale.

Valerie McKenna Arnold, Sascha, McKenna & Alexander Arnold live in North Phoenix

272

Mark, Marion & Matt??

What is going on in the kitchen behind my back?

The North Anthem Rosbrook's

Cindy & Matt Rosbrook

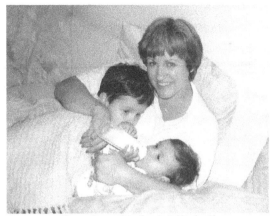

Brandon, Cindy & Mitchell

Brandon, Fluffy & Mitch

Kevin, Mark, Matt (who can not believe his eyes) Rosbrook & Todd
Brooke, who is Cindy's brother ready for Matt & Cindy's wedding.

The Carolina Puerto Rico Castillo's

Cindy Castillo Baker, Kristina, Valerie, Linda, Cara Rosbrook Castillo & Ramon Jimmy Castillo

Valerie, Cara, Jimmy & Cindy, Sunrise AZ

**Kiana, Our Son Kevin, Lisa Marie, Tasia, Brandon & Barrett, Parker
(holding a picture of Spencer Who Is In Taiwan) & Jensen**

Tasia Cleaning Sink

Eric Baker & Cindy Castillo Baker Family

No Room At The Hospital For Cindy

On Cindy's birthday on July 07 2002 Caroline and I were both in Puerto Rico celebrating our 45th wedding anniversary which was on July 13, 1957. It was Cindy's 19th birthday and we were at Cara and Jimmy's home awaiting Cindy and a group of Cindy's friends who were coming there for a pool party. Cindy and her friend were on there way to the house separately. It was raining, Cindy was a passenger in her friends car and nearly to the house when a cat ran in front of the car. Her friend slammed on the brakes and the car slide into a large palm tree crushing the passenger car door where Cindy was sitting. The rest of the party was following and came upon the scene right after the accident happened. Cindy was trapped in the car and one of the party called Cara to tell about the nearby accident.

Grandma stayed with the children at home while Cara, Jimmy and I rushed to the accident scene. We got there just as the police arrived. Some of the boys were trying to get Cindy out of the car when the police told them to get out of the way. Cindy was in terrible pain and the boys didn't want to stop helping.

A minor dispute erupted between the boys and the police just as the EMT's arrived. They then took took over complete control of the accident. Cindy was then transported by ambulance to the nearest hospital where we soon found out that she needed to go to a class-one trauma center because of her injuries. She was then put into another ambulance and transported to the trauma one hospital that was extremely busy. There we found out that Cindy's number one rib, the one closest to her heart, was broken along with a broken hip and collar bone. This was discovered while the three of us were allowed into the x-ray room. There was one tech there while we watched him do the x-rays. At one point the tech handed me the three x-rays and pointed to the display box whereupon I shoved the x-ray up into the clips that hold the the film on to the display. I saw doctors do that in many TV shows, but I had to be shown where the fractures were by the tech and he said "very bad sir." Cindy was heavily sedated at this time and after she was x-rayed she was taken back to the emergency room.

We were escorted to the "over filled" waiting room. We found out that only one person at a time could go into see the patient. Then we found out that they put Cindy in the hallway outside the emergency room where there were also several other patients parked there.

Cara was the first to see her, and she said she was cold. They were out of blankets, so Cara went home to get two for her while her Dad went to see her. Finally they sent Cindy home by ambulance at 2:00 a.m.. The only thing they could do for her was put her arm in a sling, put a collar on her neck and taping her rib's. This is about all that can be done for these type of injuries.

The next day the hospital sent over a regular hospital bed. A nurse visited her every day for a few weeks. It took a few months before she was completely mended. Now she is as good as new and is the proud mother three beautiful young adventurous daughters.

Eric & Cindy Wedding Picture

*Cindy, Anna Sophia, Sara & Megan
Baker*

Cindy Castillo Baker & Eric Baker

Rachel La Grange Ransford Nelson

Caroline's Mom Rachel At A Phoenix "All Indian Pow Wow"

Rachel at Matt & Cindy's Wedding David Ransford Caroline's Brother, Ramon, Cara Castillo, Mark, Marion Rosbrook, Lisa, Kevin, Rachel, Cindy,Matt,Caroline, Me & Sascha Arnold

Rachel was not just my mother in-law but a very good friend as well, to the point that I wanted to give the my only eulogy to date, for her, at her funeral. Being a somewhat emotional person, the only way I could do it was to deliver my memories/message in a more or less humorous fashion. Afterwords I received many congratulations for what I said from some people that I did not know. She died when she was 94 and her La Grange ancestry line goes back to Omie La Grange who died when he was 106 on 26 Apr 1731 in New Scotland, Albany, NY.

All of Omie's direct descendant line died in their eighties or nineties except one. Omie was born in Normandy France and his whole family were intertwined with Dutch wives and husbands through time. Rachel's first husband, Edmond Ransford Sr., Caroline, David and Edmond Junior's father, was electrocuted on a power pole when he worked for the Niagara Mohawk Power Company. Her second husband, Ivan Nelson, Benny's and Maureen's father, died soon after a tractor overturned on him on a side hill on his farm in Couse Corners

NY. Caroline's brother saw the accident ran to the scene and with pure adrenalin lifted the tractor off of his stepfather. Ivan rolled free from under the tractor but died at work from a heat attack at General Electric in Schenectady NY.

Maureen Nelson Niggli, Caroline's Sister

Reenie

Bo, Samantha, Kathy & Ben

Ben, Caroline's Brother & Kathy Daughter's Wedding.

The Ransford's

JUNE & ED RANSFORD II

Lori, Ron, Jason, Chad, Corrissa & Joe Peets. Lori is Ed & June Ransford II's daughter.

Laurie, Robert, Edmond Ransford III, Caroline's Nephew & Shannon. Colonel Ransford is a graduate of the US Air Force Academy.

Mrs. Pauline Fitsimmons Rosbrook Bergren's wedding reception at 3 Columbia Drive East Greenbush NY

"The Luau" Ladies, Caroline & Diane

Our first born, Mark Alden Rosbrook with Godparents Vince & Marie Colona

At the Carefree Movie Studio, we were cast members for a movie called Silver Sally's Saloon. What A Blast!

Caroline, Jennifer Coleman, Mark, Me,
Lisa, Kevin, Matt & Cindy

When the water line finally came to our home it was time to put down old 54. I didn't have the heart to do it so I had my friend & neighbour Ron Hunkler do it for me.

The Burns/Komar Girls: Suzie Burns Baker, Tiffany Komar Call, Darice Burns Terry, Lisa Burns Rosbrook, Sandy Burns Reed, & Michelle Komar Owers

Our family had a visitor from Germany (upper left) that played the piano for us as we all sang Christmas carols. What a wonderful gift. 1985

The Rapps

Jackie Rapp, Me, Caroline & Joe Rapp

Mom Being Irish!

The last time I talked with my Mom "I told her that she was getting more and more beautiful." She snapped right back with a big smile on her face and said," "Well!........... That's not my fault!" Mom, Pauline Mary Fitzsimmons Rosbrook Bergren

Rob Fitzsimmons, My Grandfather, With His New Furnace Sept, 1967

Rob at 84 , Sold Bait Fish From His Basement, In Redwood NY Rob & Jennie both passed away in their 71st year of marriage. Jennie was 18 and Rob was 17 when they married on Sept 24, 1902 They had 4 girls and 3 boys.

Me, Fred & Richard Rosbrook

In Guelph Ontario Canada, about three months after this picture was taken, Fred would tragically die from cancer on September 13, 1987 at the age of 46 years. Our family was there to celebrate Frederick Terrance Rosbrook, Jr's, marriage. It was truly a wonderful weekend party that will be remembered always.

Mom's Great, Great Grandchildren. Sara, Megan & Anna Sophia who Live In Carolina Puerto Rico.

The Last Straw

In spite of everything that we saw that was a negative, we bought the ranch anyway and have never regretted it one time since February 1986 when we moved into El Rancho de Santanna

Our property backs up to a small mountain in San Tan Mountain Regional Park. Our back property line ends about half way a steep slope to the Park fence.

Before we met our neighbors, the Hunkler's, their relatives, some visiting from Ohio, had made a big banner that they were holding over the road leading up to the Hunkler's home with a surprise Happy Birthday wish from them. The Hunkler's were a few minutes behind us and our work van. Their relatives were holding the banner with long poles that were not quite high enough for our truck to go under. Thinking we could clear it, they motioned us on after I stopped, but the banner got tangled up with the roof of the truck anyway. I was so embarrassed when all eight of these people that we did not know told me what they were trying to do. So we all hurried to get the banner unstuck and we only hoped that we did not ruin their surprise.

What a way to start a good neighbor relationship! There were no hard feelings because of that because these folks have a great sense of humor, which we would find out after we got settled into our new home.

There were only two other homes up near us then, located hundreds of feet to the north and east of our place. We live on the western edge of a horseshoe of mountains that nearly surrounded our home. The views that we have are wonderful. Some of the wild animals that we co-exist with are, at times, a challenge but we have adapted to their territory very well. All our neighbors are our partners in the security of our properties and homes. We watch out for each other and have fun doing so.

The large pool at our house was a magnet for all our family until they all grew older. Our daughter used to send her daughters up from Puerto Rico for our Camp Shaky Snakes which included races between them almost every day in the pool. With our basketball backboard at one end of the pool, we mostly the grown-ups, would play a game called "bruiser ball", which was a game based more on football rules and less on basketball rules. There were many parties held around that pool, on our grounds and in our home.

Our biggest and one of our best parties was our famous "Luau" which was Hawaiian all the way. We had a best dressed Hawaiian contest and the best Hawaiian dance contest that was a riot. Mark, our oldest, won that one using a flaming spear that he passed through and around his grass skirt. The music was mostly the heavy drumming Polynesian style.

It doesn't seem that long ago that our boys would have timing races, going from the back of our home to the top of the small mountain behind our property--across one very deep wash and up the very steep slope to the top, in just under five minutes.

After one of our bruiser ball games, one of our oldest son's younger brothers played a practical joke on him. Mark is very competitive, especially in golf. There were a lot of people there that day and the practical joker suggested that he could hit a golf ball over the top of our back mountain, egging his older brother on. This feat would have been almost impossible because of the distance away from and the height of said mountain,. The next younger brother, who was also in on the joke, took on the challenge by claiming that he could do the job with ease. This made Mark really wanting to show off his masterful golf skills by out driving them both.

Most everyone there that day was in on the joke being played on Mark. I provided three golf balls, one of which was made out of chalk that looked exactly like a golf ball. The chalk ball was for Mark. I was designated as the umpire that set the ball on a tee. The launching pad for this practical joke was set up on a road just behind the swimming pool.

Mark was chomping at the bit by the time he got to hit. Kevin went first and hit his ball a fair way but nowhere near the top of the mountain. There were about fifteen family members and friends watching and they applauded Kevin's meager drive. Matt was up next and did about the same as Kevin and still the crowd applauded. Now it was Mark's turn and he was more than ready to show everyone how powerful he was at hitting that little golf ball. I set the chalk ball on the tee and everyone chanted, "Over the top, Mark! Over the top!"

Wow! He must have hit that thing right on the "Mark", excuse the pun, because there was a huge cloud of white powder that exploded high into the air. There was some laughter but it soon stopped when Mark appeared to be injured by hitting such a light object so hard. Mark took it extremely well and as it turned out his injury was not one that lingered very long.

In the good old days we skied at Jackson Hole, Steamboat Springs, Teton Village, Sunrise Resort and Winter Park. We all were very fortunate to be able to go to these places because everyone's business was very good at that time. One Christmas the Castillo family, with their four girls, Caroline and I spent 10 days at a condo in Teton Village. We went snowmobiling in Yellowstone among the buffalo, elk and eagles. We could ski from the top of Teton mountain all the way to our condo, where we enjoyed swimming in a hot outdoor pool after skiing when the temperatures were at 16 below zero. We burned a whole cord of wood in the fireplace during those wonderful ten days. Thanks be to God we were able to enjoy such spectacular memories.

In Yellowstone Park the speed limit is 40 MPH and the rangers have radar guns and are along the trails and if caught speeding you must leave the park. The suits are included, when you rent a snowmobile, that goes over your regular clothes and boots that go over your boots.

I previously told the story about our spiritual happening at the Mass we attended in Pittsford NY just before we moved from Rochester to Phoenix. I mentioned that this was one of two more spiritual people that I was in the presence of in my lifetime, so far.

Here Is The Story Of Those Two Other People

I did a lot of swimming every evening in the heated pool where we lived in our condominium community in Scottsdale in the eighties. I developed an earache which started slowly but soon became very severe. I went to an eye, ear and nose specialist in Scottsdale and after a brief inspection of my infected ear he gave me some prescriptions that cost me over eighty dollars. The visit with the doctor cost me another seventy, which back then was a large amount of money. In just over a week I realized that the medicine was not working at all because the pain was getting worse.

A neighbor told me about a wonderful ear specialist she knew that should be able to help me. This doctor's office was located in a poorer neighborhood in Phoenix. While I was waiting for them to answer their phone I was concerned with how long it would take to get an appointment. The receptionist asked me what my problem was and after I told her, she asked me to hold on for a minute. When she came back on the phone she told me that the doctor would see me as soon as I could get there, which I told her would be about a thirty minutes. She told me to bring the meds the other doctor prescribed for me.

I was in agony, Caroline was working and I even wondered if I could drive myself to his office, but I made it. The doctor's office was in an older single family home. When I told the receptionist who I was, she immediately excused herself, got up and walked into the back area. She came back with the doctor, an older man with white hair, who asked me to follow him. On the way to his examination room he asked his patients in his waiting room--there was about seven or eight--"Is it alright if I help this person ahead of you because he is in severe pain?"

There was a chorus of "Sure, that's OK!" from the patients. I wondered how his staff and he knew seemed to know exactly how much pain I was really in but somehow, some way, they knew.

It didn't take me long to find out how caring this soft spoken doctor was and I soon learned how he wanted to teach his patients and his nurses everything that he knew.

After looking in my ear he asked to see the meds my doctor had prescribed for me. When I gave him the meds he told me, "I am very sorry to say, and I know they cost you a lot of money, but I want you to throw them away." He then went to a big cabinet and pulled out several small boxes of his "sample" meds and handed them to me. He explained to me and his nurse exactly what my infection was and how these meds were going to help me.

Then he showed us, with the aid of a large colored chart on the wall, why the infection in my left ear happened. It seems that the bottom bone in the canal leading to my left ear drum had a bump that created a little pocket next to the ear drum where these germs festered and made it very hard to get rid of them.

The doctor told me to come to his office once a day, six days a week, for two weeks, for what he called ear wick treatments. His nurse gave me three pills to take along with a cup of water and then gave me my first ear wick treatment. When I went out front to pay I was totally amazed when the lady told me that the visit only cost me twenty dollars. I told her that she must have made a mistake but she just smiled and confirmed what she said, "twenty dollars, Mr. Rosbrook." I still had some pain but not the excruciating pain I'd come there with. I took my samples and left with a lot more questions in my mind that I just could not understand.

After twelve days of the ear wick treatments and with all pain completely gone, the doctor entered the treatment room and said that he had to grind the bone down in my left ear at an out-patient hospital facility. He showed his two nurses and me everything that he wanted to do to eliminate this from ever happening again. It was then that I remembered how many ear aches I'd had as a child.

He told me that if my insurance did not cover this operation there would be no charge. Luckily for me and for him, our Blue Cross covered just about everything. When I went to pay for the twelve ear wick treatments, the always smiling "pay to" lady handed me a statement that said "No Charge". I have never had another ear ache in over forty years. I know that this doctor is responsible for that. I will always remember this remarkable man, that I am sure has helped many hundreds or even thousands to become well and learned from him, that came before me.

Carl E. Touhey

Carl graduated from Princeton University class of 1939. He rode a bicycle throughout Europe just before World War II broke out. He then joined the Army Air Force, became a B-29 pilot who retired holding the rank of Captain in 1946 after serving four years. Carl was an avid sailor who sailed up and down the East coast and once sailed to Europe.

Carl's father bought a car dealership on a whim in 1917 on Friday the 13th which is still in operation today. It is the 15th oldest family owned Ford dealership in the USA. Carl took over the dealership after his ninety-three year old father passed away. In addition to the dealership he bought Canada Dry of Albany and built a new plant for that business next door to his car dealership. He has remained President of both companies for over fifty years. He also bought Canada Dry of Southern NY (Endicott) and Canada Dry and Seven-Up of Rochester NY along with Quevic Vichy of Saratoga Springs, NY. Carl inherited his father's entrepreneurial nature and free-spirit. He also owned a real estate development company in the Albany area.

Carl believed in me and I believed in him that day he shook my hand in 1957 after I said "When do we move?" When we had our manager's meeting every month he showed us the company's books which allowed us to learn how each of us could reap better profits for the companies we operated. It was like owning a part of the company that we directly worked in.

While he was president of the Orange Motor Company with 125 employees and he would travel to his other businesses after showing up unannounced. He liked to talk to everyone that worked for him. He was a person with kindness that everyone wanted to talk with and not one that someone you would hide from in fear.

He was at my third sales meeting in Endicott where I was giving a presentation on the ingredients of Canada Dry Ginger

Ale. I had a long table in the front of the meeting room with all the ingredients I used. Carl was sitting in the back of the room when my partner, Angelo, came up and sat on the edge of the table I was working on. Angelo proceeded to interrupt me throughout my presentation, but I was used to it--after all I was twenty and "the angel" was in his forties.

After the meeting was over and everyone had left except the three of us, Carl addressed Angelo and politely suggested that he never do what he had done to me again. Carl did a great job of reprimanding Angelo and there didn't seem to be any hard feelings between us--Angelo never did it again. Carl was a teacher to everyone he met that did business with.

He was also rather eccentric in that he would take his short trips away from his Albany area home without luggage or money. He would go out for a meal with his managers and others and they would have to buy his meal but they all had their own expense accounts to work with. When he went to a hotel he would wash his underwear in the sink in his room and hope it would be dry enough in the morning. He was very careful about what he ate, well before it was in vogue.

I had a meeting at my house with our delivery men where I served up a great steak dinner. I put some fantastic NY State sharp cheddar cheese on the salad. Carl loved salad but he especially loved my salad and wanted to know where I bought the cheese. We were outside in a backyard at our apartment home at 7:00 p.m., eating with the big boss, but being with him actually put everyone at ease. That was the part of Carl that I loved.

On Christmas the company that he directly oversaw, Orange Motors, he would give out very generous checks to all of his 125 employees. The amount of each check was exactly the same. The janitor got the same amount as the General Manager .

I discovered another part of Carl after I found out that he died at ninety-five just seven months before this book was written. I woke up one morning about a week before, thinking of him and I immediately went to my computer where I found out he had passed away.

The amounts of accolades given to him were in the hundreds. He personally gave millions of dollars to the Albany Medical Center, also giving them twenty-four million from a fund drive he chaired.

He gave two million to Saint Rose College, and he worked with a priest in one of Albany's poorest neighborhoods for five decades giving food donations and paying rent for those families that could not pay. Through his non-profit Capitol Housing Rehabilitation Company he and his son rehabilitated over 150 owner--occupied homes for low-income families. He and his son saw to the building of 100 two family housing units in the Arbor Hills area and then provided one million in grants for the poor families towards the purchase these homes.

My younger brother Fred worked directly for Carl in his soft-drink businesses. Carl taught Fred everything he needed to know to become the President of Pepsi/Seven-Up Toronto Canada. When Pepsi Company wanted to remove itself from the bottling part of the business my brother bought the company for $75,000,000. Right after the purchase was completed and because he held 51% ownership of the company after giving away 50% to his top tier employees, Fred was worth over thirty-eight million dollars.

Less than six months later he passed away in a Toronto Canada Cancer Hospital on 13 September 1987. ·In that room, on that very heart heartbreaking day after Fred passed, there then were 13 left there. I feel that because of all of Fred's suffering, the number 13 is a lucky one for us because his suffering stopped abruptly that day.

Because of Carl's mentoring to both of us and all the hundreds of others he shared his talents and fortune with, I will always share a special spiritual connection with my boss, Carl E. Touhey.

Que Dieu bénisse Carl et tout le monde!

MY LAST STAND!

We and all of our immediate neighbors feel that we are blessed with living where we do. To our south and part of our east and west is 10,000 acres of park land. Over the mountains to our west lies The Gila Indian Reservation. All those that live up here enjoy looking towards the cities in the valley that lies before us and mountains farther to our north. There is very little noise that we hear from what we are able to see except for the occasional siren or airplane in the distance or maybe a house shaking explosion that has happened only once, so far. We do have lots of Coyotes howling sometimes twice a day and an occasional, Mountain Lion scream but the only louder noises we hear are from all the birds that share this land with us. Quail, Mourning Doves, Hawks, Cactus Wren, Curved Bill Thrasher and Owls sing to us every day.

To all the people that live and work in the Town Of Queen Creek and all the rest that live in the Queen Creek zip code areas I wish you the very best in all that you do to protect our community from becoming an overgrown bedroom "ghetto".

According to Roget's Thesaurus: any mode of living, working, etc., that results from stereotyping or biased treatment: *job ghettos for women; ghettos for the elderly.* or where the vast majority of suburbanites have to drive into other better planned communities to work every day.

Je suis fini! Mon ami!

CPSIA information can be obtained
at www.ICGtesting.com
Printed in the USA
LVHW040524141222
735196LV00009B/453